Vegetarian CELEBRATIONS

Also by Nava Atlas

VEGETARIANA

AMERICAN HARVEST

VEGETARIAN SOUPS FOR ALL SEASONS

VEGETARIAN EXPRESS

Vegetarian
CELEBRATIONS

Festive Menus for Holidays
and Other Special Occasions

Updated Edition

NAVA ATLAS

Little, Brown and Company

Boston • New York • Toronto • London

Revised Edition

Library of Congress Cataloging-in-Publication Data

Atlas, Nava.
    Vegetarian celebrations : festive menus for holidays and other special occasions / Nava Atlas. — Rev. ed.
        p. cm.
    Includes index.
    ISBN 0-316-05739-8
    1. Vegetarian cookery. 2. Holiday cookery. 3. Menus
4. Low-fat diet—Recipes. I. Title.
TX837.A848 1996
641.5'636—dc20.   96-5690

10   9   8   7   6   5   4   3   2   1

MV-NY

Text design and illustration by Nava Atlas

Published simultaneously in Canada by Little, Brown & Company (Canada) Limited

PRINTED IN THE UNITED STATES OF AMERICA

For Adam,
who waited patiently

ACKNOWLEDGMENTS

Writing a cookbook devoted to celebrations confirmed my belief that sharing good food at happy occasions fosters a unique warmth and closeness between family and friends. Most of the work on this book was done at a special time for me, when I was starting a family of my own; and so the support and valuable contributions of family and friends to this book were especially appreciated.

I'd like to thank the following family members and friends, in alphabetical order, for sharing their favorite recipes for entertaining and anecdotes on holiday customs: Anne Atlas for Mushroom Matzo Farfel Pie, Mushroom, Asparagus, and Artichoke Salad, and Baked Cottage Cheese Diamonds; Toni Atlas for Baba Ghanouj and Hummus; Miriam Banin for Cold Angel Hair Pasta with Tomatoes and Basil, Ricotta Dumplings, Eggplant Caponata, and Eggplant Matzo Mina; Rose Cancelmo for Italian Easter Rice Pudding and Italian Chocolate Nut Cookies; Katherine Catts for Fresh Apple Cake; Doris Colucci for Sweet Cranberry Relish; Annie Emanuel for Millet Salad; Mary Louise Farley for Three-Cheese Spread; Andy and Vincent Frisari for the entire Christmas Eve in Southern Italy menu; Lin Garber for his recollections on Mennonite Easter, and specifically for the suggestions for Beet-dyed Eggs and Fried Potato Cakes with Tomatoes; Dora Gerber, proprietor of Swissette Herb Farm in Salisbury Mills, New York, for Herb "Butter" and Herb and Curry Dip; Yuji Hiratsuka for his information on Japanese New Year foods, with special thanks to Yuji and to Beverly Penn for teaching me how to prepare sushi; Josephine Orlando Katz for Zucchini with Mint; Ron London for Mock Chopped Liver; Ann Lovett and Neil Trager for Grainy Mustard Vinaigrette and Baked Garlic with Brie; Jon Naar for Crunchy Millet Bread; Katrina Nicosia for the many English Christmas recipes and for Wassail Bowl and Spiced Fruit Punch; Pat Reppert, proprietor of Shale Hill Farm in Saugerties, New York, for Mushrooms Rosemary; and Jan Wunderman for Oat and Wheat Bran Muffins. Some of these recipes I have fiddled with and adapted until they suited the tone of this book; I ask their contributors' forbearance and want them to know that I am grateful for the creative ideas behind the original contributions.

As always, I credit my husband, Chaim Tabak, since no recipe passes muster without his discerning stamp of approval. To my agent, Peter Elek, many thanks for having worked with me so enthusiastically on developing this project. Finally, and very importantly, it should be said that no matter how great an author's initial excitement about a project, the support and equal enthusiasm of an editor are essential; I'd like to thank Jennifer Josephy for providing both.

CONTENTS

Appendix

Vegetarian
CELEBRATIONS

INTRODUCTION

Holidays and other special occasions give us a chance to gather with loved ones, reflect on our heritage, celebrate the seasons, enjoy a respite from everyday routines, and simply rejoice. And it's hard to think of any celebration in which food isn't central to the festivities.

The idea for this book on vegetarian entertaining evolved along the lines of the old saying "necessity is the mother of invention." Knowing I'd written much about vegetarian cooking and natural foods, friends, mostly nonvegetarian, started questioning me around major holidays for suggestions on what to serve the one or two expected vegetarian guests that would harmonize with the meal's theme. Similarly, in one particular postholiday conversation, an acquaintance told me how difficult it had been to plan a Passover Seder for her new stepdaughter, a vegetarian who enjoys observing tradition. And on my end, I was being invited to write articles and teach workshops on whole food holiday meals with increasing frequency.

It began to seem as if a vegetarian or two (or more) in every crowd and every family was becoming inevitable—heartening news to me and my husband, who once felt like such oddities! But interestingly, my articles, lectures, and workshops were responded to in equal numbers by nonvegetarians or semivegetarians who have other dietary restrictions, such as low-cholesterol- and lactose-free diets. This led me to conclude that much of what the new vegetarian cuisine has to offer is applicable to those restricted regimes as well.

As growing numbers of people give up meat and overly rich foods, or drastically cut down, I predict that the goal for home entertaining will be not only to create delicious meals but also to provide for guests' specific needs and to avoid overindulgence. To that end, *Vegetarian Celebrations* strives to present seasonally balanced, meatless holiday meals that are festive and at the same time demonstrate a sense of tradition; plus, to recognize that many vegetarians, as I do, love any excuse to entertain—no matter what the special occasion—and wish to do so with style and elegance.

While this book is addressed above all to vegetarians, the menus are designed to acknowledge the needs of those who either don't use dairy products by choice or who can't use them for health reasons. Wherever possible, menus that are not dairy-free provide suggestions on easy adaptations, primarily using soy foods. Vegans (vegetarians who eat no eggs or dairy products) and those who are allergic to or can't digest dairy products will find plenty of meals that are colorful and festive without being creamy, cheesy, buttery. Those who are generally health-conscious will likewise appreciate these features.

The menus here emphasize seasonal produce and abound in grains, whole grain flours, and legumes. Of course there are the occasional rich dishes—what better time to splurge if one is going to, than at festive occasions—but, for the most part, I have attempted to remain mindful of fat and cholesterol content without compromising flavor.

The menus also offer the following features:

• Since I am loath to do a lot of cooking or putter around in the kitchen once my guests arrive, I have tried to limit, as much as possible, the dishes in any given menu that need much last-minute attention. In addition, I've provided plenty of dishes that can be made ahead of time but that won't fall apart or lose color, texture, or flavor.

• People are busy in today's hectic world and don't have days on end to prepare big meals for holidays the way Great-grandma did. However, certain occasions do warrant a good deal of preparation, especially Thanksgiving, Christmas, and Passover. For those large, multicourse meals, readers will find suggested timetables that will help them plan ahead and organize the cooking so that the preparation won't seem quite such a marathon.

If you don't have the time to create a big holiday meal yourself, why not use these menus as a guide for cooperative cooking? Split the recipes up between yourself and one or two other family members or friends. I did this for a Passover Seder and it worked beautifully.

• Similarly, some of the larger, but less elaborate, menus offer make-ahead tips so that the cook can prepare the meal with greater ease and less last-minute pressure.

• The menus were devised with a balance of simpler and more involved dishes. When one cook is preparing an entire meal from soup to nuts, not every course need have numerous steps and ingredients to be delicious and elegant.

• Vegans and those on lactose-free diets will find a handy guide to the use of eggs and/or dairy products following each menu. Whenever possible, suggestions on adapting the menu to suit those needs are provided.

• A word on the use of eggs: Though eggs are used, dishes in which eggs play a starring role are few. You'll also find recipes in which egg whites are recommended as a substitute for whole eggs, such as in cookies, casseroles, and other baked goods. In general, if a recipe has eggs as a major component, it is devised so that each portion contains at most one egg yolk.

• Where dairy products are used, the low-fat versions are used as much as possible, such as low-fat cottage cheese, milk, and yogurt. I love using buttermilk, the caloric equivalent of skim milk, in baking, for the wonderful flavor and texture it yields. Hard cheeses are used in moderation. The substitution of a wonderful, relatively new product, a soy-based hard cheese analog (available in most natural food stores), is often recommended as a substitute in the recipes to meet the needs of vegans and those on dairy-free diets. They no longer have to forgo pizza, Mexican-style dishes, and the like.

• And finally, a word on my use of margarine and not butter: First and foremost, margarine is more suitable than butter for various dietary restrictions. Though margarine has the same amount of fat and calories as butter, it contains no cholesterol, and most margarines are not as highly saturated as butter—an even more important consideration.

Look for margarines that list the highest unsaturated-to-saturated fat ratio in the nutritional table as possible—two to one or better. The first ingredient should be liquid oil. Remember, too, that the softer the margarine, the less saturated it is. I like to buy soy or safflower margarines in natural food stores because they contain no additives.

In all, I hope you enjoy these vegetarian celebrations as much as I enjoyed creating them. Entertaining without meat—easily, heathily, and deliciously—will be a pleasure for both hosts and guests!

Explanation of Nutritional Analysis

All breakdowns are based on one serving, unless specified otherwise. When there's a range in the serving amount, the average number of servings is used (i.e., when a recipe specifies 6 to 8 servings, the analysis is based on 7 servings). When more than one ingredient is listed as an option (i.e., soy margarine or butter), the first ingredient is used in the analysis. Usually, the option ingredient will not change the analysis significantly. Ingredients listed as optional, most often found at the end of the recipe, however, are not included in the analysis. When salt is listed "to taste," its sodium content is not included in the analysis.

Chapter 1

THE NEW YEAR

If you've had your fill of noisy New Year parties, why not plan instead to host a meal for a few close friends to help ring in the new? A long, lingering dinner to close out the year can be a welcome respite from the revelry and hectic pace of the holiday season just passed, and a chance to reflect with those dear to you as another page in time is turned.

Most cultures have deeply ingrained rituals and customary foods with which to greet the New Year. In our melting pot nation, though, there are few universal culinary customs, which left me a delightful flexibility in planning these menus. For two New Year's Eve dinners, I chose ethnic themes, with the thought that it would simply be a lot of fun to greet the New Year by treating friends to new and exotic foods.

You'll also find an easy, casual brunch menu for New Year's Day—to my mind, the very best way to celebrate the occasion. The often obligatory glee of New Year's Eve is notably absent; in its place is a completely relaxed mood mingled with a sincere optimism about the year that lies ahead.

For many centuries and across myriad cultures, the New Year has been designated as a feast day. Though the Hindu New Year is not celebrated at the same time as ours, I liked the idea of using an Indian menu; even a relatively simple meal includes a wide variety of dishes and condiments to sample, making the meal seem a true feast, at once exotic and highly satisfying. Interestingly, the Hindu New Year meal is typically entirely vegetarian.

The recipes in this menu have been simplified, that is, a bit Americanized, by their use of ground, rather than whole, spices, and oil or margarine instead of ghee *(clarified butter).*

A CURRY FEAST

6 to 8 servings

Chapatis

Minted Apricot Chutney

Red Lentil Dal

Cucumber Raita

Koorma Vegetable Curry

Fruited Rice

Pistachio Confections

———

Contains no eggs.
Contains dairy products. Adapt to vegan by following the recommended substitutions in the recipes.

CHAPATIS

Makes 12 to 14

An Indian bread is a must for this sort of meal, especially for scooping up the dal that follows, and to soothe the palate between bites of spicy food.

2 cups whole wheat flour
1/2 teaspoon salt

Combine the flour and salt in a mixing bowl. Work about 1/2 cup water in slowly to form a soft, but not sticky, dough. Knead gently on a floured board for 5 minutes. Place back in the bowl, cover with a towel, and let rest for 30 minutes to 1 hour.

Pinch off small pieces of dough to form 1 ½-inch balls. Roll each ball out on a well-floured board to form thin 5-inch rounds. Cook on a hot griddle or dry skillet over medium-high heat on both sides, until parts of the round puff out and light brown spots form. Place on a plate or in a basket and cover with a towel until all are done. Keep covered until serving.

Per chapati:

Calories: 62	Total fat: 0 g	Protein: 2 g
Carbohydrate: 12 g	Cholesterol: 0 g	Sodium: 84 mg

MINTED APRICOT CHUTNEY

Makes about 2 cups, 8 servings or more

A spoonful of sweet-tart chutney adds a graceful note to a curry dinner.

1 tablespoon canola oil
1 large onion, finely chopped
1 medium tart apple, peeled, cored, and diced
1 heaping cup chopped dried apricots
⅓ cup orange juice
2 teaspoons dried mint
1 teaspoon grated fresh ginger, or more to taste
juice of ½ lemon
2 tablespoons cider vinegar
cayenne pepper to taste

Heat the oil in a saucepan. Add the onion and sauté over medium heat until it is golden. Add the remaining ingredients and simmer over low heat, covered, for 35 to 40 minutes. The consistency should be moist, but not liquidy. If excess liquid remains, cook uncovered, stirring, until thickened. Let cool and store in a jar, refrigerated, until needed. Bring to room temperature to serve. Serve in small portions as a relish.

Calories: 39	Total fat: 2 g	Protein: 0 g
Carbohydrate: 6 g	Cholesterol: 0 g	Sodium: 1 mg

Make-ahead suggestions for

A Curry Feast

A day ahead:

- *Make the Red Lentil Dal. Heat through as needed before serving.*

- *The Minted Apricot Chutney can be made up to a week ahead of time. Store in a tightly lidded jar in the refrigerator and bring to room temperature before serving.*

- *Cook the rice for Fruited Rice.*

- *Make the Pistachio Confections.*

Check your spice rack! Have these herbs and spices on hand:

Dried:

  Mint
  Cumin
  Coriander
  Turmeric
  Nutmeg
  Cinnamon
  Dry mustard

Fresh:

  Cilantro and/or parsley
  Ginger

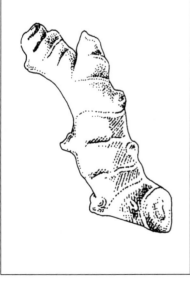

RED LENTIL DAL

6 to 8 servings

Dal, a sort of hot dip made of well-cooked legumes, is meant to be scooped up with freshly made Indian breads, such as chapatis, above. Tiny red lentils, available in natural food stores and imported food shops, cook to an appealing orange-gold color.

1 cup red lentils
1 tablespoon canola oil or soy margarine
1 medium onion, minced
2 cloves garlic, minced
1 teaspoon each: freshly grated ginger, ground cumin, and turmeric
dash of nutmeg
salt to taste

Rinse the lentils and combine them with 4 cups of water in a large, heavy saucepan. Bring to a boil, then cover and simmer until the lentils are quite mushy, about 40 minutes.

Heat the oil in a small skillet. Add the onion and garlic and sauté over moderate heat until golden. Stir into the saucepan with the cooked lentils and the remaining ingredients. Simmer over very low heat, covered, for 15 minutes. The texture should be that of a very thick soup. If making ahead, let cool and store in a covered container. Reheat before serving, transfer to 1or 2 attractive bowls, and serve hot.

Calories: 92	Total fat: 2 g	Protein: 5 g
Carbohydrate: 14 g	Cholesterol: 0 g	Sodium: 2 mg

CUCUMBER RAITA

6 to 8 servings

Raitas are yogurt-based salads that provide a refreshing contrast to spicy dishes.

2 large cucumbers, peeled, seeded, and chopped
1 ½ cups plain low-fat yogurt or soy yogurt

2 to 3 tablespoons chopped fresh cilantro or parsley
2 tablespoons minced fresh mint, or 1 teaspoon dried mint
½ teaspoon ground cumin

Combine all the ingredients in a mixing bowl. Chill before serving, then transfer to a serving container.

Calories: 46	Total fat: 1 g	Protein: 3 g
Carbohydrate: 6 g	Cholesterol: 3 g	Sodium: 40 mg

KOORMA VEGETABLE CURRY

6 to 8 servings

The term koorma refers to a Northern Indian style of cookery that utilizes yogurt. For vegans and for those who wish to adapt this to dairy-free, use soy yogurt. Do make the effort to find fresh cilantro, since it really adds a special flavor.

1 tablespoon reduced-fat margarine
1 cup chopped onion
3 to 4 cloves garlic
14- to 16-ounce can diced plum tomatoes, undrained
4-ounce can chopped mild green chiles
1 teaspoon each: grated fresh ginger, salt, ground cumin,
**   coriander, and dry mustard**
½ teaspoon each: ground turmeric, nutmeg, and cinnamon
2 large potatoes, peeled and finely diced
3 heaping cups bite-sized cauliflower pieces
2 large carrots, sliced
3 tablespoons chopped fresh cilantro
2 cups string beans, cut into 1-inch pieces
1 cup plain low-fat yogurt or soy yogurt

Heat the margarine plus 2 tablespoons of water in an extra-large skillet or, better yet, a wok, which will accommodate all the ingredients more comfortably. Add the onion and sauté over medium heat until it is translucent. Add the garlic and sauté until the onion is golden. Add the tomatoes, chiles, ginger, salt, and spices. Bring to a simmer, then stir in the potatoes, cauliflower, and carrots. Cover and simmer over medium-low heat for 20 minutes, stirring occasionally.

Stir in the cilantro, then simmer for another 5 to 10 minutes over low heat, until the vegetables are tender but still firm. While cooking, there should be enough liquid to form a sauce; if needed, add additional water, but not so much that the mixture becomes soupy.

Steam the string beans separately until they are bright green and crisp-tender (I like to add them at the last minute so they retain their color and texture). Stir into the vegetable mixture. Remove the skillet or wok from the heat, and stir in the yogurt. Serve at once.

Calories: 131	Total fat: 1 g	Protein: 5 g
Carbohydrate: 25 g	Cholesterol: 2 g	Sodium: 370 mg

FRUITED RICE

6 to 8 servings

Aromatic Basmati rice (available in natural food stores), sweet fruits, and crunchy nuts make a lovely counterpoint to the pungent curry dishes.

$\frac{1}{2}$ teaspoon salt
1 $\frac{1}{2}$ cups brown Basmati rice
   (if unavailable, substitute long-grain brown rice)
1 medium onion, finely chopped
1 large sweet apple, peeled, cored, and finely diced
$\frac{1}{3}$ cup raisins or currants
$\frac{1}{4}$ cup finely chopped dried apricots
$\frac{1}{3}$ cup chopped black (mission) figs
$\frac{1}{2}$ teaspoon each: dry mustard, turmeric, cinnamon
$\frac{1}{4}$ teaspoon nutmeg
$\frac{1}{4}$ cup apple or orange juice, or as needed
$\frac{1}{4}$ cup chopped toasted cashews

Bring 4 cups of water to a boil in a heavy saucepan. Stir in the salt and rice and return to a boil. Lower heat, cover, and simmer for 35 to 40 minutes, or until the water is absorbed. Remove from the heat.

Heat $\frac{1}{4}$ cup water in a large skillet. Add the onion and "sweat" over moderate heat, covered, until it is tender. Add the apple and sauté until it softens, about 3 to 4 minutes. Stir in the rice and all the remaining ingredients. Cook over low heat, stirring frequently, about 10 minutes. Stir in just

---

Traditional New Year Foods Around the World

The Netherlands:
Hot spiced wine with apple fritters or doughnuts

Germany:
White cabbage (symbolic of silver money)

Switzerland:
Whipped cream (symbolic of fatness and riches)

India:
Newly harvested foods, such as new rice

Bulgaria:
Cakes with holes in the center

Armenia:
Fruit and candies

enough juice to make the mixture moist. Just before serving, stir in the nuts.

Calories: 225	Total fat: 4 g	Protein: 4 g
Carbohydrate: 45 g	Cholesterol: 0 g	Sodium: 158 mg

PISTACHIO CONFECTIONS

Makes 18 to 20 1-inch balls

1 ½ cups nonfat dry milk
⅓ cup pistachio butter
⅓ cup raisins
2 tablespoons honey
½ teaspoon cinnamon
dash each: ground nutmeg, ground ginger
whole shelled pistachios, optional

Combine all the ingredients but the whole pistachios in a food processor. Process until the mixture is well blended. Drizzle water in slowly until the mixture begins to hold together as a mass.

Remove the mixture from the food processor with the help of a rubber spatula, then roll into balls no larger than 1 inch. Arrange on a plate lined with wax paper. If desired, press a whole pistachio into the top of each ball.

Refrigerate, uncovered, for several hours.

Per 1-inch piece:

Calories: 72	Total fat: 1 g	Protein: 4 g
Carbohydrate: 10 g	Cholesterol: 2 g	Sodium: 52 mg

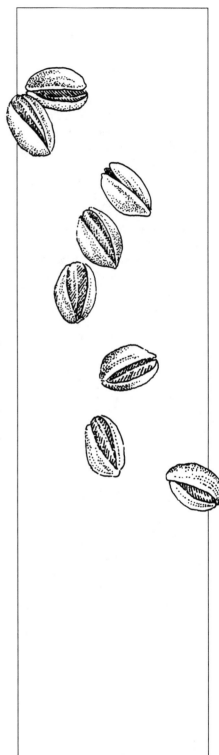

The Japanese New Year, celebrated at the same time as ours, abounds in special dishes traditional to the day. Many are vegetarian dishes, in fact, several of which have been incorporated into this menu. Though neither I nor most other American cooks can duplicate the visual beauty of a Japanese meal, the sushi does make a dramatic centerpiece. The dishes in this meal are quite easy to prepare, fortunately, since there is not much that can be done ahead of time. Sushi is the most involved, but once you get the hang of it, it is not difficult. If you've never made it, you might like to try a trial run in advance of the meal.

JAPANESE NEW YEAR

6 servings

Ozoni (New Year Soup with Rice Cakes)
Daikon and Carrot Salad
Nori-Maki Sushi
Soba Noodles
Silken Tofu Pudding

───────꒦───────

Contains no eggs or dairy products.

Note: *Look for the ingredients for this menu in Oriental groceries, natural food stores, or seafood markets.*

OZONI
(New Year Soup with Rice Cakes)

6 servings

Every region in Japan has its variation of New Year Soup; this is the Tokyo-style version. The common element among the regional variations of this soup is mochi, chewy cakes of pounded sticky rice.

Dashi (stock)
2 pieces kombu (sea vegetable), each about 3 by 5 inches
6 to 8 dried shiitake mushrooms

1 package mochi (sticky rice cakes)
1 large leek, white and palest green parts only,
    chopped and well rinsed
1 large carrot, cut into 1-inch matchsticks
½ pound fresh spinach, rinsed, stemmed,
    and coarsely chopped
2 to 3 tablespoons soy sauce or tamari, to taste

freshly ground pepper to taste
2 scallions, thinly sliced, for garnish
6 thin strips lemon peel, for garnish

Combine the kombu, mushrooms, and 6 cups of water in a soup pot. Bring to a boil, then remove from the heat and let stand, covered, for 30 minutes. Remove the kombu and discard or save for another use. Remove the mushrooms with a slotted spoon. Cut off and discard the tough stems, then slice the caps and set aside.

Break the mochi along the serrations to divide into 6 pieces. Bake in a preheated 450-degree oven or in a 500-degree toaster oven for 10 minutes, or until the cakes are puffed and lightly browned. When they are cool enough to handle, cut each cake into 4 small, square pieces and divide among 6 bowls.

In the meantime, add the leek and carrot to the dashi and bring to a boil. Simmer gently, covered, until the vegetables are crisp-tender, about 10 minutes. Stir in the spinach and sliced mushroom caps. Season to taste with soy sauce and pepper. Simmer just until the spinach is wilted.

Ladle the soup over the rice cakes in each bowl and garnish each serving with some sliced scallion and a curled strip of lemon peel. Serve at once.

Calories: 114	Total fat: 0 g	Protein: 4 g
Carbohydrate: 23 g	Cholesterol: 0 g	Sodium: 531 mg

DAIKON AND CARROT SALAD

6 servings

Matchstick-cut daikon radish and carrot make a typical Japanese salad that is served throughout the year.

1 large daikon radish, about 7 inches long,
**   scraped and trimmed (if unavailable,**
**   substitute 2 medium turnips)**
2 medium carrots
1 teaspoon salt

Dressing
2 tablespoons rice vinegar

Shopping list of special ingredients for

Japanese New Year

Here are the unusual ingredients needed for this menu, which may not be in your pantry. Look for them in Oriental groceries and in natural food shops. Many fish stores, too, carry sushi supplies such as pickled ginger, sticky rice, and even the bamboo rolling mat (sudare).

Mochi (sticky rice cakes), 12-ounce package
Kombu (sea vegetable), 3- by 10-inch piece
Shiitake mushrooms, 6 to 8
Daikon radish, two 7-inch-long radishes, or one fresh and one pickled
Rice vinegar
Sticky rice (also labeled "sweet rice" or "glutinous rice"), 2 cups
Nori (sea vegetable), pretoasted, one package, with at least 8 sheets
Wasabi powder, one package
Pickled ginger, one small jar
Sake or dry sherry
Soy sauce or tamari
Buckwheat noodles (soba), 1/2 pound
Dark sesame oil, one small bottle
Silken tofu, two 10-ounce packages

Bamboo rolling mat (sudare)

2 teaspoons sugar
1 tablespoon canola oil

Cut the daikon and carrots into 1 ½-inch-long matchsticks. Sprinkle with the salt, and let stand 30 minutes.

Combine the ingredients for the dressing in a small bowl. Let stand until the sugar dissolves. Toss with the daikon and carrot mixture and let stand, covered, another 30 minutes to 1 hour before serving.

Calories: 44   Total fat: 2 g   Protein: 0 g
Carbohydrate: 5 g   Cholesterol: 0 g   Sodium: 379 mg

NORI-MAKI SUSHI

6 servings

Many different types of sushi are commonly prepared for New Year meals in Japan. Here is a relatively simple variety, consisting of sticky rice and vegetables rolled in sheets of the sea vegetable nori. One note: Please don't substitute rice of any other type, not even short-grain—your sushi rolls simply won't hold together.

Using a bamboo mat made expressly for rolling sushi (called a sudare) will make the task considerably easier. You'll find this inexpensive item at the same places where you shop for your other supplies for this meal.

Vinegared rice for sushi
2 cups sticky rice
⅓ cup rice vinegar
1 ½ tablespoons granulated sugar
½ teaspoon salt

Soak the rice in a bowl of cold water. Swish around with your hands and drain when the water becomes cloudy. Fill with water again and repeat the procedure until the water remains clear.

Place the rice in a heavy 4-quart saucepan. Add 2 ¼ cups of water and cover with the lid. Bring the water to a boil without lifting the lid (watch for the lid jiggling). Reduce the heat to medium-high and cook for 5 minutes. Listen for a hissing or crackling sound to indicate that the water has been absorbed. Remove from the heat, and, still without lifting the lid, let the rice stand for 20 to 30 minutes.

Transfer the rice to a large bowl. Toss with a Japanese paddle or a wooden spoon until it stops steaming.

In a small bowl, combine the vinegar, sugar, and salt. Stir until the sugar is dissolved. Sprinkle into the rice, a little at a time, and toss in. Cover the vinegared rice mixture with a clean tea towel and set aside until needed (don't refrigerate it).

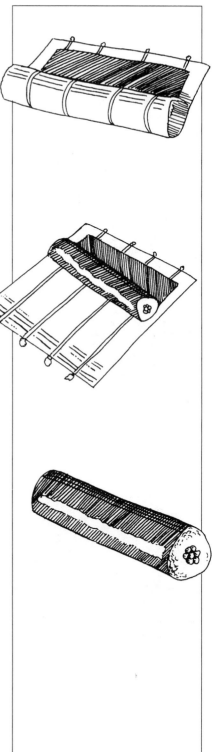

Nori and vegetables for sushi
**8 sheets nori (use pretoasted nori, specially
    made for making sushi)**

Choose from among the following vegetables:
**pickled daikon radish or raw daikon radish
cucumber, peeled, seeded, and quartered lengthwise
avocado
carrot
zucchini
3 tablespoons wasabi powder, divided
pickled ginger**

Use one sheet of nori as a guide for cutting the vegetables. The vegetables you use should be cut into very thin, very long matchsticks; their length should match the width of a sheet of nori. The exception to this is avocado, which won't be long enough, but this isn't a problem because of its soft texture. Just cut the strips lengthwise. The idea is to use about 6 strips of vegetable in each sushi roll; you may use one type of vegetable in each roll, or combine 2, for example, cucumber and avocado.

Place a tablespoon of the wasabi powder in a small bowl and combine it with enough water to make a thin paste.

Place a sheet of nori, shiny side down, on the bamboo mat discussed in the introduction to this recipe. Dampen your hands and spread $3/4$ cup of the vinegared rice over the surface of the nori, leaving a $1/2$-inch border on the end nearest you and a 2-inch border on the end farthest away.

About 1 $1/2$ inches from the side closest to you, paint a stripe of wasabi paste (use very little!) across the rice. Lay 6 or so strips of vegetable atop the stripe. Lift the side of the mat closest to you and roll it over so the nori is tightly rolled over the rice and vegetables. Wet the far end of the nori and continue the rolling motion until the result is a snugly closed roll. See the illustration facing to clarify the procedure.

Lay the rolled nori seam side down on a board, and repeat with the remaining sheets of nori.

You'll need a very sharp knife to cut the rolls. Wet the

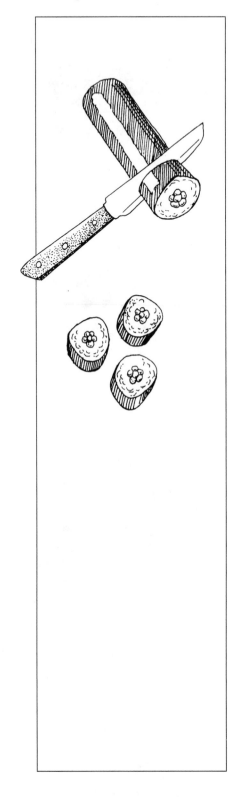

knife lightly and cut each roll into 6 equal sections. Arrange on a large platter.

In a small bowl, combine the remaining wasabi with enough water to make a fairly thick paste, thicker than what you made for the sushi rolls. Guests should take a small dab on their plates to be spread on the sushi rolls if they'd like. Put some pickled ginger in another small bowl. Let each guest take a slice or 2.

Calories: 110	Total fat: 0 g	Protein: 2 g
Carbohydrate: 24 g	Cholesterol: 0 g	Sodium: 196 mg

Dipping sauce for sushi
³⁄₄ cup Light Vegetable Stock (page 260) or water
¹⁄₂ cup soy sauce or tamari
¹⁄₄ cup sake or dry sherry

Combine the ingredients in a mixing bowl. Divide the dipping sauce among 6 small Oriental bowls and set next to each guest's plate for dipping the sushi rolls.

Calories: 35	Total fat: 0 g	Protein: 2 g
Carbohydrate: 4 g	Cholesterol: 0 g	Sodium: 1389 mg

SOBA NOODLES

6 servings

Soba, or buckwheat noodles, are a must for the Japanese New Year. Dark and nutritious, these noodles are often eaten right at midnight in the belief that they will bring good luck for the new year.

¹⁄₂ pound soba (buckwheat) noodles
2 tablespoons soy sauce or tamari, or to taste
2 tablespoons dark sesame oil
1 ¹⁄₂ tablespoons sesame seeds
2 teaspoons rice vinegar
¹⁄₂ teaspoon freshly grated ginger
3 scallions, sliced

Break the noodles in half and cook them until al dente (watch them—they cook quickly!). In a small bowl, combine the soy sauce, oil, sesame seeds, vinegar, and ginger. When the noodles are done, drain them and put in a serving container. Toss with the soy sauce mixture and scallions. Add 2 to 3 tablespoons of water, for added moistness, and toss again. Cover until ready to serve.

Calories: 110	Total fat: 5 g	Protein: 3 g
Carbohydrate: 11 g	Cholesterol: 0 g	Sodium: 338 mg

SILKEN TOFU PUDDING

6 servings

This is not a Japanese recipe, but an easy pudding made of silken tofu seems a light and appropriate finish to this meal.

1 cup chocolate syrup
2 10-ounce packages "lite" silken tofu
dash nutmeg
2 medium bananas, sliced
1 kiwifruit, sliced, for garnish

Combine the chocolate syrup, silken tofu, and nutmeg in a food processor. Process until velvety smooth.

Divide half the pudding among 6 dessert cups. Top with a layer of sliced bananas followed by the remaining pudding. Garnish each serving with a slice of kiwifruit. Chill until needed.

Calories: 230	Total fat: 3 g	Protein: 9 g
Carbohydrate: 44 g	Cholesterol: 0 g	Sodium: 108 mg

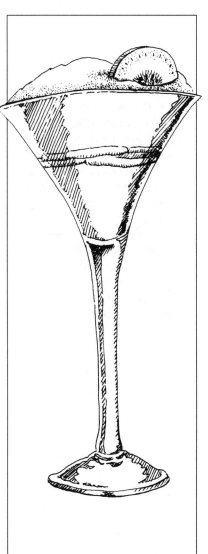

New Year's Day is a perfect time to gather with a handful of your closest friends for a brunch to toast the upcoming year. The meal must not be too early in the day, of course, nor overly taxing for the cook. Whether the guests are tired revelers or not, it's nice to keep the spirit of this get-together low-keyed and relaxed.

I immensely enjoy brunches with a Southwestern theme, and can think of no better way to greet the new year than with the zesty flavors of this cuisine.

A SOUTHWESTERN BRUNCH FOR NEW YEAR'S DAY

6 to 8 servings

Jalapeño Corn Bread

Baked Spanish Eggs

Marinated Black-eyed Peas

Grapefruit and Avocado Wedges

Pineapple, Raisin, and Rum Bread Pudding

Mimosas

Additions to the menu: Serve the Pineapple, Raisin, and Rum Bread Pudding with cinnamon-laced coffee and fresh pears.

Contains eggs and dairy products.

JALAPEÑO CORN BREAD

Makes 1 9-inch pan loaf, 9 servings

A rich-tasting, nonfat bread, almost as moist as a spoonbread. As this bakes, prepare the Baked Spanish Eggs, following. Then turn down the oven, and while the cornbread cools, bake the eggs.

1 ½ **cups yellow cornmeal**
½ **cup whole wheat flour**
1 ½ **teaspoons baking soda**
1 **teaspoon salt**
3 **egg whites, lightly beaten**
2 **cups plain low-fat yogurt**

3 tablespoons honey
1 or 2 jalapeño peppers, seeded and minced, to taste
    (see Note, below)
½ cup grated, reduced-fat cheddar or Monterey Jack
    cheese, optional
½ cup thawed frozen corn kernels

Preheat the oven to 400 degrees.

Combine the first 4 ingredients in a mixing bowl. In another bowl, combine the egg whites, yogurt, and honey. Make a well in the center of the dry ingredients and pour in the wet mixture. Stir together vigorously until smoothly blended. Stir in the jalapeños, optional cheese, and corn kernels.

Oil a 9- by 9-inch baking pan and pour in the batter. Bake for 20 to 25 minutes, or until the top just begins to turn golden and a knife inserted into the center tests clean. Allow the bread to cool in the pan. Cut into squares and serve while still warm.

Note: Whether using 1 jalapeño or 2, the result will be quite a spicy bread. You may want to wear rubber gloves while chopping them to protect your skin from irritation. For a milder version, substitute a 4-ounce can of chopped mild green chiles.

Calories: 172	Total fat: 0 g	Protein: 8 g
Carbohydrate: 34 g	Cholesterol: 1 g	Sodium: 353 mg

BAKED SPANISH EGGS

6 servings

In the Southwest, dishes infused with olive oil, garlic, peppers, and tomatoes are considered Spanish-influenced.

3 corn tortillas, cut into l-inch squares
1 tablespoon olive oil
2 medium onions, quartered and thinly sliced
2 cloves garlic, minced
1 medium green bell pepper, diced
2 medium tomatoes, diced
6 eggs, beaten
3 tablespoons low-fat milk
4-ounce can chopped mild green chiles

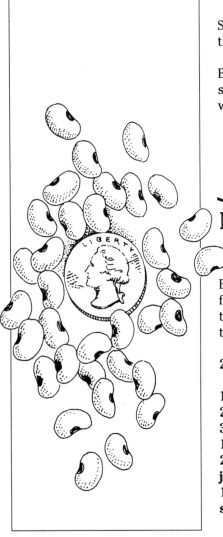

$^{1}/_{2}$ **teaspoon ground cumin**
$^{1}/_{2}$ **teaspoon dried oregano**
2 to 3 tablespoons minced fresh cilantro or parsley
salt and freshly ground pepper to taste

Preheat the oven to 350 degrees.

Heat a large skillet. Toast the cut tortillas on the dry skillet over moderate heat, stirring occasionally, until they are crisp. Transfer to a plate to cool.

Heat the oil in the same skillet. Add the onions and sauté over moderate heat until translucent. Add the garlic and pepper and sauté until the onion turns golden and the peppers soften. Add the tomatoes and sauté for another 2 to 3 minutes, just until they soften a bit.

Combine the beaten eggs with the milk in a mixing bowl. Stir in the mixture from the skillet, the tortilla bits, and all the remaining ingredients.

Oil 2 9-inch pie tins and divide the mixture between them. Bake for 25 to 30 minutes, or until set and golden on top. Let stand for 10 minutes before serving, then cut each into 6 wedges to serve, allowing 2 wedges per serving.

Calories: 170	Total fat: 8 g	Protein: 9 g
Carbohydrate: 14 g	Cholesterol: 213 g	Sodium: 80 mg

MARINATED BLACK-EYED PEAS

6 servings

Black-eyed peas are one of the few truly American good-luck foods for New Year's Day. Eating them on this day is traditional in the South, where a coin is sometimes cooked with the peas, foretelling riches throughout the coming year.

2 cups cooked or canned black-eyed peas
    (see Bean Basics, page 261)
1 medium red bell pepper, cut into narrow l-inch strips
2 scallions, minced
3 tablespoons minced fresh parsley
1 tablespoon olive oil
2 tablespoons apple juice or cider
juice of $^{1}/_{2}$ to 1 lemon, to taste
1 clove garlic, crushed, optional
salt and freshly ground pepper, to taste

dark green lettuce leaves

Combine all the ingredients except lettuce leaves in a mixing bowl and let stand, covered, for an hour or 2, refrigerated, before serving, or, better yet, make a day ahead. Stir occasionally. Before serving, remove the garlic. Line a shallow serving bowl with lettuce leaves and top them with the marinated mixture.

Calories: 95	Total fat: 2 g	Protein: 4 g
Carbohydrate: 14 g	Cholesterol: 0 g	Sodium: 3 mg

GRAPEFRUIT AND AVOCADO WEDGES

6 servings

2 pink grapefruits, peeled and sectioned
2 medium firm, ripe avocados
curly parsley for garnish

The grapefruits may be prepared ahead of time and stored in an airtight plastic container until needed. Just before serving, peel the avocados and cut them in half lengthwise. Remove the pits and cut into 1/2-inch-thick slices crosswise. Arrange on a round serving platter, alternating with the grapefruit wedges in overlapping circular rows. Garnish with curly parsley.

Calories: 138	Total fat: 8 g	Protein: 2 g
Carbohydrate: 14 g	Cholesterol: 0 g	Sodium: 5 mg

PINEAPPLE, RAISIN, AND RUM BREAD PUDDING

6 to 8 servings

A warm, satisfying finale to this or any winter meal, and so simple to put together.

20-ounce can crushed pineapple, with liquid

"The flesh of pineapple melts into water and it is so flavorful that one finds in it the aroma of the peach, the apple, the quince and the muscat grape. I can call it with justice the king of fruits because it is the most beautiful and best of all those on earth."

—Père du Tertre, 1595

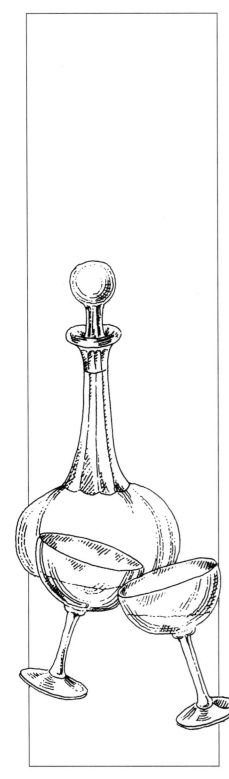

½ cup low-fat milk
**5 cups firmly packed Italian or French bread,
    torn into approximately 1-inch chunks**
⅔ **cup golden raisins**
½ **cup firmly packed light brown sugar**
1 tablespoon reduced-fat margarine, melted
1 tablespoon rum
1 teaspoon vanilla extract
½ **teaspoon cinnamon**

Glaze
1 teaspoon reduced-fat margarine
2 tablespoons rum
1 tablespoon light brown sugar
2 tablespoons sliced almonds

Preheat the oven to 350 degrees.

Combine the pineapple, milk, and bread in a mixing bowl. Stir together and let stand 10 minutes. Stir in the remaining ingredients. Pour the mixture into a lightly oiled 9- by 9-inch baking pan.

For the glaze, melt the margarine in a small skillet. Add the rum and brown sugar and stir just until the sugar is dissolved. Spoon in a thin layer over the top of the pudding. Bake for 25 minutes, then top with the almonds. Bake for another 15 to 20 minutes, or until the top is golden brown and beginning to turn crusty. Serve warm.

Calories: 279	Total fat: 1 g	Protein: 5 g
Carbohydrate: 56 g	Cholesterol: 1 g	Sodium: 215 mg

MIMOSAS

chilled orange juice
chilled champagne

What could be easier—simply fill each guest's champagne or wine glass with equal proportions of orange juice and champagne, and toast the new year!

Per 1-cup serving:

Calories: 138	Total fat: 0 g	Protein: 1 g
Carbohydrate: 14 g	Cholesterol: 0 g	Sodium: 10 mg

Chapter 2

VALENTINE'S DAY

A romantic Valentine's Day dinner for your sweetheart is sure to be even more so if you infuse your recipes with foods purported to have legendary powers to provoke desire. This chapter will show you how.

Forget about oysters and Spanish fly—many of the foods long considered aphrodisiac are in the vegetarian realm. For instance, you'll find in Cupid's cupboard a supply of eggs, onions, and garlic, three of the foods most often mentioned in historic health and advice manuals as having stimulating effects. And seemingly innocent veggies such as asparagus, carrots, and tomatoes supposedly have the ability to enhance prowess. Ancient Chinese, Arabic, and Indian writings (such as the *Kamasutra*) encouraged their readers to use such foods in the pursuit of love, and even provided recipes.

You'll find many such legendary ingredients in the menus given here. Whether or not they live up to their claims is up to you—after all, the power of suggestion is the most potent aphrodisiac of all!

ROMANCE BEGINS AT HOME

2 servings

Avocado and Orange Salad
Three-Onion Pie with Feta or Goat Cheese
Twice-baked Buttermilk Potatoes
Baked Tomatoes

———※———

Additions to the menu: Choose one of the chocolate desserts following these menus, pages 30 to 34

Contains eggs and dairy products.

The avocado, native to South America, was introduced to Europe by Cortez and his conquistadors from Spain. It quickly became a favorite throughout the bawdy palaces in Europe. Louis XIV called the green fruit "la bonne poire," "the good pear," and partook of it in his later years, believing that it stimulated his waning prowess.

AVOCADO AND ORANGE SALAD

2 servings

1 small, sweet seedless orange, such as a clementine, peeled and sectioned
½ medium-firm, ripe avocado, diced
½ cup diced jicama or turnip
½ cup loosely packed watercress leaves
red-leaf lettuce, torn, as needed

Dressing
2 teaspoons walnut oil or other aromatic nut oil
½ to 1 tablespoon lemon or lime juice to taste
½ teaspoon dried mint
½ teaspoon honey
freshly ground black pepper to taste

Combine the salad ingredients in a serving bowl. In a small bowl, stir together the dressing ingredients. Pour over the salad and toss to coat. Serve at once.

Calories: 171	Total fat: 11 g	Protein: 2 g
Carbohydrate: 17 g	Cholesterol: 0 g	Sodium: 27 mg

THREE-ONION PIE WITH FETA OR GOAT CHEESE

Makes 1 10-inch pie, 6 to 8 servings

This is a quiche-sized pie, so there will be leftovers after serving 2. You won't mind, though, as it reheats nicely.

2 tablespoons dry white wine
1 large yellow onion, chopped
1 large red onion, quartered and thinly sliced
2 large leeks, white parts only, cut into $^1/_4$-inch rings
  and well rinsed
2 eggs plus 1 egg white, beaten
3 tablespoons chopped fresh parsley, divided
1 tablespoon chopped fresh dill, or 1 teaspoon dried dill
1 teaspoon dried tarragon
4 ounces crumbled feta or dry goat cheese
freshly ground pepper to taste
1 ripe plum tomato, thinly sliced crosswise
fine dry bread crumbs

Heat the wine plus 2 tablespoons of water in a large skillet. Add the yellow and red onions and "sweat" over moderate heat, covered, for 5 minutes. Add the leeks. Sauté for another 15 minutes, stirring frequently, or until the onions are golden and the leeks are limp. Remove from the heat.

Preheat the oven to 350 degrees.

In a mixing bowl, combine the beaten eggs with 2 table-spoons of the parsley, the dill, tarragon, feta cheese, and pepper. Stir in the onion mixture.

Spray a 10-inch tart pan with cooking oil spray and line the bottom generously with bread crumbs. Pour in the onion mixture. Ring the outside edge of the pie with tomato slices, then sprinkle the remaining parsley in the center. Sprinkle a

Onions and eggs, combined in this luscious savory pie, are two of the foods most frequently mentioned as aphrodisiacs in ancient manuals. Eggs seem to have held a particularly strong allure in this realm, very likely because of their symbolic association with fertility. Hundreds of years ago, a French bride would break an egg upon entering her new home in order to ensure her own fertility. Shaykh Nefzawi, the four-teenth-century author of the classic Arabian manual The Perfumed Garden, *gave numerous omeletlike recipes, combining eggs with spices, asparagus, and, in one concoction, onions. The latter promises "invalu-able vigor for the coitus, if [he] will partake of this dish for several days."*

light layer of bread crumbs over the entire top. Bake for 40 to 45 minutes, or until the mixture is set and the top is golden. Let stand for 5 to 10 minutes, then cut into wedges and serve.

Calories: 126	Total fat: 5 g	Protein: 6 g
Carbohydrate: 12 g	Cholesterol: 75 g	Sodium: 244 mg

TWICE-BAKED BUTTERMILK POTATOES

2 servings

2 large baking potatoes
2 teaspoons reduced-fat margarine, melted
1/3 cup buttermilk
1 tablespoon fresh minced chives or 1 teaspoon dried chives
salt and freshly ground pepper to taste
paprika for garnish

Bake or microwave the potatoes until tender but still firm. Let cool (at room temperature, they have less chance of falling apart when you scoop them out), then scoop out the centers, leaving a firm, 1/4-inch-thick shell. Mash the potatoes in a small bowl, then stir in the melted margarine, buttermilk, and chives. Season to taste with salt and pepper, then fill the shells. Dust the tops with paprika. Bake at 350 degrees for 15 to 20 minutes, or until well heated through. Serve hot.

Calories: 146	Total fat: 2 g	Protein: 3 g
Carbohydrate: 29 g	Cholesterol: 1 g	Sodium: 57 mg

BAKED TOMATOES

2 servings

Winter tomatoes leave much to be desired, but I've found that plum tomatoes are acceptable, even out of season. I put them in a paper bag in a dark place for 2 days or so to improve their color and flavor.

2 good-sized plum tomatoes
fine bread crumbs
grated fresh Parmesan cheese
dried thyme

Cut each tomato in half and arrange cut side up on a baking dish. Sprinkle each half lightly with bread crumbs, Parmesan cheese, and thyme. Bake for 15 to 20 minutes.

Calories: 56	Total fat: 1 g	Protein: 2 g
Carbohydrate: 10 g	Cholesterol: 2 g	Sodium: 87 mg

Though tomatoes were for many centuries suspected of being poisonous, since the plant is a member of the deadly nightshade family, they also carried amorous connotations. In France, the tomato was once called "pomme d'amour," "apple of love." When it first reached England, it was known as "pome amoris," "love apple."

"For this was on Saint Valentine's day, When every bird cometh there to choose his mate."

—Geoffrey Chaucer
(ca. 1342-1400)
Parliament of Fowls

A VEGAN VALENTINE
2 servings

Plum Tomatoes with Olive Oil and Herbs

Asparagus Crêpes with Mushroom-Dill Sauce

Saffron-Sesame Rice with Pine Nuts

Steamed Baby Carrots

Additions to the menu: For dessert, choose one of the chocolate desserts following these menus, pages 30 to 34. Quite appropriate to this egg- and dairy-free dinner would be the Poached Pears with Chocolate Drizzle, page 32.

Contains no eggs or dairy products.

PLUM TOMATOES WITH OLIVE OIL AND HERBS
2 servings

See the note on improving the flavor of winter tomatoes under the recipe for Baked Tomatoes, page 25.

2 to 3 ripe plum tomatoes
1 to 2 tablespoons minced fresh herbs
1 teaspoon olive oil
freshly ground pepper to taste

Slice the tomatoes crosswise and arrange on 2 small individual plates. Sprinkle with the herbs and drizzle with a few drops of olive oil. Add a grinding of pepper and serve.

Calories: 45	Total fat: 2 g	Protein: 1 g
Carbohydrate: 5 g	Cholesterol: 0 g	Sodium: 11 mg

ASPARAGUS CRÊPES WITH MUSHROOM-DILL SAUCE

2 servings

Spring asparagus is not yet in season, but bunches of young, slender stalks are usually available—a bit expensive, but as a treat for two, well worth the splurge.

Crêpes
1/2 cup whole wheat pastry flour
1/4 teaspoon salt
3/4 cup soymilk
1 teaspoon canola oil

Sauce
2 teaspoons reduced-fat margarine
1 small onion, quartered and thinly sliced
1 clove garlic, minced
1 cup small white mushrooms, sliced
1 tablespoon plus 1 teaspoon unbleached flour
3/4 cup soymilk
2 tablespoons fresh minced dill
1/2 teaspoon dried tarragon
2 teaspoons lemon juice
salt and freshly ground pepper to taste

Filling
24 slender asparagus stalks

Combine the flour and salt in a mixing bowl. Make a well in the center and pour in the soymilk and oil. Beat together until smooth. Heat a 6- or 7-inch nonstick skillet. When hot enough to make a drop of water sizzle, pour in 1/4 cup of the batter and tilt the skillet until evenly coated. Cook over moderate heat until lightly browned on the bottom, then flip and brown the other side. Remove and set on a plate. Repeat

"[Asparagus] being taken after fasting several mornings together, stirreth up bodily lust in man or woman, whatever some have written to the contrary."

—Nicolas Culpeper
(1616-1654)
Culpeper's Complete Herbal

Delicate Saffron-Sesame Rice dishes out a double dose of ingredients that inspire love. Saffron was mentioned in the Arabian Nights *as a stimulant so powerful that it would cause women to swoon. Sesame seeds are mentioned in the* Kamasutra *several times, with one recipe promising men unflagging prowess.*

with the remaining batter, yielding 6 crêpes.

For the sauce, heat the margarine in a small saucepan. Add the onion and garlic and sauté over moderate heat until the onion is golden. Add the mushrooms, cover, and cook until they are limp and juicy. Sprinkle in the flour and stir until it disappears. Slowly pour in the soymilk, stirring. Bring the mixture to a simmer, then stir in the dill and tarragon. Cook at a simmer until the liquid thickens. Stir in the lemon juice and season to taste with salt and pepper. Remove from heat and cover.

Trim off about 1/2 inch from the bottoms of the asparagus stalks, and scrape off any skin from the bottom third that looks tough. Cut the stalks in half. Steam in a vegetable steamer or in a saucepan with a little water on the bottom, covered, just until crisp-tender.

To assemble, place 6 asparagus stalks in the center of each crêpe, letting the tips protrude from the top and overlapping the halved stalks in the center if necessary. Spoon a very small amount of the sauce over the asparagus. Fold one end of the crêpe in toward the center, and fold the other end over it. Arrange the crêpes, folded side down, in an oiled, shallow baking dish. Spoon the remaining sauce evenly over the crêpes. Bake in a preheated 350-degree oven just until heated through, then serve at once.

Calories: 280	Total fat: 8 g	Protein: 13 g
Carbohydrate: 39 g	Cholesterol: 0 g	Sodium: 333 mg

SAFFRON-SESAME RICE WITH PINE NUTS

4 servings

When cooking a rice dish, I like to make extra to have as leftovers. You'll get about 2 extra servings from this recipe.

1 vegetable bouillon cube
2/3 cup long-grain brown or brown Basmati rice
1/2 teaspoon saffron threads (see Note)
1/4 cup pine nuts
2 scallions, minced
juice of 1/2 lemon
1 1/2 tablespoons tahini (sesame paste)
1/4 cup minced fresh parsley

1 tablespoon sesame seeds
freshly ground pepper to taste

Combine 2 cups of water and the bouillon cube in a heavy saucepan. Bring to a boil, stir in the rice, then cover and simmer until the water is absorbed, 35 to 40 minutes. Remove from heat and cover.

Combine the saffron with $1/4$ cup hot water in a small container and let steep until needed.

In a small, dry skillet, toast the pine nuts over moderate heat until they are lightly browned, about 5 minutes. Remove from heat.

Stir the saffron water and saffron into the cooked rice, followed by the scallions, lemon juice, and tahini. Add more water if the mixture seems dry. Stir in the pine nuts, parsley, and sesame seeds, and season to taste with pepper. Serve at once.

Note: If saffron is unavailable, substitute an equal amount of turmeric.

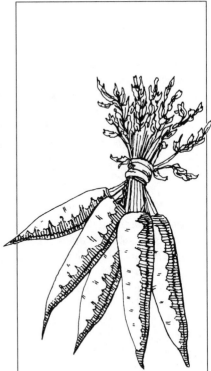

Calories: 206	Total fat: 9 g	Protein: 5 g
Carbohydrate: 26 g	Cholesterol: 0 g	Sodium: 5 mg

STEAMED BABY CARROTS

2 servings

16 baby carrots, scraped if need be
$1/4$ cup apple juice
$1/8$ teaspoon freshly grated nutmeg or
    dash of ground nutmeg

Cook the baby carrots in a saucepan with the apple juice until crisp-tender, about 4 minutes. Drain and toss with the nutmeg. Allowing 8 carrots for each serving, arrange them on the plates in a fan shape with the narrow tips pointing down.

Calories: 47	Total fat: 0 g	Protein: 1 g
Carbohydrate: 11 g	Cholesterol: 0 g	Sodium: 36 mg

Could the humble carrot really be an aphrodisiac? According to John Gerarde's Herball *(1636), "The carrot serveth for love matters . . . the use thereof winneth love." And as a bonus, the carrots in this recipe are subtly flavored with nutmeg, which appears on Aristotle's list of aphrodisiacs.*

Chocolate—"sweets to the sweet"—is perhaps associated with Valentine's Day more than any other food. The immediate pleasure of its irresistible flavor is accompanied by an overall sense of well-being (albeit tempered by a bit of guilt). Some studies, in fact, have postulated that eating chocolate releases the same bodily chemicals released when one is in love. In this selection of chocolate desserts you'll find some recipes that balance the chocolate with some redeemingly healthy ingredients and others that use less fattening cocoa and strive to keep the fat content at a minimum.

SOME SLIGHTLY SINFUL CHOCOLATE DESSERTS

Chocolate Chip Oat Cookies

Cocoa Drops

Chocolate-Peanut Butter Fudge

Poached Pears with Chocolate Drizzle

Buttermilk Chocolate-Hazelnut Cake

CHOCOLATE CHIP OAT COOKIES

Makes about 30

Chewy and chunky with oats, sunflower seeds, and chocolate, these cookies make a great gift to pack in a box for your sweetie.

½ cup (1 stick) reduced-fat margarine, softened
⅔ cup packed brown sugar
1 egg, beaten
1 teaspoon vanilla extract
1 ½ cups whole wheat pastry flour
1 cup rolled oats
1 teaspoon baking powder
¼ teaspoon salt
1 cup semisweet chocolate chips
¼ cup toasted sunflower seeds

Preheat the oven to 375 degrees.

In a mixing bowl, cream together the margarine and sugar. Beat in the egg and vanilla until fluffy and smooth. In another bowl, combine the flour, oats, baking powder, and salt. Work in the margarine mixture, using hands. Work in the chocolate chips and sunflower seeds. Drop onto 1 or 2 baking sheets in rounded, slightly flattened tablespoonfuls.

Bake 10 to 12 minutes, or until the bottoms of the cookies are lightly golden. Remove from the sheets gently with a spatula and cool on plates.

Per cookie:

Calories: 98	Total fat: 4 g	Protein: 2 g
Carbohydrate: 14 g	Cholesterol: 7 g	Sodium: 48 mg

~~~~~~

COCOA DROPS

Makes about 2 dozen

These little cookies can be enjoyed with a minimum of guilt. They have a moist, almost brownie-like texture, yet they are completely cholesterol-free and quite low in fat. They'll be appreciated by those who really can't splurge too much.

3 egg whites, at room temperature
1 cup light brown sugar
2 tablespoons canola oil
1 teaspoon vanilla extract
1 cup whole wheat pastry flour
1/2 cup unsweetened cocoa powder
1 teaspoon baking powder
dash nutmeg

Preheat the oven to 325 degrees.

Beat the egg whites with an electric mixer until stiff. Gradually beat in the sugar, oil, and vanilla.

In a small mixing bowl, combine the remaining ingredients. Work into the whipped egg white mixture to form a stiff dough.

Drop by rounded teaspoonfuls onto a nonstick baking sheet. Bake for 10 minutes, or until the tops of the cookies feel set.

Cool on a rack, then store in an airtight container.

Per cookie:

Calories: 70	Total fat: 1 g	Protein: 1 g
Carbohydrate: 13 g	Cholesterol: 0 g	Sodium: 9 mg

"Chocolate is not only pleasant to taste, but it is a veritable balm of the mouth, for the maintaining of all glands and humours in a good state of health."

—Dr. Blancardi, 1705

CHOCOLATE-PEANUT BUTTER FUDGE

Makes 5 to 6 dozen 1-inch pieces

Pack squares of this fudge in an attractive container to give as a rich, gooey gift to someone you love.

**1 cup (6 ounces) semisweet chocolate chips,
    or 6 ounces semisweet baking chocolate**
¼ cup light brown sugar
2 tablespoons low-fat milk
½ cup oatmeal or quick-cooking oats
⅓ cup reduced-fat peanut butter, at room temperature

Combine the chocolate, sugar, and milk in the top of a double boiler or in a small aluminum bowl perched atop a saucepan filled with a small amount of water. Cook over low heat until smoothly melted. Stir in the oatmeal. Drop the peanut butter in by rounded teaspoonfuls. Swirl it in until evenly distributed throughout but not blended in.

Line a small, shallow baking dish with wax paper. Pat the chocolate mixture in with the help of a cake spatula. Refrigerate for several hours until chilled and firmly set. Cut into l-inch squares.

Per 1-inch piece:

Calories: 26	Total fat: 1 g	Protein: 1 g
Carbohydrate: 3 g	Cholesterol: 0 g	Sodium: 6 mg

POACHED PEARS WITH CHOCOLATE DRIZZLE

2 servings

Chocolate is most compatible with pears as a winter treat.

2 large, firm bosc pears
3 tablespoons white wine
3 tablespoons apple juice
½ teaspoon vanilla extract
¼ teaspoon cinnamon

dash each: allspice, nutmeg
1 teaspoon cornstarch
¼ cup semisweet chocolate chips

Core the pears and cut each into 8 sections lengthwise. Combine the wine, juice, vanilla, and spices in a saucepan. Put in the pears and bring to a simmer. Cover and simmer over low heat until the pears are just done—fork-tender but still firm. Combine the cornstarch with just enough water to dissolve it. Stir into the liquid in the saucepan and simmer, uncovered, until thickened. Remove from the heat. Let cool until just warm.

Just before serving, combine the chocolate chips and about 1 tablespoon of water in the top of a double boiler or a small aluminum bowl perched atop a saucepan filled with a small amount of water. Heat until smoothly melted. Arrange the pear slices in 2 dessert bowls. Divide the cooking liquid between them. Dip a teaspoon into the melted chocolate and drizzle over the pears in a zigzag pattern, repeating until the chocolate is used up. Serve at once.

Calories: 236	Total fat: 6 g	Protein: 1 g
Carbohydrate: 38 g	Cholesterol: 0 g	Sodium: 6 mg

BUTTERMILK CHOCOLATE-HAZELNUT CAKE

Makes 1 9-inch cake, 9 servings

Despite its rich taste, this cake's sinful qualities are minimized by using prune butter in place of oil, egg whites instead of whole eggs, and cocoa powder instead of baking chocolate. Buttermilk, which is quite low in fat, makes for a wonderfully tender crumb.

1 cup buttermilk
⅓ cup prune butter (see Note)
2 egg whites
1 teaspoon vanilla extract
1 cup light brown sugar
1 cup whole wheat pastry flour
½ cup unsweetened cocoa powder
1 teaspoon baking soda

"It has been shown as proof-positive that carefully prepared chocolate is as healthful a food as it is pleasant . . . that it does not cause the same harmful effects to feminine beauty which are blamed on coffee but is on the contrary a remedy for them; that it is above all helpful to people who must do a great deal of mental work, to those who labor in the pulpit or in the classroom, and especially to travellers. . . ."

—Jean-Anthèlme Brillat-Savarin
La Physiologie du Goût,
1825

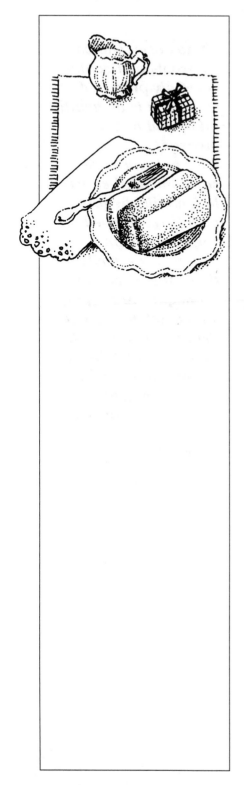

1 teaspoon baking powder
¹/₄ teaspoon salt
¹/₂ cup finely chopped hazelnuts

Preheat the oven to 350 degrees.

Combine the first 5 ingredients in a mixing bowl and beat together with an electric mixer. Combine the remaining ingredients except the hazelnuts in another bowl. Sprinkle into the wet mixture a bit at a time and beat in with the mixer until velvety smooth.

Lightly oil a 9-inch round or square cake pan. Sprinkle the bottom with flour. Pour in half of the batter, then sprinkle it evenly with half of the hazelnuts. Pour in the remaining batter and top with the remaining hazelnuts. Bake for 25 to 30 minutes, or until a knife inserted into the center tests clean. Cool in the pan, then cut into squares or wedges to serve.

Note: Prune butter, a wonderful substitute for fats or oils in baking, is available in the jam and jelly section of most supermarkets.

Calories: 230	Total fat: 6 g	Protein: 6 g
Carbohydrate: 38 g	Cholesterol: 1 g	Sodium: 98 mg

Chapter 3

EASTER AND ST. PATRICK'S DAY

The movable Christian festival of Easter, celebrated on the Sunday following the paschal full moon, is above all a day of rejoicing. The parades, the hunts for colorful, decorated eggs, festooned bonnets, among other symbols of the holiday, all add up to the marvelous certainty that spring has arrived.

In celebrating the resurrection of Christ, Easter carries many connotations of renewal of life. Brightly painted eggs are symbols of the seed of life, representing fertility; the Easter rabbit, purported to have laid the eggs that children search for in the grass, originated from the idea that rabbits are prolific and, thus, also appropriate symbols of fertility.

The festive meal following Easter services marks the end of the austere Lenten period. Though the centerpiece of the traditional American Easter dinner, the ham, will be notably absent from the vegetarian table, the fresh produce of early spring is emphasized in these menus. This will enliven the palate dulled during the lull between the early winter holidays and the eagerly awaited arrival of this holiday.

In choosing menus for Easter, I wanted to include one with a basic American theme; and down-to-earth Pennsylvania Dutch cookery fills the bill nicely. A friend who grew up as an Indiana Mennonite (a branch of the Dutch with more progressive ways than the Amish, yet still a solid, salt-of-the-earth people), recalled that the meal following church services was not terribly out of the ordinary save for the ham. The latter has been eliminated from this menu, of course, but included are some very typical Dutch dishes that he remembers as likely accompaniments. The only dish related to Easter per se, here, is the first, Beet-dyed Eggs, in which the magenta color of the egg whites plainly states that this day is out of the ordinary.

A PENNSYLVANIA DUTCH EASTER LUNCH

6 to 8 servings

Beet-dyed Eggs

Buttermilk Biscuits

Fried Potato Cakes with Tomatoes

Dutch Cucumber Salad

Corn Relish

Shoofly Pie

Contains eggs and dairy products.

BEET-DYED EGGS

6 to 8 servings

6 to 8 hard-boiled eggs, peeled
beet juice from canned beets, or from cooked beets
curly parsley for garnish

Place the whole, peeled eggs in a shallow container and cover with beet juice. Cover and refrigerate overnight. To serve, cut the eggs open (the white will be stained a glorious red, as will be part of the yolk) and arrange on a plate. Garnish with the parsley.

Calories: 80	Total fat: 6 g	Protein: 7 g
Carbohydrate: 1 g	Cholesterol: 213 g	Sodium: 71 mg

BUTTERMILK BISCUITS

Makes 12 to 16

2 $\frac{1}{4}$ cups whole wheat pastry flour
2 teaspoons baking powder
$\frac{1}{2}$ teaspoon baking soda
1 teaspoon salt
$\frac{1}{4}$ cup ($\frac{1}{2}$ stick) reduced-fat margarine,
    at room temperature, cut into bits
1 cup buttermilk

Preheat the oven to 425 degrees.

Combine the first 4 ingredients in a mixing bowl. Work the margarine in with a pastry blender or with fingertips until blended throughout. Work in the buttermilk, a bit at a time, first with a wooden spoon and then with hands, to form a soft dough. If the dough is too sticky, add a bit more flour.

Pinch the dough off in small balls, enough to allow 2 biscuits per guest (i.e., 12 balls for 6 guests, etc.). Flatten the balls slightly to form nice biscuit shapes, and arrange on a lightly oiled baking sheet. Bake for 10 to 12 minutes, or until the tops are golden. Transfer to a plate and serve hot.

Per biscuit:
Calories: 83	Total fat: 1 g	Protein: 3 g
Carbohydrate: 14 g	Cholesterol: 1 g	Sodium: 188 mg

FRIED POTATO CAKES WITH TOMATOES

6 to 8 servings

Large tomatoes aren't wonderful at this time of year, but to improve the flavor of those hothouse tomatoes, I suggest buying them a few days in advance, placing them in a paper bag, and storing in a cool, dry place for 2 or 3 days.

Potato cakes
4 large or 5 medium potatoes
2 eggs plus 1 egg white, beaten
2 tablespoons low-fat milk
2 tablespoons unbleached flour

"The Dutch are a potato-loving people, and why not, when they can cook them so well—as in their unique fried potatoes."

—J. George Frederick
The Pennsylvania Dutch and Their Cookery, 1935

Make-ahead suggestions for

A Pennsylvania Dutch Easter Lunch

A day ahead:

• *Make the Beet-dyed Eggs.*

• *Make the Corn Relish.*

• *Prepare the Basic Pastry Crust (page 260) for the Shoofly Pie. Wrap tightly and refrigerate.*

1 small onion, finely grated
2 tablespoons minced fresh parsley
salt and freshly ground pepper to taste

Fried tomatoes
²⁄₃ cup cornmeal
¹⁄₄ teaspoon dried thyme
salt and freshly ground pepper to taste
4 large tomatoes, sliced ¹⁄₄ inch thick

Cook or microwave the potatoes until they are about half done (a knife can be inserted with some resistance). Peel and then grate them in a food processor or on a coarse hand grater. In a mixing bowl, combine them with the eggs, milk, flour, onion, parsley, and salt and pepper to taste. Mix thoroughly.

Spray the bottom of a heavy, nonstick skillet or griddle with cooking oil spray. Spoon enough of the potato mixture onto the skillet to make 3-inch cakes. Fry on both sides over medium heat until golden brown and crisp. Drain on paper towels and keep warm in a covered casserole dish as the rest are being made.

Combine the cornmeal and thyme and season to taste with salt and pepper. Spray additional oil into the same skillet. Dredge the tomato slices in the cornmeal mixture and fry over moderate heat on both sides until the breading is golden brown. Drain on paper towels.

Arrange the potato cakes and tomato slices on a platter, either in overlapping rows or on opposite sides of the platter. Serve warm.

Calories: 196	Total fat: 2 g	Protein: 6 g
Carbohydrate: 38 g	Cholesterol: 61 g	Sodium: 44 mg

DUTCH CUCUMBER SALAD

6 to 8 servings

2 large cucumbers, peeled and sliced
salt
1 small onion, minced, or 2 scallions, thinly sliced
2 tablespoons apple cider vinegar
³⁄₄ cup reduced-fat sour cream or plain low-fat yogurt

1 teaspoon dried tarragon
freshly ground pepper

Place the cucumber slices in a colander. Salt them lightly and let them stand for 30 minutes. Pour them out onto several thicknesses of paper towels, and pat out as much moisture as possible. Combine the cucumbers with the remaining ingredients in a mixing bowl and toss to combine thoroughly. Transfer to a serving container to serve.

Calories: 46	Total fat: 2 g	Protein: 2 g
Carbohydrate: 5 g	Cholesterol: 9 g	Sodium: 324 mg

CORN RELISH

Makes about 2 cups

Relishes are a constant feature of Pennsylvania Dutch meals, and are part of the "sweets and sours," condiments that are intrinsic to this cuisine.

1 ½ cups cooked fresh or thawed frozen corn kernels
    (from about 2 medium ears)
¼ cup minced red onion
1 small red bell pepper, minced
3 tablespoons honey
3 tablespoons cider vinegar
½ teaspoon dry mustard
¼ teaspoon dill seed, optional
salt and freshly ground pepper to taste

Combine all the ingredients in a mixing bowl and stir until thoroughly mixed. Pack into 1 or 2 glass jars with lids. Make up to 2 days ahead of time, or at least 2 hours before serving.

Calories: 55	Total fat: 0 g	Protein: 1 g
Carbohydrate: 13 g	Cholesterol: 0 g	Sodium: 2 mg

". . . To make a company table groan properly with heartiness, there must be **seven sweets and seven sours.** *The Pennsylvania Dutch cuisine has always insisted that a dinner is quite incomplete . . . without several types of sours and preserves."*

—J. George Frederick
The Pennsylvania Dutch and Their Cookery, 1935

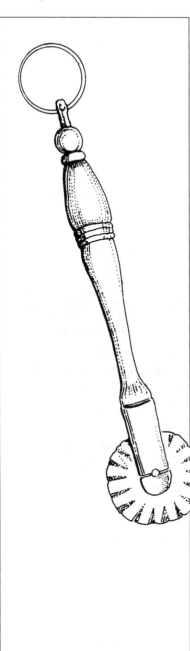

SHOOFLY PIE

Makes 1 9-inch pie, 6 to 8 servings

The quintessential Pennsylvania Dutch dessert.

Crumb mixture
**3 tablespoons reduced-fat margarine, softened and
    cut into bits**
$^3/_4$ cup whole wheat pastry flour
$^1/_3$ cup firmly packed light brown sugar
1 teaspoon cinnamon
**$^1/_4$ teaspoon each: ground ginger, ground cloves,
    and salt**

$^1/_2$ cup molasses
$^1/_2$ teaspoon baking soda
1 recipe Basic Pastry Crust (page 260)

Preheat the oven to 375 degrees.

In a mixing bowl, combine the ingredients for the crumb mixture. Work the margarine into the mixture with a pastry blender or the tines of a fork until the mixture resembles a coarse meal.

In another bowl, dissolve the molasses in $^1/_2$ cup of boiling water. Sprinkle in the baking soda and stir until it dissolves. Add about $^2/_3$ of the crumb mixture and stir together until the crumbs are moistened; the mixture need not be smooth. Pour into the prepared crust and top with the remaining crumbs. Bake for 30 to 35 minutes, or until the crust and crumbs are golden and the filling is set. Serve warm or at room temperature.

Calories: 264	Total fat: 5 g	Protein: 4 g
Carbohydrate: 51 g	Cholesterol: 0 g	Sodium: 294 mg

AN EASTER LUNCH OR DINNER TO CELEBRATE THE SPRING

6 to 8 servings

Cream of Leek and Asparagus Soup

Zucchini, Tomato, and Red Onion Salad

Lemony Bulgur with String Beans and Walnuts

Spring Vegetable Pie

Roasted Potatoes and Tomatoes with Rosemary

Almost-Spring Fruit Bowl

Italian Easter Rice Pudding

Additions to the menu: Hazelnut-stuffed Mushrooms (page 236) make a nice appetizer for this meal. Serve fresh bread or rolls of your choice with the soup.

Contains eggs and dairy products. Lemony Bulgur with String Beans and Walnuts is provided as an alternative main dish for vegans and those on dairy-free diets. Follow suggestions within the other recipes to adapt to vegan, and omit rice pudding.

To welcome spring, this vegetarian Easter menu celebrates the new season with the delicate green flavors so long absent—pale green leeks, new asparagus, young string beans, and a vegetable-filled pie enlivened by the tang of feta or goat cheese.

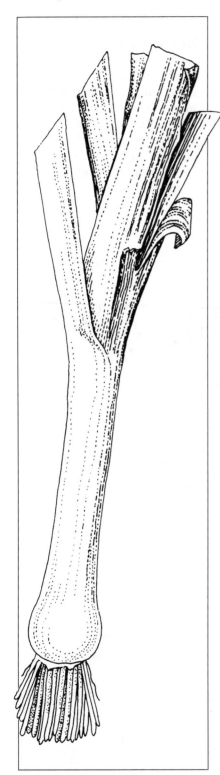

CREAM OF LEEK AND ASPARAGUS SOUP

6 to 8 servings

This delicate spring soup tastes even better if made a day ahead.

1 tablespoon canola oil
1 cup chopped onion
2 large celery stalks, diced
1 ½ pounds asparagus
6 large leeks, white and palest green parts only,
**   chopped and well rinsed**
2 medium potatoes, peeled and finely diced
Light Vegetable Stock (page 260) or water with
**   2 vegetable bouillon cubes**
½ teaspoon each: dried tarragon and dried basil
¼ cup chopped fresh parsley
1 to 1 ½ cups low-fat milk or soymilk, as needed
salt and freshly ground pepper to taste

Heat the oil in a large soup pot. Add the onion and celery and sauté over moderate heat until the onion is golden.

Trim about 1 inch from the bottoms of the asparagus stalks. Scrape the skin from the bottom half of the stalks and cut them into l-inch pieces. Set aside the tips and add the remaining pieces to the soup pot along with the leeks, potatoes, dried herbs, and just enough stock or water to barely cover (if using water, add the bouillon cubes as well). Bring to a boil, then lower heat and simmer, covered, until the vegetables are tender, about 20 to 25 minutes.

Puree the soup in batches and return to the soup pot. Return to low heat. Stir in the parsley and enough milk to achieve a slightly thick consistency. Season to taste with salt and pepper. Simmer over very low heat for 10 minutes. If time allows, let the soup stand for several hours off the heat, or, if making ahead, let cool and refrigerate until needed.

Just before serving, steam the reserved asparagus tips until bright green and crisp-tender. Stir into the soup and serve.

Calories: 168	Total fat: 3 g	Protein: 5 g
Carbohydrate: 30 g	Cholesterol: 2 g	Sodium: 61 mg

ZUCCHINI, TOMATO, AND RED ONION SALAD

6 to 8 servings

2 medium-small zucchinis, about $3/4$ pound total,
    thinly sliced
1 pound ripe plum tomatoes, sliced crosswise
$2/3$ cup thinly sliced red onion
$1/4$ cup chopped fresh parsley
1 tablespoon olive oil
juice of $1/2$ lemon, or more to taste
dash ground cumin
salt and freshly ground pepper to taste
curly red- or green-leaf lettuce
$1/4$ cup sliced black olives

Combine all the ingredients except the last 2 in a mixing bowl. Toss well and cover. Refrigerate for an hour or 2, but not more, before serving.

Arrange curly-edged lettuce on a large serving platter (an oval-shaped plate works nicely). Arrange the salad over the lettuce, then sprinkle with the olives.

Calories: 51	Total fat: 2 g	Protein: 1 g
Carbohydrate: 5 g	Cholesterol: 0 g	Sodium: 44 mg

LEMONY BULGUR WITH STRING BEANS AND WALNUTS

6 to 8 servings

The bulgur is filling and hearty, but the lemony flavor and the young string beans give this dish its touch of spring.

$3/4$ cup raw bulgur (presteamed cracked wheat)
1 tablespoon olive oil
1 large onion, quartered and sliced
2 cloves garlic, minced
1 cup sliced mushrooms
1 cup canned or cooked navy beans
    (see Bean Basics, page 261)

Make-ahead suggestions for

An Easter Lunch or Dinner to Celebrate the Spring

A day ahead:

- *Make the Cream of Leek and Asparagus Soup.*

- *Cook the bulgur for Lemony Bulgur with String Beans and Walnuts.*

- *Precook or microwave the potatoes for Roasted Potatoes and Tomatoes with Rosemary.*

- *Cook the rice for Italian Easter Rice Pudding.*

2 cups slender string beans, cut into 1-inch lengths
   and steamed crisp-tender
3 tablespoons finely chopped walnuts
2 to 3 tablespoons minced fresh dill
juice of 1 lemon, more or less to taste
2 tablespoons soy sauce or tamari, or to taste
freshly ground pepper to taste

Place the bulgur in a heatproof dish. Pour 1 ½ cups of boiling water over it and cover until the water is absorbed, about 30 minutes. Fluff with a fork.

Heat the oil in a large skillet or wok. Add the onion and sauté until translucent. Add the garlic and continue to sauté until the onion is lightly browned. Add the mushrooms; cover and "sweat" until they are wilted. Stir in the bulgur and all remaining ingredients and cook over low heat, stirring frequently, for 10 minutes. Transfer to a covered casserole dish to serve.

Calories: 164	Total fat: 4 g	Protein: 6 g
Carbohydrate: 26 g	Cholesterol: 0 g	Sodium: 292 mg

SPRING VEGETABLE PIE

6 to 8 servings

A crustless pie filled with the flavors of spring and the tang of sharp cheese.

2 medium carrots, quartered lengthwise and sliced
1 cup finely chopped cauliflower
3 scallions, minced
½ cup steamed fresh or thawed frozen green peas
2 tablespoons minced fresh parsley
3 eggs, beaten
2 tablespoons low-fat milk
4 ounces crumbled feta or crumbly goat cheese
¼ teaspoon dried thyme
freshly ground pepper
½ cup fine fresh bread crumbs

Preheat the oven to 375 degrees.

Heat ¼ cup water in a large saucepan. Add the carrots and cauliflower and steam, covered, over moderate heat. Lift the lid and stir occasionally until crisp-tender. Stir in the scallions and steam for another minute or so, just until they become slightly limp. Stir in the peas and parsley and remove from the heat.

In a mixing bowl, combine the beaten eggs with the milk, feta or goat cheese, and thyme. Stir in the skillet mixture and add a few grindings of pepper.

Oil a 10-inch tart pan. Line the bottom with half the crumbs and pour the vegetable mixture in. Top with the remaining crumbs. Bake for 20 to 25 minutes, or until set and the top is golden. Let stand for 10 minutes before serving, then cut into 6 to 8 wedges to serve.

Calories: 108	Total fat: 6 g	Protein: 6 g
Carbohydrate: 7 g	Cholesterol: 106 g	Sodium: 241 mg

In Ireland, a meal of eggs at dawn on Easter breaks the fast of Lent.

Egg-rolling parties have long been popular the world over and have for many years been an annual event on the White House lawn in Washington, D.C.

ROASTED POTATOES AND TOMATOES WITH ROSEMARY

6 to 8 servings

Roasted potatoes, flavored with rosemary, were a traditional dish of the old Roman Easter. Here is a contemporary interpretation of this dish.

6 medium potatoes, preferably long and narrow
4 to 6 firm ripe plum tomatoes, sliced crosswise
olive oil
1 tablespoon minced fresh rosemary, or 1 teaspoon dried
minced chives
salt and freshly ground pepper to taste

Preheat the oven to 375 degrees.

Cook, bake, or microwave the potatoes in their skins until done but still nice and firm. Peel and slice crosswise ½ inch thick.

Oil a large, shallow baking dish. Alternate the potato

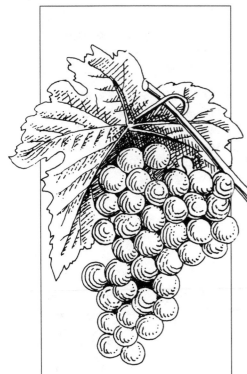

slices with the tomato slices in rows. Drizzle lightly with olive oil, then sprinkle with the rosemary, chives, salt, and pepper. Bake for 20 to 25 minutes, or until the potatoes begin to turn golden and crisp around the edges.

Calories: 134	Total fat: 1 g	Protein: 2 g
Carbohydrate: 27 g	Cholesterol: 0 g	Sodium: 13 mg

ALMOST-SPRING FRUIT BOWL

6 to 8 servings

It's not quite time for the fruits of spring, but this salad makes the most of this in-between season for a luscious and refreshing finale to the meal.

3 bosc pears, quartered, cored, and diced
2 small oranges, sectioned and seeded
1 cup green or red seedless grapes
$\frac{1}{2}$ cup chopped dried apricots
l-pound can unsweetened pineapple chunks, drained
$\frac{1}{4}$ cup maple syrup
$\frac{1}{2}$ teaspoon grated fresh ginger
2 teaspoons lemon juice

Combine the first 5 ingredients in a serving container. In a small bowl, stir together the maple syrup, ginger, and lemon juice. Toss with the fruits. Cover and refrigerate until needed. Serve on dessert plates alongside squares of Rice Pudding (recipe follows).

Calories: 167	Total fat: 0 g	Protein: 1 g
Carbohydrate: 39 g	Cholesterol: 0 g	Sodium: 4 mg

ITALIAN EASTER RICE PUDDING

8 servings

The contributor of this recipe remembers this as an Eastertime favorite when her family was growing up.

²/₃ cup raw brown rice, preferably medium-grain
1 pound part-skim ricotta cheese
²/₃ cup firmly packed light brown sugar,
   more or less to taste
¹/₄ cup low-fat milk
1 teaspoon vanilla extract
dash nutmeg
cinnamon for topping

Bring 2 cups of water to a boil in a small saucepan. Stir in the rice. Bring to a gentle simmer, then cover and cook until the water is absorbed, about 35 minutes.

Preheat the oven to 350 degrees.

Combine the rice with the remaining ingredients except the cinnamon in a mixing bowl and stir together. Pour into a lightly oiled, square 9- by 9-inch casserole dish, preferably glass. Bake for 1 to 1 ¹/₄ hours, or until the top and sides are golden and slightly crusty. Let cool and serve slightly warm or at room temperature.

| Calories: 235 | Total fat: 4 g | Protein: 9 g |
| Carbohydrate: 39 g | Cholesterol: 18 g | Sodium: 83 mg |

"'Twas Easter Sunday. The full blossomed trees
Filled all the air with fragrance and with joy."

—Henry Wadsworth
   Longfellow (1807-1882)
   "The Spanish Student"

In America, the holiday honoring St. Patrick, the patron saint of Ireland, is noted with parades, decorating everything from shop windows to clothing with green shamrocks, and drinking ale in saloons. Traditionally, however, St. Patrick's Day in Ireland is a considerably lower-keyed religious holiday that includes church services.

This menu highlights several fascinating and flavorful traditional Irish dishes. The Irish cuisine is a very basic and homey one, seasoned with a rich historic legacy rather than savory spices. Though it does not utilize a wide variety of vegetables, its use of bland and basic ones such as potatoes, leeks, cabbages, and cauliflower is satisfying and hearty.

IRISH CLASSICS FOR ST. PATRICK'S DAY

6 servings

Irish Soda Bread

**Slane Salad
(Watercress, Apples, Carrots, and Bitter Greens with Garlicky French Dressing)**

Cauliflower, Cheddar, and Bread Panada

Colcannon

Apple and Oat Crisp

---

*Contains eggs and dairy products.
To adapt to vegan, follow the suggested alternatives within the recipes. Only Soda Bread cannot be adapted, since buttermilk is essential to its character.*

IRISH SODA BREAD

Makes 2 loaves

2 ½ cups whole wheat flour
2 ½ cups unbleached white flour
2 ½ teaspoons baking soda
1 ½ teaspoons salt
1 tablespoon granulated sugar
2 cups buttermilk
⅓ cup canola oil
low-fat milk

Preheat the oven to 400 degrees.
Combine the first 5 ingredients in a mixing bowl. Make a

well in the center and pour in the buttermilk and oil. Work together, first with a wooden spoon, then with hands to form a dough. Add additional flour if necessary until the dough loses its stickiness. Knead for 2 to 3 minutes on a well-floured board. Divide in half and shape into rounds. Score a shallow cross down the centers with a sharp knife and brush the tops with milk.

Arrange the dough rounds on a floured baking sheet. Bake for 45 to 50 minutes, or until the tops are nicely browned and a knife inserted into the center tests clean. Cool on a rack. Wrap the extra loaf tightly in foil, then plastic, until needed.

Per $^3/_4$-inch-thick slice:

Calories: 178	Total fat: 6 g	Protein: 5 g
Carbohydrate: 28 g	Cholesterol: 1 g	Sodium: 217 mg

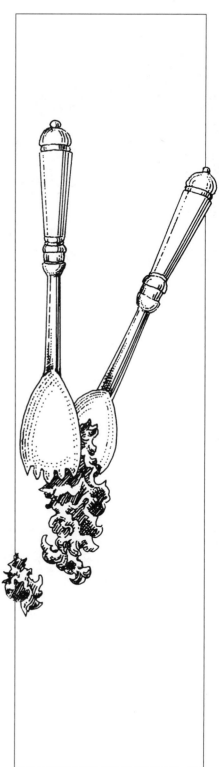

SLANE SALAD
(Watercress, Apples, Carrots, and Bitter Greens with Garlicky French Dressing)

6 servings

This salad is traditionally made with sorrel; however, sorrel is rarely available in March in this country, and not everyone likes its sour taste. As a substitute, use dark, sharp greens—chicory is quite bitter, and escarole is milder—just enough bite without being overpowering.

1 cup firmly packed watercress leaves
2 medium carrots, sliced
2 medium Granny Smith apples, peeled and
    diced
sorrel, escarole, or chicory as needed
French Dressing, as needed (page 257)

Combine the salad ingredients in a serving bowl. Pour enough dressing over the salad to moisten it. Toss together well and serve at once.

Calories: 76	Total fat: 3 g	Protein: 1 g
Carbohydrate: 11 g	Cholesterol: 0 g	Sodium: 46 mg

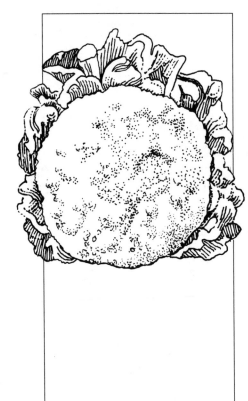

CAULIFLOWER, CHEDDAR, AND BREAD PANADA

6 servings

A panada is a savory pudding made with bread crumbs. You can make this one without the eggs; the flavor won't suffer at all, but the texture will be less cohesive.

1 tablespoon canola oil
1 cup finely chopped onion
2 cloves garlic, minced
3 cups finely chopped cauliflower
4 cups fresh bread crumbs
1 $3/4$ cups low-fat milk or soymilk
1 $1/2$ cups grated reduced-fat cheddar cheese
    or cheddar-style soy cheese
1 egg plus 1 egg white, beaten, optional
2 tablespoons minced fresh parsley
1 teaspoon dry mustard
dash of cayenne pepper
salt to taste

Preheat the oven to 375 degrees.

Heat the oil in a large skillet. Add the onion and sauté over moderate heat until translucent. Add the garlic and continue to sauté until the onion is golden. Stir in the cauliflower along with just enough water to moisten the bottom of the skillet. Cover and "sweat" until the cauliflower is crisp-tender. Remove from the heat.

In a mixing bowl, combine the bread crumbs and milk. Stir in the cheese and optional beaten eggs. Add the cauliflower mixture, parsley, and seasonings. Stir together thoroughly. Pour into an oiled, shallow 9- by 13-inch baking casserole or a 13-inch round casserole. Bake for 35 to 40 minutes, or until the top begins to turn crusty. Let stand 5 to 10 minutes, then cut into wedges or squares and serve.

Calories: 244	Total fat: 10 g	Protein: 14 g
Carbohydrate: 24 g	Cholesterol: 25 g	Sodium: 401 mg

COLCANNON

6 servings

In this Irish classic, the combination of potatoes and cabbage, browned in a skillet and embellished with lots of scallions, becomes uncommonly tasty.

1 tablespoon canola oil
2 cups finely chopped white cabbage
6 scallions, white and green parts, sliced
4 large potatoes, cooked, peeled, and coarsely mashed
1 cup low-fat milk or soymilk
2 tablespoons minced fresh parsley
salt and freshly ground pepper to taste

Heat the oil in a large skillet. Add the cabbage and sauté, covered, over moderate heat. Lift the lid and stir occasionally, until it is limp. Add the scallions and sauté, uncovered, until the cabbage begins to turn golden. If the skillet becomes dry, add small amounts of water as needed.

Combine the potatoes and milk in a mixing bowl and stir together. Turn the heat up to moderately high and stir the potatoes and parsley in with the cabbage mixture in the skillet. Sauté without stirring until the bottom of the mixture gets nicely browned. Fluff with a wooden spoon, then season to taste with salt and pepper and serve.

Calories: 161	Total fat: 2 g	Protein: 3 g
Carbohydrate: 31 g	Cholesterol: 2 g	Sodium: 32 mg

APPLE AND OAT CRISP

6 servings

The use of oats in Irish desserts is widespread. This is not much different from the apple crisps familiar to most Americans.

4 to 5 medium apples, peeled, cored, quartered,
    and thinly sliced
1/4 cup finely chopped pecans or walnuts
1/2 teaspoon each: cinnamon, ground ginger
dash nutmeg

3 tablespoons apple juice concentrate

Topping
1 tablespoon reduced-fat margarine
³⁄₄ cup oatmeal
¹⁄₄ cup light brown sugar
¹⁄₂ teaspoon cinnamon
frozen vanilla nonfat yogurt, or nondairy frozen dessert

Preheat the oven to 350 degrees.

Combine the apples, nuts, spices, and juice concentrate in a mixing bowl and toss until the spices coat the apples evenly. Transfer to a 9- by 9-inch baking pan.

Melt the margarine in a skillet. Stir in the oats until evenly coated with the margarine. Remove from the heat and stir in the sugar and cinnamon. Sprinkle the topping evenly over the apples.

Bake for 45 minutes, or until the topping is golden brown and the apples are tender. Serve warm over frozen yogurt or nondairy dessert.

Calories: 291	Total fat: 4 g	Protein: 6 g
Carbohydrate: 56 g	Cholesterol: 0 g	Sodium: 92 mg

Chapter 4

PASSOVER

One of the most ancient of religious festivals still celebrated, Passover is also the most widely observed Jewish holiday. Commemorating the deliverance of the Jews from slavery in Egypt, Passover lasts for eight days and most often falls in April, according to the dates of the Hebrew calendar.

The central event of the holiday, the Seder, is a service and feast in which families gather around the table and recount the story of the Exodus as told by the *Haggadah* (Passover prayer book). The sampling of many symbolic foods and the drinking of wine are major components of this ritual.

Passover, or Pesach, as it is called in Hebrew and Yiddish, is also known as the "Feast of the Unleavened Bread." The holiday's most symbolic food, the matzo, represents the bread made by the Jews just before they fled Egypt, when there was no time to let it leaven. Before the Passover holiday begins, observant households are cleared of bread and any other leavened products, and during the week, only matzo may be eaten.

Though there is flexibility in what may be served for the meal itself, following the reading of the *Haggadah*, there are also many restrictions. Many Jews avoid, aside from bread-related products, any other grains and legumes—not an easy task for vegetarians. However, since Passover once had a strong seasonal festival aspect, produce heralding the arrival of spring is most welcome and used in abundance.

The two menus given here incorporate various traditions of Ashkenazic (Eastern European) and Sephardic (Far, Near, and Middle Eastern) Passover Seders.

"Today you go forth in the month of Spring, for lo, the winter is past, the rain is over and gone. The flowers are seen in the land: The time of the nightingale is come and the turtle-dove is heard in our land. The fig-tree perfumes its green figs and the vines with young grapes are fragrant."

—Song of Songs

AN EASTERN EUROPEAN (ASHKENAZIC) SEDER

8 to 10 servings

**Mock Chopped Liver
(Cashew, Onion, and String Bean Pâté)**

Haroset

Salted Eggs

Spring Vegetable Soup with Matzo Balls

Leek and Potato Gratin

Mushroom Matzo Farfel Pie

Carrot-Apple Pudding

Fruit Compote

Dessert of your choice from Passover Baking and More (pages 66 to 70)

Additions to the menu: Though this is a large and filling meal, a simple lettuce and tomato salad may be added.

Contains eggs and dairy products.

MOCK CHOPPED LIVER
(Cashew, Onion, and String Bean Pâté)

Makes about 2 cups

This spread resembles chopped liver in an uncanny way, but its delicious flavor is something else and will not be off-putting to vegetarians who don't care for imitation meat flavors. Serve with raw vegetables or with matzo crackers.

1 ½ tablespoons canola oil
1 ½ cups chopped onions
²/₃ cup toasted cashews
1 cup steamed fresh string beans, cut into l-inch lengths,
    or 1 cup thawed frozen string beans
1 tablespoon lemon juice
salt and freshly ground pepper to taste

Heat the oil in a small skillet. Sauté the onions slowly over moderately low heat, stirring frequently, until nicely browned.

Combine the onions with the remaining ingredients in the container of a food processor. Process until smoothly pureed, scraping down the sides as needed. Store in a jar until needed, and bring to room temperature before serving.

Per 2-tablespoon serving:
Calories: 53	Total fat: 4 g	Protein: 1 g
Carbohydrate: 4 g	Cholesterol: 0 g	Sodium: 2 mg

HAROSET

Makes about 2 cups

Eastern European-style haroset is always made of essentially the same few ingredients, though proportions may be varied to taste. One of the important symbolic dishes of Passover, haroset represents the bricks used by the Jewish slaves to build Pharaoh's cities.

2 large sweet apples, peeled, cored, and diced
²/₃ cup walnuts
¼ cup sweet Passover wine

Suggested timetable for

An Eastern European (Ashkenazic) Seder

A day ahead:

- *Make the Mock Chopped Liver. Store in an airtight container, refrigerated, and bring to room temperature before serving.*

- *Hard-boil the eggs for Salted Eggs.*

- *Make the Spring Vegetable Soup. Cool, then refrigerate, covered, until needed.*

- *Make the Matzo Balls according to package directions on matzo meal. Store, refrigerated, separately from the soup, and add to the soup while it heats.*

- *Bake or microwave the potatoes for Leek and Potato Gratin.*

(timetable continues . . .)

Same day, morning:

- *Make the Fruit Compote. Refrigerate, covered, until needed.*

- *Make any dessert from Passover Baking and More (pages 66 to 70), if desired.*

- *Make the Haroset. Refrigerate, covered, until needed.*

Starting about 3 hours before serving:

- *Make the Carrot-Apple Pudding and bake.*

- *Assemble the Leek and Potato Gratin.*

- *Assemble the Mushroom Matzo Farfel Pie.*

- *Remove Mock Chopped Liver from the refrigerator.*

1 to 2 teaspoons honey, to taste
1 teaspoon cinnamon
dash each: nutmeg, allspice

Combine all the ingredients in the container of a food processor. Process until coarsely pureed. Store in an airtight container until needed.

Per 2-tablespoon serving:

Calories: 49	Total fat: 3 g	Protein: 1 g
Carbohydrate: 5 g	Cholesterol: 0 g	Sodium: 1 mg

SALTED EGGS

8 to 10 servings

Another important symbolic dish in the Seder, eggs represent the eternal memory of the loss of the Holy Temple, and the salt water represents the tears shed by the Jewish people.

6 hard-boiled eggs, chopped
2 scallions, minced
salt to taste

Combine the ingredients with 6 cups of water in a serving container. Cover and refrigerate until needed. Serve each guest a small portion in a small, shallow bowl.

Calories: 53	Total fat: 4 g	Protein: 4 g
Carbohydrate: 0 g	Cholesterol: 142 g	Sodium: 46 mg

SPRING VEGETABLE SOUP WITH MATZO BALLS

8 to 10 servings

Matzo ball soup is served at many Jewish festivities, but never more appropriately than at Passover. Most often, the soup is the classic Jewish chicken soup, but here we substitute a light soup chock-full of spring vegetables.

1 ½ tablespoons canola oil

1 large onion, finely chopped
2 medium celery stalks, finely diced
1 medium potato, peeled and finely diced
2 medium carrots, finely diced
2 vegetable bouillon cubes
handful of celery leaves
1 cup canned diced tomatoes
½ teaspoon ground cumin
2 cups finely chopped cauliflower
salt and freshly ground black pepper to taste
1 cup firmly packed, finely shredded lettuce
1 cup steamed fresh or thawed frozen green peas
1 tablespoon minced fresh dill, or more, to taste
2 scallions, minced
matzo balls (see Note, following)

Heat the oil in a large soup pot. Add the onion and celery and sauté over moderate heat until golden. Add the potato, carrots, bouillon cubes, celery leaves, tomatoes, and cumin. Cover with 6 cups of water and bring to a boil. Simmer gently over medium heat, covered, for 15 minutes, or until the vegetables are nearly tender. Add the cauliflower and continue to simmer for 10 minutes more, or until it is crisp-tender.

Season to taste with salt and pepper and remove from the heat. Let the soup cool, then refrigerate overnight to allow time for it to develop flavor. Just before serving, heat the soup through. Add the remaining ingredients and simmer over very low heat for 10 to 15 minutes. Add more water if the vegetables seem crowded, then adjust the seasonings.

Note: For the matzo balls, you will need a box of Passover matzo ball mix on which you'll find a standard recipe for matzo balls. Increase the recipe so that there will be 3 or 4 matzo balls for each serving of soup. If you'd like, substitute an extra egg white for 1 or 2 of the egg yolks called for in the recipe. Vegans, substitute a sprinkling of matzo farfel (coarse crumbs made of matzo flour, available in boxes from the supermarket), since matzo balls are made with eggs.

Per serving with 3 matzo balls:
Calories: 211	Total fat: 6 g	Protein: 10 g
Carbohydrate: 28 g	Cholesterol: 142 g	Sodium: 91 mg

Starting about 1 hour before serving:

- *Assemble the Seder plate (sidebar, page 58).*

- *Bake the Leek and Potato Gratin.*

- *Bake the Mushroom Matzo Farfel Pie.*

- *Serve Mock Chopped Liver to any guests already present.*

- *Make the Salted Eggs.*

30 minutes before serving:

- *Heat the Spring Vegetable Soup with Matzo Balls.*

The Passover Table and Seder Plate

With the service and the meal, a plate of matzos is served and replenished as needed, as is plenty of Passover wine. Central to the table is the Seder plate, a round dish with designated spots for placement of the symbolic foods to be sampled during the reading of the Haggadah. The foods are not eaten from this plate, but everyone gets a sampling of the foods to be tasted from separate platters; the Haggadah acts as a guide. Here are the foods included on the Seder plate:

- Karpas: *A mild green vegetable or herb, such as celery or parsley. This symbolizes the new growth of spring. It is sometimes dipped into salt water or vinegar as a reminder of the tears of the enslaved Jews.*

- Maror: *A bitter herb, usually horseradish for Ashkenazic Jews or a bitter green such as escarole for Sephardic Jews. This represents the bitterness of slavery suffered by the Jews in Egypt.*

LEEK AND POTATO GRATIN

8 to 10 servings

Since so many staples, including grains other than wheat, and legumes, are forbidden during Passover, an astonishing number of dishes have developed that are made in some way from matzos. This is an elegant example.

2 tablespoons reduced-fat margarine
2 large leeks, white parts only, chopped and well rinsed
1 small red bell pepper, finely diced
3 matzos, broken
4 medium potatoes, baked, peeled, and sliced
6 ounces evaporated skim milk
salt and freshly ground pepper to taste
1 cup grated mild white cheese, such as Monterey Jack or Muenster
minced chives or scallions for topping

Preheat the oven to 350 degrees.

Heat the margarine in a medium-sized skillet. Add the leeks and sauté, covered, until they are wilted. Add the red pepper and sauté another 5 minutes.

In the meantime, combine the matzos with 1 cup of hot water in a bowl and soak for 3 to 5 minutes until soft. Drain and squeeze out excess water with hands.

Combine the leek mixture and matzos with all the remaining ingredients except cheese and chives in a mixing bowl. Stir together until thoroughly mixed. Pour into an oiled, shallow 2-quart casserole. A round dish is particularly attractive. Sprinkle the cheese over the top, followed by the chives. Bake for 35 to 40 minutes, or until the top is golden. Let stand for 5 to 10 minutes, then cut into squares or wedges to serve.

| Calories: 184 | Total fat: 4 g | Protein: 7 g |
| Carbohydrate: 27 g | Cholesterol: 12 g | Sodium: 122 mg |

MUSHROOM MATZO FARFEL PIE

6 to 8 servings

I always liked this tasty dish that my sister-in-law makes for her Seders, and now include it in mine.

1 teaspoon seasoned salt
1 box (1 pound) matzo farfel (coarse crumbs
    made of matzo flour)
1 tablespoon reduced-fat margarine
1 cup finely chopped onion
1 pound mushrooms, chopped
1 medium zucchini, quartered lengthwise and sliced
3 egg whites, beaten
seasoned salt to taste
freshly ground pepper to taste

Preheat the oven to 350 degrees.

Stir the seasoned salt into 1 cup of hot water. Combine with the matzo farfel in a heatproof mixing bowl and let soak.

In the meantime, heat the margarine in a large skillet. Add the onion and sauté over moderate heat until golden. Add the mushrooms and zucchini and sauté until the mushrooms are wilted.

Drain any excess water from the matzo farfel. Add the mushroom mixture and the beaten egg whites. Season to taste with additional seasoned salt, if desired, and freshly ground pepper. Pour into an oiled 9-inch glass pie plate or 10-inch tart pan. Bake, covered, for 30 minutes. Uncover and bake another 15 minutes, or until the top is browned. Let stand for 5 to 10 minutes, then cut into wedges to serve.

Calories: 302	Total fat: 1 g	Protein: 10 g
Carbohydrate: 61 g	Cholesterol: 0 g	Sodium: 342 mg

- Haroset: *This mixture of nuts, wine, and apples, as Ashkenazic Jews make it, or nuts, wine, and dried fruits, as Sephardic Jews make it, has a bricklike color that symbolizes the bricks used by the Jewish slaves to build Pharaoh's cities.*

- Hazeret: *Another bitter herb or green, such as watercress or chicory. Some believe that two bitter herbs should be tasted, though this component of the Seder plate is optional.*

- Zoreah: *A shank bone, this represents the paschal lamb whose blood was said to be on the doorsteps of the homes of the Israelites on the eve of the Exodus. Not likely to be an item that a vegetarian family would include on their Seder plate, and, quite honestly, I've been to many a Seder where this item has not been included at all.*

- Baytzah: *An egg, hard-boiled and roasted. Eggs symbolize the eternal mourning for the loss of the Holy Temple.*

CARROT-APPLE PUDDING

6 to 8 servings

5 large carrots, grated
2 medium apples, peeled, cored, and grated
¹⁄₃ cup raisins
3 egg whites, lightly beaten
2 tablespoons canola oil
¹⁄₄ cup sweet Passover wine
¹⁄₄ cup packed brown sugar
1 teaspoon cinnamon
¹⁄₄ teaspoon each: ground allspice, nutmeg, and ginger

Preheat the oven to 325 degrees.

Combine all the ingredients in a mixing bowl. Pour into an oiled 9- by 5- by 3-inch loaf pan. Cover and bake for 45 minutes. Uncover and bake another 40 to 45 minutes, or until the top is nicely browned and crusty. Let cool. Slice and serve warm or at room temperature.

Calories: 136	Total fat: 3 g	Protein: 2 g
Carbohydrate: 21 g	Cholesterol: 0 g	Sodium: 52 mg

FRUIT COMPOTE

6 to 8 servings

A compote of cooked fruit is a common way to end a festive Jewish holiday meal. It acts as a palate refresher and a prelude to dessert—for those who still have room!

3 medium firm pears, peeled, quartered, cored, and sliced
3 medium tart apples, peeled, cored, quartered, and sliced
1 cup apple juice
¹⁄₄ cup dry white or red kosher wine
1 stick cinnamon
6 whole cloves
¹⁄₂ cup golden raisins
1 tablespoon lemon juice

Combine all but the last 2 ingredients in a saucepan. Bring to a simmer, then cover and cook over moderate heat until the fruit is soft, about 15 to 20 minutes. Stir in the raisins and lemon juice and let cool, then chill, covered, until needed. Bring to the table in individual dessert bowls or parfait glasses.

Calories: 130	Total fat: 0 g	Protein: 1 g
Carbohydrate: 29 g	Cholesterol: 0 g	Sodium: 5 mg

A SEPHARDIC SEDER

8 to 10 servings

Date Haroset

Long-cooked Eggs (*Huevos Haminados*)

Lemony Leek and Mushroom Soup

Eggplant Matzo Mina

Potatoes with Parsley Sauce

Sautéed Carrots with Almonds

Dessert of your choice from Passover Baking and More (pages 66 to 70)

Additions to the menu: The Mock Chopped Liver from the previous menu, though Eastern European in character, is nonetheless a great Passover appetizer, and I would recommend making some as a premeal "nosh" for this menu, too. As in the first menu, you might add a simple tossed salad. For dessert, the Sephardic Wine and Fruit Pudding is particularly fitting with this menu's theme.

Long-cooked Eggs are the only eggs used in this meal. Can be made dairy-free by following the suggested substitutions in the recipes.

Suggested timetable for

A Sephardic Seder

A day ahead:

- *Make the Date Haroset. Refrigerate, covered.*

- *Make the Long-cooked Eggs.*

- *Make the Lemony Leek and Mushroom Soup.*

- *Make the parsley sauce for Potatoes with Parsley Sauce. Refrigerate, covered.*

- *Make a dessert from Passover Baking and More (pages 66 to 70), if desired.*

Starting 2 1/2 to 3 hours before serving:

- *Assemble the Eggplant Matzo Mina.*

- *Cook, bake, or microwave the potatoes in their skins for Potatoes with Parsley Sauce. Keep covered at room temperature until needed.*

- *Remove the Mock Chopped Liver from the refrigerator, if serving.*

(timetable continues . . .)

Starting 1 ½ hours before serving:

- *Assemble the Seder plate (see sidebar, page 58).*

- *Peel the Long-cooked Eggs and arrange on a platter.*

- *Finish preparing the Potatoes with Parsley Sauce.*

Starting 1 hour before serving:

- *Remove Date Haroset from the refrigerator.*

- *Bake the Eggplant Matzo Mina.*

- *Make the Sautéed Carrots with Almonds.*

- *Serve the Mock Chopped Liver, if desired, to guests already present.*

Starting 30 minutes before serving:

- *Heat the Lemony Leek and Mushroom Soup.*

DATE HAROSET

8 to 10 servings

Sephardic harosets vary widely according to culture and use a far greater variety of ingredients than the Eastern European counterpart. One of the hallmarks is the use of dried fruits. This recipe is an amalgam from several cultures.

1 cup pitted dates
½ cup dried apricots
⅓ cup walnuts
⅓ cup almonds
1 teaspoon cinnamon
¼ teaspoon ground ginger
⅓ cup orange juice
2 tablespoons sweet red Passover wine

Combine all the ingredients in the container of a food processor. Process until finely chopped. Pat into a serving container, then cover until needed.

| Calories: 135 | Total fat: 4 g | Protein: 2 g |
| Carbohydrate: 20 g | Cholesterol: 0 g | Sodium: 2 mg |

LONG-COOKED EGGS
(Huevos Haminados)

Commonly served at many Sephardic holiday meals, these are particularly typical at Sephardic Seders. The eggs are cooked or baked for many hours, turning the white a pale brown and giving the entire egg a rather creamy texture.

1 egg per guest

Place as many eggs as needed in a single layer in a large pot and cover with at least 3 times their volume in water. Bring to a boil, then cover and simmer at the lowest possible heat for 8 hours. Or, you may place the pot in a 200-degree oven overnight. Cool, then peel and arrange on a platter to serve.

| Calories: 79 | Total fat: 6 g | Protein: 7 g |
| Carbohydrate: 1 g | Cholesterol: 213 g | Sodium: 69 mg |

LEMONY LEEK AND MUSHROOM SOUP

8 to 10 servings

Leeks are a favorite vegetable among Sephardic Jews and, heightened with the lemony flavor, welcome spring in this Greek-influenced soup.

Stock
1 cup chopped onion
green tops from 2 leeks, well washed
4 sprigs parsley
1 large celery stalk, coarsely chopped
2 vegetable bouillon cubes

2 tablespoons olive oil
4 large leeks, white and lightest green parts only,
**   chopped and well rinsed**
2 medium turnips, peeled and cut into ½-inch dice
1 large celery stalk, diced
2 bay leaves
14- to 16-ounce can diced tomatoes, undrained
12 ounces white mushrooms, sliced
juice of 1 lemon, or more to taste
salt and freshly ground pepper to taste
2 to 3 tablespoons minced fresh parsley
2 to 3 tablespoons minced fresh dill
matzo farfel (coarse crumbs made of matzo flour)
**   for garnish, optional**

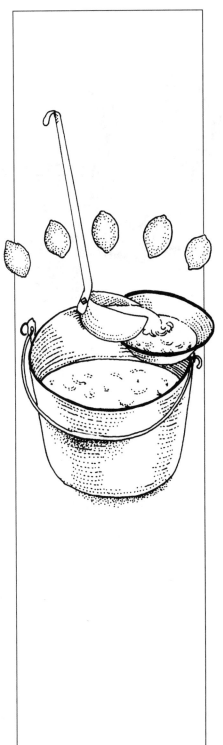

Combine all the ingredients for the stock with 7 cups of water in a soup pot. Bring to a boil, then cover and simmer for 30 minutes. Let stand until needed, then strain before using.

Heat the oil in a large soup pot. Add the chopped leeks and sauté over moderate heat, stirring frequently, until the leeks just begin to go limp. Add the stock, turnips, celery, and bay leaves. Bring to a boil, then cover and simmer for 10 minutes. Add the tomatoes and mushrooms and continue to simmer until the vegetables are tender, another 15 to 20 minutes. Season to taste with lemon juice, salt, and pepper. Remove from the heat.

Allow the soup to stand for several hours, or cool and refrigerate overnight. Before serving, heat through as needed. Stir in the parsley and dill. If the vegetables seem crowded,

adjust the consistency with more water, then adjust the seasonings and lemon juice. Top each serving with a sprinkling of matzo farfel if desired.

Calories: 111	Total fat: 2 g	Protein: 2 g
Carbohydrate: 18 g	Cholesterol: 0 g	Sodium: 53 mg

EGGPLANT MATZO MINA

8 to 10 servings

I first heard of matzo minas, which are layered casseroles or pies, from a woman from Bologna, Italy, who described them as matzo lasagnas. A fitting description, though later I discovered that many variations are made by Sephardic Jews of various cultures. This one is of definite Italian influence, and will certainly remind you of an eggplant lasagna.

2 medium eggplants, about 2 pounds total
2 tablespoons olive oil, divided
1 medium onion, finely chopped
2 cloves garlic, minced
15-ounce can tomato sauce
14- to 16-ounce can diced tomatoes, lightly drained
2 to 3 tablespoons minced fresh parsley
1/2 teaspoon each: dried oregano, dried basil,
    and paprika
salt and freshly ground pepper to taste
6 matzos
12 ounces part-skim mozzarella cheese or
    mozzarella-style soy cheese, grated (see Note)

Preheat the broiler.
Cut the eggplants into 1/2-inch slices and peel. Brush lightly with some of the oil and broil on each side until tender.
Heat the oil in a deep saucepan. Add the onion and garlic and sauté until golden. Add the tomato sauce, tomatoes, parsley, and seasonings. Bring to a simmer and cook over low heat, covered, for 15 minutes.
Break each matzo into 3 strips. Fill a shallow casserole dish with lightly salted water. Place the matzo strips in it for 2 to 3 minutes until pliable but not mushy. Remove carefully to a plate.
Preheat the oven to 350 degrees.

Lightly oil a large, shallow baking casserole and layer as follows: a thin layer of sauce, a layer of eggplant, a layer of matzo, and a layer of cheese. Repeat. Bake for 35 to 40 minutes, or until the cheese is touched with brown spots.

Note: The use of soy cheese is allowed here, unlike in the previous Passover menu. That is because many Sephardic cultures continue to use beans (and, as you know, soy cheese is derived from soybeans) during Passover, whereas the Ashkenazic tradition does not.

Calories: 262	Total fat: 8 g	Protein: 13 g
Carbohydrate: 31 g	Cholesterol: 22 g	Sodium: 496 mg

POTATOES WITH PARSLEY SAUCE

8 to 10 servings

Parsley, often the *karpas* on the Seder plate that symbolizes the new growth of spring, is used in abundance in this warm potato salad.

6 large potatoes, preferably red-skinned, scrubbed

Sauce
1 cup firmly packed fresh parsley
3 tablespoons olive oil
1 cup chopped cucumber
juice of 1/2 large lemon
2 tablespoons minced fresh dill
2 scallions, coarsely chopped
salt and freshly ground pepper to taste
poppy seeds for topping
1/4 pound crumbled feta or goat cheese for topping, optional

Cook, bake, or microwave the potatoes in their skins until done but still firm. When cool enough to handle, quarter them lengthwise and slice 1/2 inch thick.

Place the ingredients for the sauce in a food processor and process until the mixture is a smooth, thick paste. Toss at once with the potatoes. Season to taste with salt and pepper. Transfer the mixture to a shallow serving container.

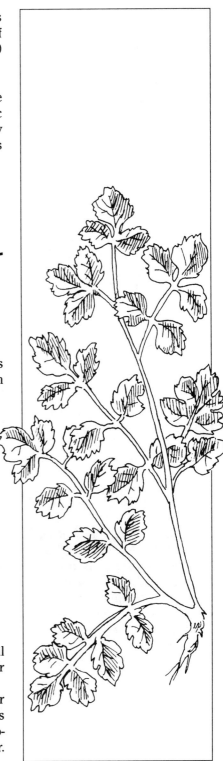

Sprinkle the top with poppy seeds and the optional feta or goat cheese. Serve warm.

Calories: 125	Total fat: 4 g	Protein: 1 g
Carbohydrate: 20 g	Cholesterol: 0 g	Sodium: 8 mg

SAUTÉED CARROTS WITH ALMONDS

8 to 10 servings

2 tablespoons reduced-fat margarine
$1/4$ cup apple juice, or more as needed
2 pounds carrots, thinly sliced
1 tablespoon lemon juice
2 to 3 tablespoons minced chives
$1/4$ cup sliced almonds
dash salt

Heat the margarine and apple juice in a large skillet. Add the carrots and sauté over moderate heat, stirring frequently, until crisp-tender and beginning to turn golden, about 10 to 15 minutes. If the skillet begins to turn dry, sprinkle in additional apple juice while sautéeing. Continue to sauté, stirring, until the carrots are just tender. Stir in the remaining ingredients, then transfer to a serving container.

Calories: 83	Total fat: 3 g	Protein: 1 g
Carbohydrate: 12 g	Cholesterol: 0 g	Sodium: 88 mg

Passover baking represents a distinct challenge, since flour and leavening agents are forbidden. Instead, products like matzo meal and matzo cake meal (a course and a fine meal, respectively, ground from matzo) are used. Here are a handful of baked goods with this unique Passover character.

PASSOVER BAKING AND MORE

Pineapple Crumble
Sephardic Wine and Fruit Pudding
Almond Macaroons
Passover Onion Biscuits
Matzo Brei

PINEAPPLE CRUMBLE

8 or more servings

Matzo meal makes a perfect crumble topping.

16-ounce can unsweetened crushed pineapple, drained
2 medium pears or apples, peeled, cored, and finely diced
1 teaspoon vanilla extract
$\frac{1}{2}$ teaspoon cinnamon
dash nutmeg

Crumb topping
2 tablespoons reduced-fat margarine
$\frac{2}{3}$ cup matzo meal
$\frac{1}{3}$ cup finely ground walnuts
$\frac{1}{2}$ cup light brown sugar
$\frac{1}{2}$ teaspoon cinnamon

vanilla nonfat frozen yogurt or nondairy frozen dessert

Preheat the oven to 350 degrees.
Combine the first 5 ingredients in a mixing bowl, then pat into a 9-inch square baking pan.
Melt the margarine in a skillet, then remove from the heat. Stir in the remaining topping ingredients until evenly coated with the margarine. Sprinkle evenly over the top of the pineapple mixture. Bake for 25 to 30 minutes, or until the crumb topping is lightly golden. Serve warm over vanilla frozen yogurt or nondairy frozen dessert.

Calories: 275	Total fat: 4 g	Protein: 5 g
Carbohydrate: 54 g	Cholesterol: 0 g	Sodium: 100 mg

"A cup of deliverance we raise to commemorate the Exodus from Egypt; from subservience to freedom, from dispersion to redemption; to life and deliverance!"

—from the Passover *Haggadah*

SEPHARDIC WINE AND FRUIT PUDDING

Makes 24 or more little squares

1/2 cup chopped dried apricots
1/2 cup chopped dates
1/3 cup raisins
3/4 cup sweet Passover wine
2 eggs plus 2 egg whites, beaten
1/4 cup honey
3/4 cup matzo cake meal
1 teaspoon cinnamon
2 tablespoons canola oil
2/3 cup finely chopped walnuts

Combine the dried fruits with the wine in a small mixing bowl. Let soak overnight or for the good part of a day, then drain off any excess wine.

Preheat the oven to 350 degrees.

Combine the remaining ingredients in a mixing bowl, then stir in the soaked fruits. Pour into an oiled 9- by 13-inch baking pan. Bake, covered, for 45 minutes, then uncover and bake for 15 minutes more, or until the pudding looks dark but still moist and springs back at a gentle touch. Cool, then cut into small squares or diamonds to serve.

Per square:
Calories: 93	Total fat: 3 g	Protein: 2 g
Carbohydrate: 12 g	Cholesterol: 18 g	Sodium: 12 mg

ALMOND MACAROONS

Makes about 3 dozen

Macaroons are traditional to Passover, but don't limit the use of these light and crisp cookies to Passover only. These nutty treats, which have no added fat and no egg yolks, are nice to have on hand anytime. When making them at other times, you can use regular flour instead of the potato starch or matzo cake meal.

1/2 pound (about 2 cups) lightly toasted almonds

¹⁄₄ cup matzo cake meal or potato starch
3 egg whites, at room temperature
²⁄₃ cup firmly packed light brown sugar
1 teaspoon vanilla extract
¹⁄₂ teaspoon cinnamon
dash salt

Preheat the oven to 325 degrees.

Place the almonds in the container of a food processor and process until they resemble a coarse meal.

Beat the egg whites until stiff. Beat in the sugar, vanilla, cinnamon, and salt. Gently fold in the ground almonds. Drop by tablespoonfuls on an oiled baking sheet or 2. Bake for 15 minutes, or until the edges are golden. Remove carefully with a spatula and set gently to cool on plates. The cookies will be soft at first, but become crisp once cool. Store in an airtight container.

Per cookie:

Calories: 56	Total fat: 3 g	Protein: 1 g
Carbohydrate: 6 g	Cholesterol: 0 g	Sodium: 7 mg

PASSOVER ONION BISCUITS

Makes 20 to 22

These moist little biscuits are great with soups.

1 tablespoon canola oil
1 cup finely chopped onion
¹⁄₄ cup canola oil
2 cups matzo meal
2 eggs plus 1 egg white, beaten
1 teaspoon salt
1 tablespoon chopped fresh dill, or 1 teaspoon dried dill
2 teaspoons poppy seeds

Preheat the oven to 350 degrees.

Heat the oil in a small skillet. Add the onion and sauté over moderate heat, stirring frequently, until lightly browned. Remove from heat.

Combine 1 cup of boiling water and the oil in a mixing bowl. Stir in the matzo meal, a little at a time, until smoothly combined with the water and oil. Stir in the eggs, followed by the onions, and all the remaining ingredients.

Form into 1 ½-inch-diameter balls. Flatten slightly and arrange on an oiled baking sheet or 2. Bake for 25 to 30 minutes, or until golden. Cool on a rack. Serve warm. Store any not used immediately in a tightly sealed plastic container.

Per biscuit:

Calories: 75	Total fat: 3 g	Protein: 2 g
Carbohydrate: 8 g	Cholesterol: 20 g	Sodium: 111 mg

MATZO BREI

2 to 3 servings

Matzo brei, a sort of skillet pie made of matzo and eggs, is a standard Passover breakfast treat. It's usually eaten plain, but you can serve it with maple syrup or applesauce.

3 matzos, crumbled
3 eggs, beaten
salt to taste
1 tablespoon reduced-fat margarine for frying

Combine the matzos with 1 cup of boiling water in a mixing bowl and let stand for 10 minutes or so, until softened. Pour in the beaten eggs and salt and stir until the matzos are evenly coated. Season to taste with salt.

Heat just enough margarine to coat the bottom of a 9- or 10-inch nonstick skillet. When it is hot enough to make a drop of water sizzle, pour in the matzo mixture. Turn to moderate heat and cover. Cook until the bottom is golden brown and the top is fairly set. Loosen with a spatula, then slide out onto a flat plate. Invert the skillet over the plate, then flip over so that the uncooked side is now on the bottom of the skillet. Cook, uncovered, until the underside is golden brown. Cut in half to serve 2, or into 3 wedges to serve 3.

Calories: 255	Total fat: 8 g	Protein: 11 g
Carbohydrate: 32 g	Cholesterol: 256 g	Sodium: 119 mg

Chapter 5

MOTHER'S DAY AND FATHER'S DAY

Mother's Day in America originated early this century as the result of one woman's desire to honor her mother; Father's Day started soon after, coming more from the idea of paying tribute to fatherhood in general. Both holidays rapidly became national institutions, and regardless of the differing sentiments behind their origins, we all celebrate them as personal homage to our own moms and dads.

When mom and dad live close by, or are visiting, a meal is an inevitable part of our gift to them (or theirs to us). While going out to eat is a typical way to celebrate, a home-cooked meal is an even more heartfelt gesture.

Today, many of our mothers and fathers are striving to control their intake of cholesterol and fats, while boosting their intake of complex carbohydrates, including fiber, as part of a fit lifestyle. Those of us who are parents ourselves are also more than ever aware of the importance of these goals in order to preserve our future health and, by example, that of our children. With that in mind, I designed several celebrations that the generations can enjoy together— colorful, sustaining meals that are far from austere, for which the toast "To your health!" is most appropriate.

Since many cholesterol-conscious folks have drastically cut down on eggs, I thought it particularly fitting to forgo the traditional special-occasion breakfast omelet for Mother's Day and Father's Day. Instead, I present a pair of menus filled with whole grains and the glorious first fruits of summer.

This first, fruit-filled menu is a special tribute to my own mom, whose favorite food, bar none, is fruit.

A FRUITFUL MOTHER'S DAY OR FATHER'S DAY BREAKFAST

4 to 6 servings

Oat and Wheat Bran Muffins

Composed Fresh Fruit Plates

Tropical Yogurt

❧

Contains egg whites.
Contains dairy products.

OAT AND WHEAT BRAN MUFFINS

Makes 1 dozen

1 cup whole wheat pastry flour
1/4 cup wheat germ
1/2 cup oat bran
1/2 cup wheat bran
1 teaspoon baking soda
1 teaspoon baking powder
2 egg whites, lightly beaten
3/4 cup buttermilk
3/4 cup applesauce
2 tablespoons molasses
2 tablespoons honey
3 tablespoons canola oil
1 teaspoon grated lemon or orange rind
1/4 cup toasted sunflower seeds
1/2 cup golden raisins

Preheat the oven to 350 degrees.

Combine the first 6 ingredients in a mixing bowl. In another bowl, combine the next 7 ingredients and beat together until smooth. Make a well in the center of the dry ingredients and pour in the wet mixture. Stir vigorously until thoroughly combined. Stir in the sunflower seeds and raisins. Divide the batter among 12 oiled or paper-lined muffin tins. Bake 20 to 25 minutes, or until a toothpick inserted in the center of a muffin tests clean.

Per muffin:

Calories: 169	Total fat: 5 g	Protein: 5 g
Carbohydrate: 25 g	Cholesterol: 1 g	Sodium: 24 mg

COMPOSED FRESH FRUIT PLATES

4 to 6 servings

Here quantities are not so important as arrangement—and of course, the fruit should be ripe and luscious. Since these are individually composed plates rather than one big fruit salad, each plate should be attractively arranged and filled without being overloaded.

2 medium bananas, sliced
strawberries, hulled and halved, and/or blueberries
Tropical Yogurt (recipe follows)
cantaloupe, peeled and cut into wedges
honeydew, peeled and cut into wedges
papaya or mango, peeled and cut into long, narrow slices
pineapple, cut into chunks
sliced almonds for garnish
fresh mint leaves for garnish, optional

In a small mixing bowl, combine the sliced bananas with the berries. Add just enough of the Tropical Yogurt to lightly coat the fruit and stir together. Reserve the remaining Tropical Yogurt. Place a small amount of the banana and berry mixture on the side of each guest's plate.

Arrange a few overlapping slices of cantaloupe and honeydew on each plate. Arrange a few slices of papaya or mango along the side of each plate, and next to that, a few pineapple chunks. Leave an opening in the center of each plate, and

> *"In the summer and when they are obtainable, always have a vase of freshly-gathered flowers on the breakfast table, and when convenient, a nicely-arranged dish of fruit; when strawberries are in season, these are particularly refreshing . . . and it is well known that breakfast time is the most wholesome one to partake of fruit."*

—Isabella Beeton
Mrs. Beeton's Everyday Cookery and Housekeeping Book, 1892 edition

spoon into that some of the Tropical Yogurt. Sprinkle the yogurt with some sliced almonds, and garnish each plate with the optional mint leaves.

| Calories: 360 | Total fat: 4 g | Protein: 7 g |
| Carbohydrate: 72 g | Cholesterol: 3 g | Sodium: 74 mg |

TROPICAL YOGURT

4 to 6 servings

1 cup vanilla nonfat yogurt
1 cup diced papaya or mango
1 cup pineapple chunks
1 to 2 tablespoons honey, to taste
dash nutmeg

Place all the ingredients in the container of a food processor. Pulse on and off until the fruit is reduced to tiny pieces but not pureed. Serve with the composed fruit plates as instructed.

| Calories: 80 | Total fat: 1 g | Protein: 3 g |
| Carbohydrate: 17 g | Cholesterol: 1 g | Sodium: 36 mg |

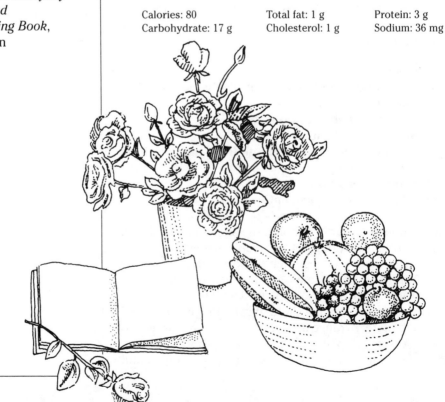

PANCAKE BREAKFAST FOR MOM OR DAD

4 to 6 servings

Cinnamon-Apple Pancakes
Strawberry-Buttermilk Pancakes

———— ༨༩ ————

Additions to the menu: Serve maple syrup, applesauce, and yogurt with the pancakes, plus fresh fruit or fruit salad of your choice.

Contains egg whites.
Contains dairy products. Can be made dairy-free by following the suggested substitutions in the recipes.

Pancakes for breakfast—the very thought makes eyes widen with anticipation. And so much the better, when they're made from scratch, tantalizing the palate with the flavor of fruit cooked right into them. You can choose one of the two pancakes given here, or make half a batch of each to serve together for variety.

CINNAMON APPLE PANCAKES

Makes about 24 3- to 4-inch pancakes, 4 to 6 servings

1 cup whole wheat flour
1 cup unbleached white flour
1 teaspoon baking powder
1 $\frac{1}{2}$ teaspoons cinnamon
2 egg whites, lightly beaten
3 tablespoons light brown sugar
1 $\frac{1}{2}$ cups applesauce
$\frac{1}{4}$ cup low-fat milk or soymilk, or as needed
3 tablespoons finely chopped walnuts
extra applesauce and cinnamon

Combine the first 4 ingredients in a mixing bowl. In another bowl, combine the beaten egg whites with the brown sugar and stir until the sugar is dissolved. Stir in the applesauce and milk. Make a well in the center of the flour mixture and

pour in the wet ingredients. Stir together until thoroughly combined, but do not overbeat. Add more milk if the batter seems too thick. Stir in the walnuts.

Spray just enough cooking oil spray on a nonstick griddle to coat it lightly. Ladle the batter on in scant $1/4$ cupfuls. Cook over moderate heat on both sides until golden brown. These need to brown a bit more slowly than do most griddle-cakes to be cooked all the way through. Keep them warm in a covered casserole dish in a 200-degree oven until all are done. Serve hot with extra applesauce and a dusting of cinnamon.

Calories: 263	Total fat: 3 g	Protein: 8 g
Carbohydrate: 50 g	Cholesterol: 1 g	Sodium: 34 mg

STRAWBERRY-BUTTERMILK PANCAKES

Makes about 24 3- to 4-inch pancakes, 4 to 6 servings

I've called for soymilk as a substitute for buttermilk for those of you who'd like to make these pancakes dairy-free, but please note that the buttermilk yields better flavor and texture.

1 $3/4$ cups whole wheat pastry flour
$1/4$ cup cornmeal
1 teaspoon baking soda, if buttermilk is used,
    or 1 teaspoon baking powder if soymilk is used
$1/4$ teaspoon cinnamon
dash nutmeg
2 egg whites, beaten
2 cups buttermilk or soymilk
1 teaspoon vanilla extract
1 $1/2$ cups firm, ripe strawberries, hulled, halved, and
    thinly sliced
small whole strawberries for garnish
maple syrup

Combine the first 5 ingredients in a mixing bowl. Make a well in the center and pour in the beaten egg whites, butter-milk, and vanilla. Stir until thoroughly combined, but do not overbeat. If the batter seems a bit thick, add some water or low-fat milk. Gently stir in the strawberries.

Heat a nonstick griddle and drop the batter on it in scant

"On strawberries: Doubtless God could have made a better berry, but doubtless God never did."

—William Butler, 1600

$1/4$ cupfuls. Cook over moderate heat on both sides until golden brown. Keep warm in a covered casserole dish in a 200-degree oven until all are done. Garnish each plate with 2 or 3 small whole strawberries. Serve warm with maple syrup.

Calories: 224	Total fat: 2 g	Protein: 11 g
Carbohydrate: 41 g	Cholesterol: 4 g	Sodium: 73 mg

AN ORIENTAL-FLAVORED DINNER FOR MOM

4 to 6 servings

Chinese Cabbage and Bean Curd Soup with Mushrooms

Udon Noodles with Asparagus and Cashews

Citrus-flavored Spinach and Baby Corn Salad

Amaretto Strawberries

Additions to the menu: If this is to be a leisurely dinner, you may consider serving Mung Bean Sprout and Mushroom Spring Rolls (page 234) as an appetizer. Have frozen vanilla or fruit nonfat yogurt or nondairy frozen dessert on hand to serve with the Amaretto Strawberries.

Contains no eggs or dairy products, unless frozen yogurt is used with the dessert. Use a nondairy frozen dessert if you wish to keep the meal dairy-free.

Waist-watching mothers will appreciate this light, colorful meal, in which the presence of asparagus and strawberries announces that spring has really arrived.

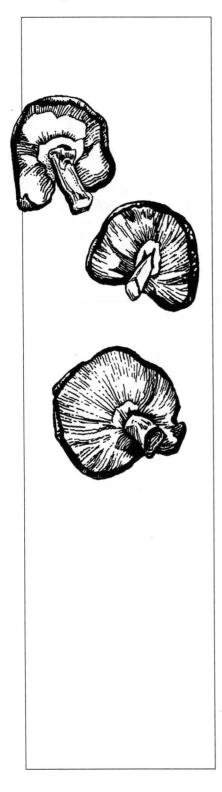

CHINESE CABBAGE AND BEAN CURD SOUP WITH MUSHROOMS

4 to 6 servings

Mushroom stock
1 small onion, halved
2 cloves garlic, halved
8 to 10 dried shiitake mushrooms
2 tablespoons soy sauce or tamari, or to taste

1 tablespoon canola oil
1 large onion, quartered and thinly sliced
2 ½ cups finely shredded Chinese or savoy cabbage
1 cup small mushrooms, thinly sliced
½ cup sliced water chestnuts
2 tablespoons dry sherry or white wine
½ pound tofu (bean curd), cut into ½-inch dice
scallions, green part only, thinly sliced, for garnish

Combine all the stock ingredients in a large heavy saucepan with 6 cups of water and bring to a simmer. Simmer over moderate heat, covered, for 15 minutes. Remove from the heat and let stand another 15 minutes, then strain the stock. Reserve the mushrooms. Trim and discard their tough stems and slice the caps.

Heat the oil in a large soup pot. Add the onion and sauté over low heat until it is golden. Cover with the stock, then add the remaining ingredients except the tofu and the scallions. Bring to a boil, then cover and simmer over low heat for 10 minutes. Remove from the heat. Stir in the tofu and let the soup stand for 30 minutes. Heat through before serving, and top each portion with a bit of the scallion garnish.

Calories: 141	Total fat: 4 g	Protein: 6 g
Carbohydrate: 16 g	Cholesterol: 0 g	Sodium: 416 mg

UDON NOODLES WITH ASPARAGUS AND CASHEWS

4 to 6 servings

Thick, hearty noodles are intertwined with delicious cashews and young asparagus in a light sauce.

¹/₂ pound whole wheat udon noodles (see Note)
1 tablespoon canola oil
1 teaspoon dark sesame oil
1 to 2 cloves garlic, minced
1 ¹/₂ pounds slender asparagus, bottoms trimmed,
    scraped if necessary, and cut into l-inch pieces
1 cup snow peas, trimmed
2 tablespoons dry sherry
2 tablespoons soy sauce or tamari, or to taste
1 ¹/₂ teaspoons cornstarch
¹/₄ cup chopped cashew pieces

Cook the noodles al dente in rapidly simmering water, then drain and transfer to a covered serving casserole.

In the meantime, heat the oils in a wok or large skillet. Add the garlic and stir-fry for 1 minute. Add the asparagus along with 2 tablespoons or so of water and stir-fry until it is bright green. Add the snow peas, sherry, and soy sauce. Continue to stir-fry until the snow peas and asparagus are crisp-tender.

Dissolve the cornstarch in ¹/₄ cup cold water. Pour over the vegetables and stir in quickly. Let the liquid bubble until thickened. Pour over the noodles and toss together. Add the cashews and toss again. Serve at once.

Note: Whole wheat udon noodles are usually available in natural food stores. Oriental markets carry udon also, but not always the whole-grain variety. If you can't find udon noodles, substitute linguine.

Calories: 200	Total fat: 7 g	Protein: 7 g
Carbohydrate: 24 g	Cholesterol: 0 g	Sodium: 414 mg

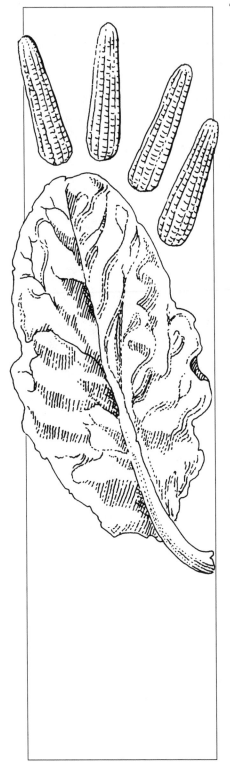

CITRUS-FLAVORED SPINACH AND BABY CORN SALAD

4 to 6 servings

3 cups washed and stemmed fresh spinach, torn
16-ounce can baby corn, drained
1 heaping cup peeled, diced white turnip
2 medium carrots, sliced diagonally
2 tiny seedless oranges, such as small clementines, sectioned
2 tablespoons minced fresh chives

Dressing
2 tablespoons lemon or lime juice
2 teaspoons dark sesame oil or unrefined peanut oil
2 tablespoons orange juice
2 teaspoons honey
freshly ground pepper to taste

Combine the salad ingredients in a serving bowl and toss together. Combine the dressing ingredients in a small bowl and stir together. Pour over the salad just before serving and toss well.

Calories: 151	Total fat: 2 g	Protein: 3 g
Carbohydrate: 31 g	Cholesterol: 0 g	Sodium: 61 mg

AMARETTO STRAWBERRIES

4 to 6 servings

This dessert is almost embarrassingly simple, yet luscious, low-fat, and elegant. I rely on it often during strawberry season.

1 pint sweet, ripe strawberries, hulled
¼ cup amaretto liqueur
vanilla nonfat frozen yogurt or nondairy frozen dessert
fresh mint leaves for garnish, optional

Cut the strawberries into quarters and place them in a wide, shallow container. Crush them lightly, then stir in the amaretto. Cover and allow to soak for several hours, refrigerated. Serve in small bowls or pudding glasses over frozen yogurt or nondairy frozen dessert, garnished with mint leaves.

Calories: 150	Total fat: 0 g	Protein: 5 g
Carbohydrate: 30 g	Cholesterol: 0 g	Sodium: 86 mg

A HEARTY LUNCH FOR DAD

6 servings

Warm Leek and Potato Salad

Succotash

Creamy Tangy Coleslaw

Chilled Berry Soup

Additions to the menu: Serve fresh bagels and a plate of sliced tomatoes, cucumbers, and green peppers.

Contains no eggs.
Contains dairy products. Can be made dairy-free by following the suggested substitutions in the recipes.

Prove to Dad that a meal can be filling without being fattening! This menu concentrates on hearty produce—potatoes, leeks, corn, cabbage—just the kind of basic, homey vegetables that many men seem to relish.

WARM LEEK AND POTATO SALAD

6 servings

Adapted from Barbara Batcheller's wonderful *Lilies of the Kitchen*, this goes far beyond ordinary potato salad.

6 medium red-skinned potatoes, scrubbed
6 slender leeks or 3 large leeks, white parts only

1 tablespoon olive oil
6-ounce jar marinated artichoke hearts, with liquid
1 small sweet red pepper, cut into narrow, l-inch strips
1/2 cup fresh green peas, steamed crisp-tender
Grainy Mustard Vinaigrette (page 256), as needed
salt and freshly ground pepper to taste
dark green lettuce leaves
halved cherry tomatoes
snipped fresh chives
minced fresh parsley

Cook or microwave the potatoes in their skins until done but still firm. When cool enough to handle, but still warm, cut in half lengthwise and slice 1/2 inch thick. Place in a mixing bowl and cover.

Trim the leeks and cut in half lengthwise. Cut 1/4 inch thick crosswise, then rinse well to rid them of grit. Heat the olive oil in a skillet along with 2 tablespoons of water. Cover and steam until crisp-tender, stirring occasionally.

Add the leeks to the potatoes. Cut the artichoke hearts in half and add them along with their liquid to the potato-leek mixture, followed by the sweet pepper and peas. Add enough vinaigrette to moisten the salad. Season to taste with salt and pepper and toss well.

To serve, line a large platter with lettuce leaves. Top them with the potato salad. Surround with cherry tomatoes and sprinkle with the minced herbs. Serve at once.

Calories: 267	Total fat: 7 g	Protein: 4 g
Carbohydrate: 46 g	Cholesterol: 0 g	Sodium: 86 mg

SUCCOTASH

6 servings

1 tablespoon canola oil
1 large Sweet Vidalia onion, chopped
2 cloves garlic, minced
2 cups chopped ripe, juicy tomatoes
1/2 teaspoon each: dried tarragon, summer savory, and
    dry mustard
2 cups cooked corn kernels, preferably fresh
1 cup string beans, cut into l-inch lengths and steamed
1 cup frozen baby lima beans, thawed

2 teaspoons cider vinegar
salt and freshly ground pepper to taste

Heat the oil in a large skillet. Add the onion and sauté over moderate heat until translucent. Add the garlic and continue to sauté until the onion is lightly golden. Add the tomatoes, dried herbs, and mustard and cook, stirring occasionally, for 5 minutes. Add the remaining ingredients and cook, covered, over very low heat, for 10 minutes, until heated through. Transfer to a serving container and serve at once.

Calories: 124	Total fat: 2 g	Protein: 4 g
Carbohydrate: 22 g	Cholesterol: 0 g	Sodium: 18 mg

CREAMY TANGY COLESLAW

6 servings

Low-fat cottage cheese and yogurt stand in for heavier and more caloric mayonnaise that is typically used to dress coleslaw. Those who wish to keep this menu dairy-free can dress the slaw with Tofu Mayonnaise (page 257). A hint of horseradish gives extra zest.

4 cups firmly packed shredded white cabbage,
    or 2 cups each red and white cabbage
1 large carrot, grated
1 scallion, minced
¼ cup finely diced green bell pepper
¼ cup finely diced half-sour pickle
1 tablespoon minced fresh parsley
1 teaspoon prepared horseradish
salt and freshly ground pepper to taste

Dressing (alternatively, use 1 cup
Tofu Mayonnaise, page 257)
⅔ cup low-fat cottage cheese
⅓ cup plain low-fat yogurt
1 tablespoon lemon juice
1 teaspoon prepared mustard
1 teaspoon honey

Combine the salad ingredients in a mixing bowl and toss together. Combine the dressing ingredients in the container

of a food processor. Process until completely smooth. Pour over the salad and toss well. Cover and refrigerate for 30 minutes to an hour to allow the flavors to blend. Transfer to a serving container to serve.

Calories: 58	Total fat: 0 g	Protein: 5 g
Carbohydrate: 8 g	Cholesterol: 3 g	Sodium: 140 mg

CHILLED BERRY SOUP

6 servings

1 pint blueberries
1 pint strawberries, hulled and coarsely chopped
1 cup raspberries
2 medium peaches or nectarines, chopped
4 cups raspberry or cranberry juice
    (made from concentrate)
$\frac{1}{3}$ cup dry red or white wine
juice of $\frac{1}{2}$ lemon
1 teaspoon cinnamon
$\frac{1}{2}$ teaspoon ground allspice
$\frac{1}{4}$ teaspoon ground nutmeg
brown sugar to taste, if needed
sliced strawberries for garnish

Combine all the ingredients except the last 2 in a large soup pot. Bring to a simmer, then simmer gently, covered, over medium heat for 10 to 15 minutes, or until the fruit is tender. Taste to see whether a bit more sweetness is needed, and add brown sugar accordingly—depending on the sweetness of the fruit and the fruit juice, you may not wish to add additional sweetness at all, or very little. Allow the soup to cool, then chill thoroughly.

Garnish each serving with a few slices of strawberry.

Calories: 162	Total fat: 0 g	Protein: 1 g
Carbohydrate: 35 g	Cholesterol: 0 g	Sodium: 12 mg

Chapter 6

MEMORIAL DAY AND BEYOND: Picnic Pleasures

Designating a chapter for Memorial Day and beyond is in no way intended to trivialize the true meaning of the holiday itself—the commemoration of soldiers whose lives were sacrificed to war. It's an easy tendency to view every holiday as a joyous occasion, whether warranted or not.

So, although this chapter is not intended to make Memorial Day itself a celebratory occasion, the passing of this weekend is deeply ingrained in our national consciousness as the mark of the unofficial start of summer. The arrival of warm weather and the anticipated enjoyments it brings with it are what is celebrated here.

The Pleasures of Picnics

Sometime around mid-May, when the lilacs are in bloom, I get the urge to pack a delicious lunch and head for a spot with a breathtaking view. After having lived in New York City for some years, I nearly forgot how much fun picnics could be. But once I moved to a more rural region I rediscovered this pastime with great pleasure.

Food always tastes better alfresco, especially when accompanied by the intoxicatingly scented air of late spring and early summer and enhanced by a lovely vista. I feel lucky to live in a region full of stunning picnic spots within an hour of home.

FILLING FARE ALFRESCO

6 servings

Mushroom, Asparagus, and Artichoke Salad

White Bean and Sun-dried Tomato Pâté (page 242)

Herbed Potato Salad

Peanut Butter-Carrot Cookies

———— ꡑ ————

Additions to the menu: Take along a basket of cherry tomatoes and a loaf of fresh bread. A whole wheat Italian or French loaf pairs nicely with the pâté. Include a pint of strawberries to eat with, or instead of, the cookies.

Contains egg whites in cookies only.
Contains dairy products. Can be made dairy-free by following the suggested substitutions in the recipes.

MUSHROOM, ASPARAGUS, AND ARTICHOKE SALAD

6 servings

My sister-in-law, from whose recipe I adapted this delicious salad, serves this dish as an appetizer. The strong flavor has a great deal of staying power, and I find it's perfect for taking along for an outdoor meal.

½ pound small button mushrooms
½ pound slender asparagus
10-ounce package frozen artichoke hearts, thawed

and cut in half
1 small zucchini, quartered lengthwise and sliced
1 large half-sour dill pickle, chopped
2 tablespoons minced fresh dill
2 tablespoons minced fresh parsley
**1/3 cup plain low-fat yogurt plus 1/3 cup reduced-fat or
    soy mayonnaise, or 2/3 cup Tofu Mayonnaise
    (page 257)**
juice of 1/2 lemon
salt and freshly ground pepper to taste

Wipe the mushrooms clean and trim the stem bottoms if they look dark or fibrous. If the mushrooms are larger than button size, cut them in half. Place in a skillet with just enough water to keep moist; cover and steam over moderate heat for 2 minutes, then drain and let cool.

Trim the bottoms of the asparagus, then cut the stalks into l-inch pieces. Using the same skillet, add just enough water to keep the bottom moist, cover, and steam until the asparagus is bright green and crisp-tender. Drain and rinse with cool water.

Combine the mushrooms and asparagus in a serving container. Add the artichoke hearts, zucchini, pickle, and herbs. In a small bowl, mix the yogurt, mayonnaise, and lemon juice until smoothly combined. Pour over the vegetables and toss well. Add salt and pepper to taste and toss again. Refrigerate until needed. Pack into a tightly lidded plastic container to transport.

Calories: 80   Total fat: 3 g   Protein: 3 g
Carbohydrate: 9 g Cholesterol: 1 g   Sodium: 121 mg

HERBED POTATO SALAD

6 servings

Serving potato salad is a great way to announce that summer has arrived!

**4 medium red-skinned potatoes, scrubbed, cooked,
    cooled, and diced**
2 medium celery stalks, finely chopped
1 cup steamed fresh or thawed frozen green peas
1/2 cup minced green bell pepper
1/3 cup chopped black olives

Don't just pack your basket and head for the nearest crowded park or beach—consider where you are headed as carefully as you plan the picnic meal itself. Delve into your surroundings—is there a rushing stream you'd like to sit by, a meadow of rolling lawns, a spread of sand dunes, or a historic home? A perfect spot adds much to the enjoyment of a picnic; the experience is transformed from merely eating lunch outdoors to a revitalization of the spirit and an awakening of all the senses.

Picnic Tips

- *No matter what theme I'm planning for a picnic, I like to keep things fairly simple and think along the lines of a variety of cold dishes, fresh breads, and refreshing beverages.*

- *Sandwiches are a common offering for picnics, but I find them boring, since that's what I generally have for lunch at home. I find pâtés and spreads (meatless in my case, of course), served with fresh breads, far more enticing.*

- *Marinated salads have great staying power, as do salads with some mayonnaise in them. Dishes that are well seasoned or that contain generous amounts of herbs also hold up very well.*

(picnic tips continue . . .)

2 tablespoons chopped fresh parsley
2 tablespoons minced fresh dill
1 scallion, minced
2 tablespoons toasted sunflower seeds
⅓ cup Grainy Mustard Vinaigrette (page 256),
  or as needed to moisten
salt and freshly ground pepper to taste

Combine all the ingredients in a mixing bowl and toss together thoroughly. Cover and refrigerate until needed. Pack into a tightly lidded plastic container to transport.

Calories: 194	Total fat: 10 g	Protein: 3 g
Carbohydrate: 24 g	Cholesterol: 0 g	Sodium: 143 mg

PEANUT BUTTER-CARROT COOKIES

Makes about 30

Tiny flakes of carrot add color and texture to these substantial, spiced cookies.

1 cup whole wheat pastry flour
½ cup oat bran or fine oatmeal
1 teaspoon baking powder
½ teaspoon cinnamon
¼ teaspoon each: salt, ground nutmeg, ginger,
  and allspice
¼ cup (½ stick) reduced-fat margarine,
  at room temperature
½ cup reduced-fat peanut butter, at room temperature
⅔ cup light brown sugar
2 egg whites, lightly beaten
½ cup firmly packed, finely grated carrot
½ cup raisins

Preheat the oven to 350 degrees.

Combine the first 3 ingredients in a mixing bowl and stir in the spices.

In another bowl, cream together the margarine, peanut butter, and brown sugar. Stir the egg in vigorously until the mixture is smooth, then stir in the grated carrot and raisins. Work the wet mixture into the dry to form a stiff dough.

Drop heaping teaspoonfuls onto 1 or 2 baking sheets and flatten with a fork. Bake for 12 to 15 minutes, or until the edges begin to turn golden. Cool on a rack. Pack into a tightly lidded flat plastic container to transport.

Per cookie:

Calories: 77	Total fat: 2 g	Protein: 2 g
Carbohydrate: 12 g	Cholesterol: 0 g	Sodium: 56 mg

SAVORY SAMPLINGS IN THE OPEN AIR

6 servings

Marinated Wild Rice with Mushrooms
Zucchini, Red Onion, and Feta Tartlets
Beet, Cucumber, and Orange Salad
Fig Bars

Additions to the menu: Sesame breadsticks make a nice accompaniment to the tartlets. Pack fresh grapes to complement the Fig Bars.

Contains eggs and dairy products.

• *While the weather is still cool, and if the picnic area is close to home, brown-bagging your meal or packing it in a knapsack if you'll be hiking is sufficient if foods are well packed. Wicker picnic baskets are a nice alternative and infinitely more romantic than brown bags. Once things warm up a bit, though, coolers and thermoses are in order.*

• *Flat, rectangular plastic storage containers are perfect for the kind of cold dishes I like to take on picnics. They stack nicely, and once the food is gone, they can be stacked one inside the other for more compact storage.*

(picnic tips continue . . .)

- *For beverages, take along a thermos of fruit juice with some ice added. Wine coolers are nice, too. Or you might prefer to buy individual bottles of fruit juice once you are near your picnic location, if that's possible.*

- *Don't forget to pack paper plates and disposable utensils, plus plenty of napkins. It might not be as ecological or elegant as bringing real plates and utensils, but if you'd like to do some additional hiking, swimming, or just relaxing, it's nice to dispose of as much as possible after the meal.*

- *My favorite picnic dessert is fruit with some cookies. Cookies pack well and hold up better than many desserts that get soft and gooey. However, even cookies are not absolutely necessary, and you may find that some refreshing fruit is sufficient after so filling a lunch.*

MARINATED WILD RICE WITH MUSHROOMS

Makes 6 servings

A cold dish suffused with nutty, sophisticated flavors.

1 vegetable bouillon cube
1/2 cup wild rice
1/2 cup long-grain brown rice
4 ounces fresh shiitake or porcini mushrooms
1 cup sliced small white mushrooms
1 cup carrot, cut into 1 1/2-inch-long matchsticks
3 tablespoons minced fresh parsley
2 tablespoons minced fresh chives or scallions
1/4 cup finely chopped walnuts
1/3 cup Nutty Vinaigrette (page 256)
salt and freshly ground pepper to taste

Combine 3 cups of water and the bouillon cube in a heavy saucepan and bring to a boil. Stir in the wild and brown rice and return to a boil. Lower the heat, cover, and simmer until the water is absorbed, about 45 minutes. Let the rice cool to room temperature.

Trim the tough stems off the shiitakes, if using. Slice the shiitakes or porcinis into narrow strips. Heat a nonstick skillet. Combine the wild and white mushrooms in the skillet, cover, and "sweat" them over moderate heat until just wilted. Combine in a large mixing bowl with the rice and all the remaining ingredients. Cover and marinate for 2 hours or so before serving. If making this ahead, marinate in the refrigerator, then take out about an hour before serving to bring to room temperature.

Calories: 258	Total fat: 8 g	Protein: 7 g
Carbohydrate: 38 g	Cholesterol: 0 g	Sodium: 97 mg

ZUCCHINI, RED ONION, AND FETA TARTLETS

Makes 1 dozen, 2 per serving

For the purpose of a picnic, I wanted these miniature egg tarts to have a firm texture, and baking them in muffin tins does the trick nicely.

1 tablespoon canola oil
1 ½ cups chopped red onion
½ pound zucchini (about 1 medium),
    coarsely grated
1 teaspoon dried tarragon
1 teaspoon dried summer savory
4 eggs, plus 2 egg whites, beaten
2 tablespoons low-fat milk
4 ounces feta cheese, finely crumbled
3 tablespoons cornmeal
freshly ground pepper to taste

Preheat the oven to 350 degrees.

Heat the oil in a large skillet. Add the red onion and sauté over moderate heat until golden. Stir in the grated zucchini and dried herbs and add 2 to 3 tablespoons water to moisten. Cook, covered, until the zucchini is wilted but still somewhat crisp, about 4 to 5 minutes. Remove from heat.

In a mixing bowl, beat the eggs together with the milk. Stir in the feta cheese, cornmeal, and the onion-zucchini mixture. Season to taste with pepper.

Line 12 muffin tins with aluminum muffin-tin liners. Divide the mixture among the 12 tins. Bake for 35 to 40 minutes, or until the tops are golden. Let cool to room temperature, then pack in a wide, shallow plastic container to transport for a picnic. If making ahead of time, refrigerate, covered, after cooling, then bring to room temperature before serving.

Calories: 82	Total fat: 4 g	Protein: 5 g
Carbohydrate: 4 g	Cholesterol: 79 g	Sodium: 139 mg

BEET, CUCUMBER, AND ORANGE SALAD

6 servings

I'm very fond of beets and am always happy to devise new and different ways of preparing them. They're wonderful combined with the crunch of cucumber and the sweetness of citrus.

**4 to 5 medium fresh beets, rinsed and cooked or
    microwaved until tender, or substitute 1-pound
    can sliced beets, drained
1/2 medium cucumber, peeled, seeded, and sliced
2 small sweet seedless oranges, such as small
    clementines, sectioned
1 tablespoon minced fresh dill
1 tablespoon minced fresh chives
1 to 2 tablespoons minced fresh mint (if unavailable,
    substitute 1 to 2 teaspoons dried mint)
juice of 1 lemon
1 tablespoon honey
1/2 teaspoon horseradish
salt and freshly ground pepper to taste**

Peel the cooked beets, then quarter them and slice them about 1/8 inch thick. Combine them in a mixing bowl with the cucumber, orange, and herbs. In a small bowl, combine the lemon juice, honey, and horseradish and mix well. Pour over the beet mixture. Season to taste with salt and pepper. Pack in a tightly lidded container and chill until needed.

Calories: 49	Total fat: 0 g	Protein: 1 g
Carbohydrate: 11 g	Cholesterol: 0 g	Sodium: 20 mg

FIG BARS

Makes about 2 dozen

Moist and chewy, these cookies hark back to those fig cookies you enjoyed as a child.

Dough
2 cups whole wheat pastry flour
1 teaspoon baking powder
1/2 teaspoon salt
1/2 cup (1 stick) reduced-fat margarine, softened
1/2 cup light brown sugar
1 egg, beaten

Filling
12 ounces black (mission) figs
1/3 cup walnuts
1/2 cup apple juice
1 teaspoon vanilla extract
1 teaspoon cinnamon
1/4 teaspoon each: ground cloves, allspice

Combine the first 3 ingredients in a mixing bowl. In another bowl, cream the margarine and sugar. Beat in the egg until the mixture is smooth. Combine the 2 mixtures and work together with hands. Sprinkle in enough water (about 1/4 to 1/3 cup) so that the mixture holds together as a soft dough. Wrap the dough tightly and refrigerate for at least 30 minutes.

In the meantime, combine the ingredients for the filling in the container of a food processor. Process until finely ground.

Once the dough is chilled, preheat the oven to 350 degrees. Divide the dough into 2 equal parts. On a well-floured board, roll each out into a rectangular shape to fit a 9- by 13-inch baking pan. Oil and flour the bottom of the pan, then fit one of the dough rectangles into the bottom and trim the sides. With the help of a cake spatula, spread the filling evenly over it. Cover with the remaining dough rectangle and trim.

Bake for 35 to 40 minutes, or until the top is lightly golden. Let cool and cut into 24 2-inch-square pieces. You may, if you'd like, cut smaller pieces. To transport, pack in a tightly lidded flat plastic container.

Per bar:
Calories: 116	Total fat: 3 g	Protein: 2 g
Carbohydrate: 20 g	Cholesterol: 9 g	Sodium: 82 mg

Things Not to Be Forgotten at a Picnic

"A stick of horseradish, a bottle of mint sauce, well-corked, a bottle of salad dressing, a bottle of vinegar, made mustard, pepper, salt, good oil, and pounded sugar. If it can be managed, take a little ice. It is scarcely necessary to say that plates, tumblers, wine-glasses, knives, forks, and spoons must not be forgotten; as also teacups and saucers, 3 or 4 teapots, some lump sugar, and milk, it this last-named article cannot be obtained in the neighbourhood. Take 3 corkscrews.

"Beverages—3 dozen quart bottles of ale, packed in hampers; ginger-beer, soda-water and lemonade, of each 2 dozen bottles; 6 bottles of sherry, 6 bottles of claret, champagne a discretion, and any other light wine that may be preferred, and 2 bottles of brandy. Water can usually be obtained, so it is useless to take it."

—Isabella Beeton
The Book of Household Management, 1859-1861

A SLIGHTLY SOUTHWESTERN SOJOURN

6 servings

Olive-Rice Salad
Pinto Beans with Watercress
Cheddar Corn Muffins
Tomato Salsa ($\frac{1}{2}$ recipe, page 201)
Cocoa Drops (page 31)

Additions to the menu: Pack some peeled, sliced jicama or kohlrabi in a shallow, covered container. Sprinkle with a bit of water or pack with a damp paper towel to keep moist. Take some good-quality reduced-fat or fat-free tortilla chips to scoop up the salsa. Fresh oranges go well with the Cocoa Drops and end the meal on a refreshing note.

Contains egg whites and dairy products in the Cheddar Corn Muffins and egg whites in the Cocoa Drops. To adapt to vegan, replace the muffins with a whole wheat or rye bread, and the cookies with a dessert or fruit of your choice.

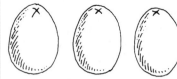

"Except the vine, there is no plant which bears a fruit of as great an importance as the olive."

—Pliny the Elder
Naturalis Historia, 79 B.C.

OLIVE-RICE SALAD

6 servings

$\frac{3}{4}$ **cup raw medium-grain brown rice**
1 cup cooked corn kernels
$\frac{1}{3}$ **cup chopped black olives**
$\frac{1}{3}$ **cup chopped green olives**

1 medium red bell pepper, finely diced
1 ½ cups finely shredded white cabbage
⅓ cup chopped fresh parsley
2 scallions, minced
1 tablespoon olive oil
juice of ½ lemon, or more to taste
freshly ground pepper to taste

Bring 2 cups of water to boil in a saucepan. Stir in the rice, return to a boil, then lower the heat and simmer, covered, until the water is absorbed, about 35 minutes. Fluff the rice with a fork, then let it cool completely.

Combine the rice with the remaining ingredients in a mixing bowl and toss together thoroughly. Pack in a securely lidded plastic container to transport.

Calories: 146	Total fat: 5 g	Protein: 3 g
Carbohydrate: 24 g	Cholesterol: 0 g	Sodium: 137 mg

PINTO BEANS WITH WATERCRESS

6 servings

2 cups canned or cooked pinto beans
    (see Bean Basics, page 261)
1 cup watercress leaves
2 medium firm, ripe plum tomatoes, finely diced
1 medium celery stalk, finely diced

Dressing
¼ cup reduced-fat or soy mayonnaise
1 tablespoon lemon or lime juice
1 teaspoon prepared mustard
½ teaspoon dried oregano
¼ teaspoon ground cumin
salt and freshly ground pepper to taste

Combine the first 4 ingredients in a mixing bowl. In a small bowl, combine the dressing ingredients and mix thoroughly. Pour over the salad and toss to combine

"At a picnic there is no get-away for anyone, as there is at an evening party or 'at home.' However dull or bored one may feel, one must stay to the bitter end of these alfresco entertainments; ergo, it is necessary, to make them successful, that the guests be well chosen."

—Isabella Beeton
Mrs. Beeton's Everyday Cookery and Housekeeping Book, 1892 edition

thoroughly. Season to taste with salt and pepper. Pack in a securely lidded plastic container to transport.

Calories: 113	Total fat: 2 g	Protein: 4 g
Carbohydrate: 17 g	Cholesterol: 0 g	Sodium: 102 mg

CHEDDAR CORN MUFFINS

Makes 1 dozen

3/4 cup whole wheat flour
3/4 cup stone-ground cornmeal
1/4 cup unbleached white flour
1 teaspoon baking soda
1/2 teaspoon baking powder
1/2 teaspoon salt
2 eggs, beaten
2 tablespoons honey
1 1/2 cups plain nonfat yogurt
1 cup grated reduced-fat cheddar cheese

Preheat the oven to 375 degrees.
Combine the first 6 ingredients in a mixing bowl.

In a smaller bowl, combine the remaining ingredients and mix thoroughly. Add the wet ingredients to the dry and stir vigorously to combine. Divide among 12 oiled or paper-lined muffin tins. Bake for 12 to 15 minutes, or until a toothpick inserted in the center of one tests clean.

Per muffin:

Calories: 137	Total fat: 2 g	Protein: 8 g
Carbohydrate: 19 g	Cholesterol: 43 g	Sodium: 193 mg

Chapter 7

INDEPENDENCE DAY: Cooking and Celebrating Outdoors

Fire up the grills! Vegetarians need no longer feel left out when America celebrates its birthday with the outdoor barbecue feasts that have become the hallmark of this holiday. Create your own fireworks with alternative protein foods and vegetables that take on an entirely new taste dimension on the grill.

Grilling is more art than science. It takes a few go-rounds to get the knack of working with whatever equipment you have, be it a fancy gas-powered unit or a simple barbecue pit in the ground. It should be said, though, that expensive equipment is not necessary to create a tasty outdoor meal. It's more a matter of learning about the coals and woods befitting your particular grill, how to light them easily, and how long to let the hot coals die down in your unit before putting the food on. Generally, it takes 30 to 45 minutes for hot coals to reach the right temperature for grilling foods.

This chapter presents fairly easy and straightforward barbecue recipes, since this is an area that many vegetarians have traditionally avoided. Once you try some of the recipes here, there's no doubt you'll be eager to experiment with your own grilling ideas.

The two menus given here demonstrate how several grilled dishes may be combined in a meal. The combinations in these menus are quite flexible, and after exploring The Vegetarian Barbecue sidebars, you might like to use them as a guide, substituting different vegetables and protein foods for the ones listed. For example, in the first menu, you could substitute Curried Grilled Tempeh for the Tofu and Potato Kebabs, and do a grilled curried vegetable platter instead of the Grilled Ratatouille.

INDEPENDENCE FEAST

6 to 8 servings

Tofu and Potato Kebabs

Red Onion Relish

Grilled Ratatouille

Millet Salad

Peaches, Cantaloupe, Honeydew, and Blueberries

───❦───

Additions to the menu: While the grill is going, you may want to serve a light appetizer such as raw vegetables with Creamy Herbed Cheese Dip (page 239). Or, if you'd like to keep the menu completely dairy-free, serve the Spinach and Cucumber Spread (page 240) with baby vegetables or any nicely composed platter of fresh, bite-sized vegetables.

Contains no eggs or dairy products except for optional Parmesan cheese in Millet Salad.

TOFU AND POTATO KEBABS

8 servings

4 medium red-skinned potatoes
2 pounds firm tofu
Sweet and Savory Grilling Sauce (page 112) or
　　Teriyaki Marinade (page 113)
2 medium sweet red bell peppers, cut into l-inch squares

Cook or microwave 4 medium red-skinned potatoes until

done but still quite firm. Allow to cool, then cut into 1-inch chunks.

Cut tofu into $^3/_4$ to 1-inch-thick slices and press as directed in sidebar on page 106. After pressing, cut into $^3/_4$ to 1-inch dice. Marinate in Sweet and Savory Grilling Sauce or Teriyaki Marinade for 30 minutes.

Alternate tofu and potato chunks with red pepper pieces on skewers.

Prepare grill. Brush the skewered ingredients with additional sauce or marinade used. Grill, turning carefully, until touched with charred spots, about 10 minutes total.

Calories: 215	Total fat: 6 g	Protein: 10 g
Carbohydrate: 28 g	Cholesterol: 0 g	Sodium: 545 mg

RED ONION RELISH

Makes about 2 cups

This flavorful relish is a great companion to grilled vegetables or any of the grilled protein foods.

2 tablespoons canola oil
2 tablespoons dry red wine
4 cups chopped red onion
3 tablespoons honey
3 tablespoons red wine vinegar
½ teaspoon each: freshly grated ginger,
    ground cinnamon, dry mustard

Heat the oil in a large skillet. Add the wine and onions and sauté, covered, over low heat, for 30 minutes, stirring occasionally. If the mixture gets dry, moisten with small amounts of water.

Stir in the remaining ingredients and cook, uncovered, over low heat, for another 15 minutes or until the onions are very tender. Let cool. Store until needed in a covered container. Serve at room temperature.

Per 2-tablespoon serving:

Calories: 42	Total fat: 2 g	Protein: 0 g
Carbohydrate: 6 g	Cholesterol: 0 g	Sodium: 1 mg

"Onion: humble kindred of the lily clan, rooted from oblivion by Alexander the Great and bestrewn by him, along with learning, to the civilised world, thus lending a touch of wisdom and sophistication to the whole."

—Della Lutes
The Country Kitchen, 1938

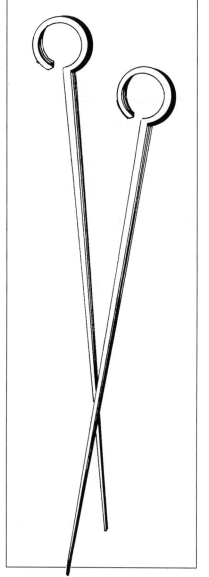

*"Cooking on skewers
. . . this primitive
form of cooking, is
still among the easi-
est and most
savoury."*

—Ambrose Heath
 Good Food, 1932

GRILLED RATATOUILLE

6 to 8 servings

A grilled version of the classic French stew, this glistening warm salad will whet appetites dulled by summer heat.

1 medium eggplant, about 1 pound
2 medium onions
1 medium zucchini or 2 small zucchinis, about
 $^{1}/_{2}$ pound total
1 large green or red bell pepper
Olive Oil-Lemon Marinade (page 113), as needed
1 large ripe tomato, diced
$^{1}/_{4}$ cup chopped black olives
2 tablespoons chopped fresh basil
2 tablespoons chopped fresh parsley
1 $^{1}/_{2}$ tablespoons olive oil
1 tablespoon wine vinegar
salt and freshly ground pepper to taste
$^{1}/_{4}$ pound crumbly goat cheese, such as Bucheron,
 optional

Cut the eggplant into l/2-inch-thick slices. Salt them and place in a colander for 30 minutes, then rinse and drain.

Peel the onions and cut in half. Steam or microwave until just tender.

Cut the zucchini in half lengthwise.

Prepare grill. Brush the vegetables lightly with the Olive Oil-Lemon Marinade. Grill the eggplant on both sides until nicely browned and quite tender, about 15 minutes total. Grill the onions and zucchini on both sides until marked with brown, and tender, about 10 to 15 minutes total. Place the bell pepper directly on the grill and turn frequently, allowing all sides to get charred. Remove and place in a paper bag to steam.

When all the vegetables are cool enough to handle, chop into fairly large chunks and combine in a serving bowl. Slip the skin off the pepper, then remove the core and seeds. Cut into small squares.

Stir in the tomato, olives, herbs, olive oil, and vinegar, and toss well. Season to taste with salt and pepper. If desired, sprinkle the top with crumbled goat cheese. Serve warm or at room temperature.

Calories: 101	Total fat: 7 g	Protein: 1 g
Carbohydrate: 10 g	Cholesterol: 0 g	Sodium: 43 mg

MILLET SALAD

6 to 8 servings

I had this unusual salad at an outdoor party at the home of a friend; not only did I love it, but I was impressed with the enthusiasm with which other guests ate it. Bland but nutritious millet, after all, is not a grain that normally causes excitement. My friend suggests that other vegetables can be substituted for the ones given here, but that fresh dill and a strong dressing are musts.

1 cup raw millet
¼ teaspoon salt
1 cup snow peas, trimmed and halved crosswise
2 medium carrots, thinly sliced
1 cup diced yellow summer squash
1 green or red bell pepper, cut julienne
½ cup sliced radishes
2 to 3 tablespoons minced fresh dill
2 scallions, minced
⅓ cup Garlic Vinaigrette (page 256)
2 tablespoons reduced-fat or soy mayonnaise
2 tablespoons grated fresh Parmesan cheese, optional
freshly ground pepper
1 heaping cup halved cherry tomatoes
¼ cup toasted sunflower seeds, optional
curly parsley and halved cherry tomatoes for garnish

Spray a nonstick skillet lightly with cooking oil spray. Add the millet and toast over medium heat, stirring frequently, for 5 to 7 minutes, or until the grain smells nutty. Pour in 2 ½ cups of water and stir in the salt. Bring to a boil, then cover and simmer over low heat until the water is absorbed, about 40 minutes. Remove from the heat, fluff with a fork, and let cool.

Steam the snow peas very briefly, just until bright green, then rinse with cool water and drain.

Combine the cooled millet with the snow peas in a large mixing bowl along with the remaining ingredients except the last 3. Toss gently but thoroughly and let the salad stand, covered, for 1 to 2 hours before serving. Just before serving, stir in the cherry tomatoes and seeds. Transfer to a serving bowl and garnish the edge, alternating halved cherry tomatoes with sprigs of curly parsley.

Calories: 214	Total fat: 9 g	Protein: 4 g
Carbohydrate: 29 g	Cholesterol: 0 g	Sodium: 136 mg

BASIC EQUIPMENT FOR GRILLING

Skewers

Best are those with flat blades; vegetables won't swivel as they're being turned.

Basting Brush

Essential for spreading marinade repeatedly on grilled foods.

Long-handled Tongs

For turning food on the grill.

Wire Mesh Grilling Screen

Look for this handy item in kitchen supply shops. It's especially useful for delicate vegetables like tomatoes, and for those likely to fall through the grill, such as string beans and carrots. The screen is also good for soft, hard-to-turn foods like tofu.

Oven Mitts

When the coals are at their hottest, mitts are necessary, especially for turning skewers.

"The arrangement of fresh fruits for the table affords play for the most cultivated taste and not a little real inventive genius . . . a raised centerpiece of mixed fruits furnishes a delicious dessert, and is an indispensable ornament to an elegant dinner table."

—*The Buckeye Cookbook*, 1883

PEACHES, CANTALOUPE, HONEYDEW, AND BLUEBERRIES

6 to 8 servings

This is not so much a recipe as a suggestion for a combination of fruits in a salad that is as appealing to the eye as it is to the palate. With fruits at their sweetest and juiciest, there's no need for a dressing or any other embellishment. Simply cut a fairly equivalent amount of peaches, cantaloupe, and honeydew into bite-sized chunks, allowing about 3/4 cup of fruit per serving. Place in an attractive bowl (a glass bowl shows the colors off nicely) and stir in about a cup of blueberries. If making ahead, cover and refrigerate until needed.

Calories: 82   Total fat: 0 g   Protein: 1 g
Carbohydrate: 18 g   Cholesterol: 0 g   Sodium: 14 mg

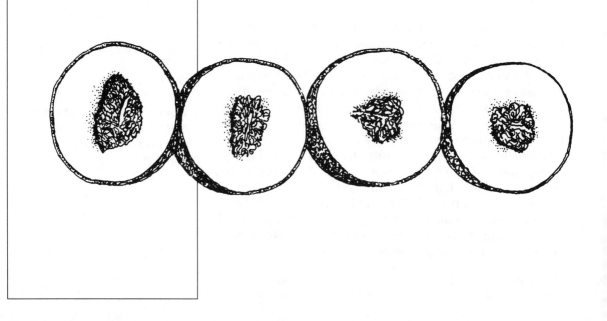

BACKYARD FIREWORKS

6 servings

**Grilled Corn on the Cob (page 109),
with Herb "Butter" (page 258)
Grilled Eggplant Teriyaki
Sweet and Savory Grilled Tofu (page 106)
Bowtie Pasta with Red Beans and
Grilled Tomatoes
Fresh Mint Sherbet**

Additions to the menu: What says Fourth of July
better than watermelon? Serve each guest a
generous wedge along with the sherbet.

Contains no eggs or dairy products.

GRILLED EGGPLANT TERIYAKI

6 servings

**2 medium-large eggplants, about 2 to 2 ½ pounds total
Teriyaki Marinade (page 113), as needed
2 scallions, green parts only, thinly sliced
½ red bell pepper, finely diced
1 tablespoon sesame seeds**

Slice the eggplants ½ inch thick and peel. Salt them and
let stand in a colander for 30 minutes, then rinse well.

Prepare grill. Brush the eggplant slices generously on
both sides with Teriyaki Marinade. Grill on each side until
nicely browned and tender (5 to 10 minutes on each side,

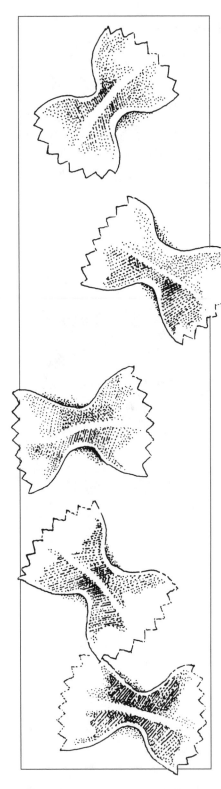

depending on the heat of the coals). Remove and let cool slightly on a cutting surface. Cut into strips and place in a serving container. Stir in the scallions. Add enough additional Teriyaki Sauce to moisten and flavor the eggplant to taste. Sprinkle the top with the red pepper dice and sesame seeds.

Calories: 86	Total fat: 2 g	Protein: 2 g
Carbohydrate: 15 g	Cholesterol: 0 g	Sodium: 177 mg

BOWTIE PASTA WITH RED BEANS AND GRILLED TOMATOES

6 to 8 servings

2 cups canned or cooked red beans (see Bean Basics, page 261)
1 tablespoon olive oil
2 tablespoons cider vinegar
¹⁄₂ pound bowtie pasta
1 ¹⁄₂ cups finely chopped broccoli florets
¹⁄₄ cup chopped fresh parsley
3 scallions, minced
2 to 3 tablespoons chopped fresh basil
Basic Vinaigrette (page 256) as needed to moisten the salad
salt and freshly ground pepper to taste
1 ¹⁄₂ pounds ripe, juicy tomatoes, grilled as directed under Tomatoes (page 111), chopped

Combine the beans in a container with the oil and vinegar, mix well, then cover and refrigerate for several hours or overnight.

Cook the pasta al dente, drain and rinse until cool. Combine in a large serving bowl with the beans and remaining ingredients except the tomatoes. Toss well and refrigerate until needed.

Once the grill is going, grill the tomatoes and toss them into the salad.

Calories: 194	Total fat: 7 g	Protein: 6 g
Carbohydrate: 26 g	Cholesterol: 0 g	Sodium: 28 mg

FRESH FRUIT SHERBET

6 servings

Icy, refreshing sherbets make a perfect finale to a meal of strong-flavored grilled foods. And they are easy to make without an ice-cream machine. Generally, recipes for fruit sherbets call for making a sugar-and-water syrup, but for added ease and flavor, I prefer using fruit juice concentrate instead. An added benefit is that if you use fruit-only juice concentrate, you can avoid refined sugar altogether. Orange juice, apple juice, and pineapple juice concentrates have no added sugar, whereas lemonade, limeade, berry juices, and mixed fruit punches are based on high-fructose corn syrup. Which you use is a matter of preference and of compatibility with the fresh fruit being used.

Use the lushest, sweetest fruit possible. Half-ripe peaches and watery cantaloupe just won't do the trick!

4 to 4 ½ cups diced fresh fruit
½ to ¾ cup frozen fruit juice concentrate, to taste
extra fruit and mint leaves for garnish, optional

Combine the fruit and juice concentrate in a food processor and process until smoothly pureed. Transfer to a shallow freezer pan and freeze for several hours until firm (but not a block of ice).

About an hour before serving, scoop out and transfer back to the food processor. Puree until smooth, then transfer back to the pan. Freeze until the sherbet is the right consistency to serve—firm, but slushy enough to scoop out.

Serve in small rounded scoops in dessert bowls, garnished with a bit of the fresh fruit or fruits from which the sherbet was made, and, if possible, a mint leaf or 2. Following are a few suggestions for combinations, but once you have the method down pat, you'll want to experiment with combinations of your own.

| Calories: 134 | Total fat: 0 g | Protein: 2 g |
| Carbohydrate: 30 g | Cholesterol: 0 g | Sodium: 17 mg |

VARIATIONS:

Honeydew-Lime: Combine 4 to 4 ½ cups ripe, sweet honeydew and ½ to ¾ cup limeade concentrate.

Peach-Papaya-Pineapple: Combine more or less equal amounts of peach and papaya chunks (if papaya is unavailable, use all peaches or combine peaches and nectarines or apricots) to equal 4 to 4 $\frac{1}{2}$ cups, and $\frac{1}{2}$ to $\frac{3}{4}$ cup pineapple juice concentrate.

Cantaloupe-Orange: Combine 4 to 4 $\frac{1}{2}$ cups cantaloupe and $\frac{1}{2}$ to $\frac{3}{4}$ cup orange juice concentrate.

The Vegetarian Barbecue

GRILLING PROTEIN FOODS

TOFU

High-protein tofu is an excellent candidate for the grill. Its spongy texture soaks up delicious marinades, and it needs only a short time to brown once it hits the grill. Because of its consistency, tofu tends to be delicate when exposed to such high temperatures. So in addition to choosing the firmest tofu possible, I strongly recommend pressing it first before marinating. This extracts excess water and gives it an even firmer texture.

To press tofu: If you'll be using the tofu for kebabs, cut it into $\frac{1}{2}$- to $\frac{3}{4}$-inch-thick slices. Otherwise, cut the tofu cutlet-style as described in the recipes. Arrange the slices on 1 or 2 layers of absorbent dish towel or several layers of paper towel. Cover with another towel or more paper towels, then with a cutting board. Place some weight, such as a heavy skillet, on the board. Allow to sit for 20 to 40 minutes.

Tofu to be used for kebabs may then be diced.

SWEET AND SAVORY GRILLED TOFU: Cut tofu into $\frac{1}{4}$- to $\frac{3}{8}$-inch-thick slices and press as directed above. Pour enough Sweet and Savory Grilling Sauce (page 112) to coat the bottom of a shallow container. Arrange the pressed tofu slices on top, then cover each with a thin layer of sauce. Marinate for 30 minutes to 1 hour. Prepare grill. Grill the tofu slices on each side for 7 to 10 minutes, or until nicely browned. Let guests pass around additional sauce to put on the tofu.

GRILLED TOFU TERIYAKI: Cut tofu into $\frac{1}{4}$- to $\frac{3}{8}$-inch-thick slices and press as directed above. In a shallow container, marinate the tofu slices in Teriyaki Marinade (page 113) for 30 minutes to 1 hour. Prepare grill. Grill tofu slices on each side for 7 to 10 minutes, or until nicely browned, brushing them with additional marinade as they grill. Delicious with Red Onion Relish (page 99) as an accompaniment.

TEMPEH

GRILLED TEMPEH TERIYAKI: Cut tempeh into pieces approximately 1 ½ by 2 inches, then cut each piece through the middle to make slices half as thick. In a shallow container, marinate the tempeh slices in Teriyaki Marinade (page 113) for 1 hour. Prepare grill. Grill tempeh slices on each side for 7 to 10 minutes, or until nicely browned, brushing them with additional marinade as they grill. Like Tofu Teriyaki, this is nice accompanied by Red Onion Relish (page 99).

SWEET AND SAVORY GRILLED TEMPEH: Cut tempeh into pieces approximately 1 ½ by 2 inches, then cut each piece through the middle to make slices half as thick. Pour enough Sweet and Savory Grilling Sauce (page 112) into a shallow container to coat the bottom. Arrange the tempeh slices on top, then cover each with a thin layer of sauce. Marinate for 30 minutes to 1 hour. Prepare grill. Grill tempeh slices on each side for 7 to 10 minutes, or until nicely browned. Let guests pass around additional sauce to put on the tempeh. These slices make a great sandwich, particularly on whole wheat rolls with shredded lettuce and rings of raw or grilled sweet red onion.

CURRIED GRILLED TEMPEH: Cut tempeh into pieces approximately 1 ½ by 2 inches, then cut each piece through the middle to make slices half as thick. In a shallow container, marinate the tempeh slices in Curry Marinade (page 114) for 1 hour. Prepare grill. Grill tempeh slices on each side for 7 to 10 minutes, or until nicely browned, brushing them with additional marinade as they grill. Basil or Parsley and Yogurt Sauce (page 114) makes a wonderful, palate-cooling accompaniment to pass around with the tempeh.

Tempeh (pronounced tem-PAY) is a traditional soy food from Indonesia. Like tofu, it has slowly gained popularity through natural food outlets. Unlike tofu, though, tempeh is not a common offering in supermarkets, and it's hard to say whether it ever will be. A super-nutritious food with even higher protein content than tofu, tempeh has a chewy texture that is quite pleasing to many, but it has a distinct taste with a slightly fermented bite. Some people love it and others just don't care for it. A case in point—I love tempeh, and my husband can easily do without it. I can honestly report, though, that he seems to enjoy if far better when grilled. The marinade and smoky flavors tone down the fermented flavor.

If you do like tempeh, you'll love it grilled. Like tofu, tempeh is a practically ready-to-eat food and needs no preparation other than cutting and marinating.

Seitan, or cooked wheat gluten, is a high-protein food that harks back to the ancient Orient. It's still used commonly in Japan, China, and Korea. Chances are good that vegetarians have had it in those mixed vegetable dishes in Chinese restaurants—it appears as small, chewy, dark-tan chunks. Your mind may have even flashed, "Goodness, was that a piece of meat?" Seitan does have a rather meatlike quality and is, in fact, sometimes called "wheat meat."

Commonly available in natural food stores, seitan is packaged in small plastic tubs. It is made from a dough of wheat and water that has been rinsed under running water until the starch and much of the bran have run out, leaving a mass of firm, stringy gluten, the most protein-packed part of wheat. The gluten is then cooked in a broth flavored with soy sauce and the sea vegetable kombu. The result is a chewy texture and a full-bodied, yet not overly distinct flavor. Seitan is somewhat salty, and I wouldn't recommend it for people who must restrict sodium intake.

On the grill, seitan becomes rather crisp on the outside and remains tender and moist on the inside.

SEITAN

GRILLED SEITAN TERIYAKI: When preparing the Teriyaki Marinade (page 113), use only half the amount of soy sauce called for, since seitan is somewhat salty to begin with. Prepare grill. Cut seitan into chunks about 2 inches square by 1 inch thick. Marinate with Teriyaki Marinade and grill, turning every 2 minutes or so, for a total of 6 to 10 minutes, or until the outside is dark brown and crisp. Serve with Basil or Parsley and Yogurt Sauce (page 114) or Red Onion Relish (page 99).

SEITAN AND GRILLED VEGETABLES TERIYAKI: When preparing the Teriyaki Marinade (page 113), use only half the amount of soy sauce, since seitan in somewhat salty to begin with. Cut seitan into chunks about 1 to 1 ½ inches square and press gently between layers of paper towel to squeeze out liquid. Alternate on skewers with vegetables of your choice. Use 3 or 4 of the following: steamed, bite-sized pieces of broccoli, cherry tomatoes, mushrooms, small eggplant dice, zucchini dice, parboiled baby onions. Prepare grill. Brush the ingredients with Teriyaki Marinade. Grill, turning carefully, until touched with charred spots, about 10 minutes total.

SWEET AND SAVORY GRILLED SEITAN: Prepare grill. Cut seitan into chunks about 2 inches square by 1 inch thick. Brush on all sides with Sweet and Savory Grilling Sauce (page 112). Grill on both sides, brushing with additional marinade as needed, about 5 minutes on each side, or until touched with charred spots. Let guests pass around additional sauce to put on the seitan.

GRILLING VEGETABLES

Depending on the theme of your meal, you may choose any of the marinades on pages 113 to 114 for vegetables that call for one in the directions. Olive Oil-Lemon Marinade is the most neutral and all-purpose of the marinades. Teriyaki Marinade gives vegetables a delicious Oriental flavor, but is not the least overpowering. Curry Marinade is the strongest and spiciest of the marinades and gives the vegetables an unusual twist. I don't recommend the Sweet and Savory Grilling Sauce for individually grilled vegetables, since it will tend to overpower their flavors. It is fine, though, used with vegetable kebabs that are combined with tofu or seitan.

BELL PEPPERS: The grill is actually the perfect place to prepare Roasted Peppers (page 258), a relish-like side dish that goes so well with so many foods. Instead of charring peppers under a broiler, set them right on a hot grill, turning on all sides until well covered with blackened spots. Let steam in a tightly shut paper bag for at least 15 minutes, then slip off the skins, core, seed, and cut into strips.

Bell peppers are also a standard ingredient in vegetable kebabs, simply cut into 1- and 1 ½-inch squares and skewered through the center. They will, more often than not, remain pretty crisp this way, since very little of their surface is exposed to heat, but this is not necessarily a drawback—since skewered vegetables tend to become rather tender, the contrasting crunch of the peppers is quite nice.

BROCCOLI: Broccoli is not often done on a grill but works quite well. Cut into approximately 3-inch pieces, including florets. Steam the broccoli until bright green and just barely crisp-tender. Rinse under cool water. Brush with Olive Oil-Lemon Marinade (page 113) or Teriyaki Marinade (page 113). Grill, turning frequently, for about 6 to 8 minutes total, or until touched with charred spots.

CARROTS: Carrots are often overlooked when it comes to grilling, but they are a treat. Peel and cut into 4- or 5-inch lengths, then cut in half lengthwise. Brush on both sides with marinade of your choice, pages 113 to 114. Grill on both sides until touched with charred spots, about 7 to 10 minutes total.

CORN: The most sophisticated way to grill corn is to carefully pull down the husks without removing them, then just as carefully remove the silk. The husks are then pulled back up around the corn and tied with a long, narrow piece of husk. I must admit that I've never gotten the hang of this. Everything seems to just fall apart for me.

This is what I do instead: Peel and husk the corn and let it soak in cold water for 1 hour. Prepare grill. Wrap the corn in aluminum foil. Grill for 20 to 30 minutes, turning every few minutes, or until it is touched with light brown spots. Alternatively, the corn can be microwaved until barely done, then set on the grill just long enough to brown lightly on all sides.

For a great summer treat, serve the corn with Herb "Butter" (page 258).

The great flavors of fresh summer vegetables turn extraordinary when exposed to the rapid, high-heat action of a grill. A slight sweetness is brought out, which, combined with slight charring, results in a most pleasant sensation. Grilling vegetables is a subtle art. It may take several tries to get the hang of just when to put them on the coals so that they don't char completely on the outside before the insides get done. In the list of good-to-grill vegetables, starting on the facing page, I give approximate times, but you will need to monitor the process carefully, as it is highly variable.

VEGETABLE KEBABS

Colorful kebabs are a festive way to serve grilled vegetables, and are quick and easy to prepare. Exact quantities of vegetables and specific recipes are unnecessary— and, in fact, detract from the fun of improvising. Just keep these general guidelines in mind:

- *Use flat-bladed skewers rather than rounded ones. The former hold the vegetables better, and the vegetables don't rotate as you turn them on the grill.*

- *Consult Grilling Vegetables (pages 108 to 111) for general information on the grilling characteristics of individual vegetables.*

- *Use 3 to 5 different vegetables, with a variety of colors.*

- *Prepare 2 skewers of vegetables per guest.*

EGGPLANT and JAPANESE EGGPLANT: Cut regular eggplant into slices 1/2 inch thick. Peel if desired. Salt lightly and place in a colander for 30 minutes, then rinse well. I highly recommend taking this extra step, since summer eggplant can be bitter, and the salting and rinsing are effective in removing much of that bitterness. Brush with the marinade of your choice, pages 113 to 114. Grill on both sides until tender and nicely browned, about 5 to 7 minutes on each side.

Tiny Japanese eggplants may simply be stemmed and cut in half lengthwise. Brush on both sides with marinade of your choice, pages 113 to 114 (it is especially good with Teriyaki Marinade), then grill on both sides until tender and the fleshy part is lightly browned, about 6 to 8 minutes total.

MUSHROOMS: Mushrooms are good grilled individually as well as part of kebabs. Choose larger mushrooms, wipe clean, and trim rough ends from the stems. Brush with marinade of your choice, pages 113 to 114. Grill for 5 to 8 minutes total, or until touched with charred spots, turning frequently and brushing with additional marinade, since mushrooms tend to dry out quickly.

ONIONS: Various types and sizes of onions call for varying treatments on the grill. Peel and cut large onions into 1/2-inch-thick slices. Brush on both sides with Olive Oil-Lemon Marinade (page 113). Grill on both sides until tender and touched with charred spots, about 10 minutes total. Try this with red onions and with Sweet Vidalia onions.

Parboil or microwave medium-sized onions until about half done (or until skewer can enter them with some resistance). Cut them in half and brush with Olive Oil-Lemon Marinade, then grill on both the cut and rounded sides for 10 to 12 minutes, or until tender and touched with charred spots. Or, half-done onions may simply be wrapped whole in foil without marinade and set on the grill for at least 20 minutes, or until very tender. This long cooking renders them very sweet and juicy.

Very small white onions are excellent for kebabs, but I still would recommend parboiling or microwaving them until half done before skewering them. All too often, I've been served kebabs with all the other vegetables tender and nicely charred, but the little onions virtually raw.

POTATOES: Potatoes, whether large or small, should be precooked or microwaved to a done, but very firm, texture before going on the grill. However, letting them cool before cutting and grilling them helps ensure that they won't fall apart. Cut large potatoes into thick slices and brush on both sides with marinade of your choice, pages 113 to 114. Grill on both sides until nicely browned, about 7 to 10 minutes total.

Cut tiny new potatoes in half, brush with marinade of your choice, pages 113 to 114. Grill on both sides until nicely browned, about 5 to 8 minutes total.

Firmly cooked potatoes, cut into 1-inch chunks, are an excellent addition to kebabs.

SCALLIONS: Whole scallions are very nice done on the grill, but must be watched carefully and taken off before the green parts get too charred. Brush with marinade of your choice, pages 113 to 114, and set on the grill for about 3 to 5 minutes total, or until beginning to brown. Scallions are especially tasty done with Teriyaki Marinade (page 113).

SQUASHES: Summer squashes are excellent candidates for the grill, since their not-too-hard, not-too-soft raw texture yields great results. As a side dish, or for a grilled vegetable platter, use tiny zucchini or yellow summer squash. Cut them in half lengthwise. Slice delicate-flavored pattypan squashes $1/4$ inch thick, crosswise. Brush them with Olive Oil-Lemon Marinade (page 113) or Teriyaki Marinade (page 113) and grill both sides until touched with charred spots, about 7 to 10 minutes total.

Larger zucchini and yellow squash, cut into 1-inch chunks, work very well in kebabs.

STRING BEANS: Grilled string beans are a surprising treat. Choose beans that are not too thin, but not so large as to be tough and gnarled. Brush raw string beans with marinade of your choice, pages 113 to 114. Grill, gently rolling them with tongs to expose all sides to the coals for about 5 to 10 minutes total, or until touched with charred spots.

TOMATOES: Tomatoes tend to get soft very quickly on the grill, and they are tricky to turn, but the results are tasty and worth the effort. I like to stick with the simple taste of Olive Oil-Lemon Marinade (page 113) for really good summer tomatoes, but tomatoes not at their peak of flavor can benefit from the stronger taste of Teriyaki Marinade or Curry Marinade (pages 113 to 114).

Slice large, firm tomatoes at least $1/2$ inch thick or cut plum tomatoes in half lengthwise and brush lightly with marinade. Grill on both sides until the edges brown, about 5 to 8 minutes total. Cherry tomatoes work well in kebabs.

- *Vegetables should be cut into approximately 1-inch chunks.*

- *Combine vegetables of consistent cooking times. Otherwise, for instance, in a kebab containing cherry tomatoes and baby onions or onion chunks, the tomatoes will be mush long before the onions have even lost their raw taste. However, there is no reason that harder vegetables can't be parboiled or microwaved and combined with softer raw vegetables.*

- *To make main-dish kebabs, add pressed, diced tofu, which is compatible with any combination of vegetables. See Grilling Tofu, page 106, for information on how to press and marinate tofu.*

- *Use one of the marinades on pages 113 to 114, and choose according to the flavor most compatible with the rest of the meal you are serving. Turn carefully on the grill, and cook until the vegetables are touched with charred spots. Most kebabs should be done in about 10 minutes.*

Here are some possible combinations for vegetable kebabs:

- *Parboiled or microwaved baby onions, tomato chunks or cherry tomatoes, green bell peppers, firm-cooked or microwaved potato chunks. Baste with Teriyaki Marinade (page 113) or Curry Marinade (page 114).*

- *Yellow summer squash, broccoli florets (steamed crisp-tender), mushrooms. Baste with Teriyaki Marinade (page 113).*

- *Zucchini, eggplant, cherry tomatoes, green or red bell peppers. Baste with Sweet and Savory Grilling Sauce (at right).*

SAUCES AND MARINADES

Sweet and Savory Grilling Sauce
Olive Oil-Lemon Marinade
Teriyaki Marinade
Curry Marinade
Basil or Parsley and Yogurt Sauce

SWEET AND SAVORY GRILLING SAUCE

Makes about 2 cups

This easy, no-cook sauce falls into that general realm of sweet and pungent tomato-based sauces generically known as "barbecue sauce."

1 ½ cups thick tomato sauce
3 tablespoons honey
1 tablespoon molasses
1 tablespoon olive oil
2 tablespoons soy sauce or tamari, or to taste
1 teaspoon each: paprika, chili powder, dry mustard, garlic powder, dried oregano

Combine all the ingredients in a mixing bowl and mix well. Cover and let stand for at least an hour to allow the flavors to combine.

Per 2-tablespoon serving:
Calories: 32   Total fat: 1 g   Protein: 0 g
Carbohydrate: 6 g   Cholesterol: 0 g   Sodium: 266 mg

OLIVE OIL-LEMON MARINADE

Makes about ½ cup

This basic marinade is excellent for grilling vegetables. The bit of lemon balances the fruity taste of the olive oil.

⅓ cup olive oil
juice of 1 lemon
1 teaspoon lemon thyme, if available
freshly ground pepper to taste

Combine all the ingredients in a small container. When brushing on vegetables, swirl the mixture around with the brush often to keep the oil and lemon combined.

Per 1-teaspoon serving:
Calories: 25	Total fat: 2 g	Protein: 0 g
Carbohydrate: 0 g	Cholesterol: 0 g	Sodium: 0 mg

TERIYAKI MARINADE

Makes about 1 cup

A highly flavored marinade, this adds exciting flavor to grilled tofu, tempeh, and seitan, and any vegetables that you wish to give an Oriental flavor on the grill— eggplant, broccoli, string beans, scallions, carrots, and mushrooms.

¼ cup soy sauce or tamari
¼ cup sake or white wine
2 tablespoons canola oil
2 teaspoons dark sesame oil
3 tablespoons light brown sugar
2 tablespoons rice vinegar or white wine vinegar
1 to 2 cloves crushed or minced garlic
1 teaspoon freshly grated ginger

Combine all the ingredients in a small container. Let stand until the sugar is dissolved. When brushing on foods, swirl the mixture often with the brush to keep combined.

Per 2-tablespoon serving:
Calories: 71	Total fat: 3 g	Protein: 1 g
Carbohydrate: 6 g	Cholesterol: 0 g	Sodium: 505 mg

GRILLED VEGETABLE PLATTERS

Here is another pleasing way to serve grilled vegetables to a group. Choose 4 to 6 different vegetables from Grilling Vegetables (pages 108 to 111). Select one of the marinades on pages 112 to 114, with the possible exception of Sweet and Savory Grilling Sauce, since you don't want to subordinate the delicate flavors of the vegetables to that of a strong sauce in this case. Grill vegetables according to the individual instructions. As they are done, arrange them aesthetically on a large platter. Don't worry if they are not all done at once. This is good served just warm or even cool. A few tips:

- *Create a platter with an Oriental theme—combine string beans, eggplant, broccoli, mushrooms, and cherry tomatoes, basted with Teriyaki Marinade. For protein, you might like to add tofu in the form of Grilled Tofu Teriyaki (page 106).*

- *Celebrate the bounty of summer with a platter of small yellow summer squash and zucchini, plum tomatoes, new potatoes, and carrots, basted with Olive Oil-Lemon Marinade (page 113). Once arranged on the platter, drizzle with a bit of additional marinade and sprinkle with crumbled goat cheese.*

- *Try a spicy curried grilled vegetable platter—choose eggplant, string beans, carrots, potatoes, and tomatoes, basted with Curry Marinade (at right). Arrange on a platter surrounding a small bowl of Basil or Parsley and Yogurt Sauce (at right) as a palate refresher.*

CURRY MARINADE

Makes about ½ cup

When it comes to grilling, a spicy marinade with a Far Eastern flavor can be a nice change of pace from the expected.

2 tablespoons canola oil
¼ cup dry white wine
juice of 1 lemon
1 tablespoon soy sauce or tamari
2 tablespoons minced shallot
1 to 2 teaspoons good curry powder, to taste

Combine all the ingredients in a small container. When brushing on foods, swirl often with the brush to keep combined.

Per 1-tablespoon serving:
Calories: 39   Total fat: 3 g   Protein: 0 g
Carbohydrate: 1 g   Cholesterol: 0 g   Sodium: 126 mg

BASIL OR PARSLEY AND YOGURT SAUCE

Makes about 1 ½ cups

Use this sauce as a refreshing counterpoint to strong or spicy marinades. It's perfect, for instance, as a sauce for Curried Grilled Tempeh.

1 ½ cups plain low-fat yogurt or soy yogurt
½ cup firmly packed fresh basil or parsley
1 tablespoon minced chives or scallion
1 ½ teaspoons honey
½ teaspoon prepared mustard
¼ teaspoon each: ground cumin, coriander

Combine the ingredients in the container of a food processor and process until all that remains of the herb is tiny flakes.

Per 2-tablespoon serving:
Calories: 24   Total fat: 0 g   Protein: 2 g
Carbohydrate: 3 g   Cholesterol: 2 g   Sodium: 29 mg

Chapter 8

LABOR DAY:
Summer's Harvest

⌣

Labor Day weekend, for most of us, marks the unofficial end of summer and is a signal for one final fling. Celebrations on this weekend carry mixed emotions: on one hand, there is the anticipation of a new school year for some, a stepping up of professional activities for others, after the relaxed pace of summer. Some people look forward to cooler weather and the spectacular show of changing leaves ahead. On the other hand, it's time to bid good-bye to long evenings, our home gardens, vacations, and visits with friends rarely seen outside of summer.

Though I enjoy that "back-to-the-real-world" ethic marked by Labor Day, I'm equally saddened to see the end of summer's relaxation, not the least of which is the pleasurable ease of preparing summer meals. Now is the time to make the most of what's left of summer's produce until the heartier riches of the fall harvest arrive.

For gardeners the end of summer means giving away overabundant tomatoes and zucchini, and using up the garden's remaining yield. People with time and patience will can and pickle what can't be used immediately. Herb gardeners will harvest long stems of herbs and hang them to dry.

In many areas, while other fresh goods are waning, local corn will be at its peak, and smart marketers will buy ears by the dozen, not only for eating off the cob, but to use fresh to make delicious dishes.

Labor Day gatherings can be a time to say good-bye to some friends and to welcome back others. In either case, this weekend should be a relaxed time to say farewell to summer's lazy days before getting back to the industrious ways that the day commemorates!

Late summer's culinary pleasures are captured in this zesty meal that works nicely as either a late lunch or a light supper. If you grow your own herbs, this will be one of your final opportunities to show them off. Most herb gardeners are diligent about harvesting their plants for drying and freezing before cool nights damage the leaves (see Making the Most of Your Herb Harvest, following pages); however, I try to put off doing so for as long as possible, since the flavors of fresh herbs—even after their peak—can't be equaled by dried or frozen herbs.

In this menu and, in fact, in those that follow in this chapter, I call for plenty of fresh dill, basil, parsley, oregano, and thyme to enhance the bounties of late summer's garden—zucchini, peppers, and tomatoes, among others. And when the flavor of summer fruit begins to wane, mint makes a welcome rescue.

AN HERB GARDEN SAMPLER

6 servings

Basil Cheese Tortellini

Navy Beans and String Beans with Fresh Herbs

Tomato Relish Salad with Oregano and Thyme

Fresh Fruit Salad with Honey-Mint Dressing

Herb "Butter" (page 258)

❧

Additions to the menu: Serve crusty rolls and pass the Herb "Butter" around to spread on them.

Contains no eggs.
Contains dairy products.

BASIL CHEESE TORTELLINI

6 servings

Use the juiciest, most flavorful late-summer tomatoes for best results.

1 pound good-quality cheese tortellini (use a mixture of white and spinach varieties, if possible)
2 pounds ripe tomatoes
2 tablespoons olive oil, divided
2 to 3 cloves garlic, minced
1/2 cup chopped fresh basil, more or less to taste
2 tablespoons chopped fresh oregano
3 tablespoons grated fresh Parmesan cheese, optional

dash hot red pepper flakes or cayenne pepper
salt and freshly ground pepper to taste
curly parsley for garnish

Cook the tortellini according to package directions, then drain.

Bring water to a boil in a large, deep saucepan. Plunge the tomatoes in and simmer for 1 minute. Drain, and when cool enough to handle, slip the skins off and chop finely.

Heat 1 tablespoon of the oil in a small skillet. Add the garlic and sauté over moderately low heat for a minute or 2, just until it begins to turn golden.

Combine the tortellini, tomatoes, garlic, and the rest of the olive oil and remaining ingredients in a mixing bowl and toss thoroughly. Transfer to a serving bowl and garnish the edges with curly parsley. Serve warm or at room temperature.

Calories: 281	Total fat: 11 g	Protein: 11 g
Carbohydrate: 37 g	Cholesterol: 22 g	Sodium: 260 mg

NAVY BEANS AND STRING BEANS WITH FRESH HERBS

6 servings

The strong flavor of fresh dill is a standout in this substantial salad.

½ pound string beans
2 cups canned or cooked navy beans
    (see Bean Basics, page 261)
1 medium Kirby cucumber, halved lengthwise and
    thinly sliced
1 small red bell pepper, finely diced
¼ cup reduced-fat or soy mayonnaise
½ cup plain low-fat yogurt
juice of ½ lemon, or more to taste
¼ cup minced fresh dill
¼ cup chopped fresh parsley
2 tablespoons minced fresh chives
1 tablespoon minced fresh tarragon
salt and freshly ground pepper to taste
dark green lettuce leaves for garnish

Trim the tips from the string beans and snap them in half. Steam until crisp-tender, then rinse under cool water. Combine in a mixing bowl with all the remaining ingredients except the garnishes and toss together well. Cover and refrigerate until needed. Before serving, line a serving bowl or wide serving plate with lettuce leaves, then arrange the salad over them. If desired, decorate the top with additional strips of red bell pepper.

Calories: 146	Total fat: 2 g	Protein: 7 g
Carbohydrate: 23 g	Cholesterol: 1 g	Sodium: 87 mg

TOMATO RELISH SALAD WITH OREGANO AND THYME

6 servings

The jewel-like colors of this simple relish salad make it especially appealing.

1 pound ripe yellow tomatoes
1 pound ripe red tomatoes
$^1/_4$ to $^1/_2$ cup minced red onion, to taste
3 tablespoons chopped oregano leaves
2 teaspoons French thyme or lemon thyme leaves
1 tablespoon olive oil
2 tablespoons red wine vinegar
1 $^1/_2$ teaspoons honey
salt and freshly ground pepper to taste

Cut the tomatoes into dice no larger than $^1/_2$ inch. Combine them in a serving bowl with the onion and herbs. In a small bowl, mix the oil, vinegar, and honey. Pour over the tomatoes and toss together. Cover and refrigerate for an hour. Before serving, season to taste, if desired, with salt and pepper.

Calories: 58	Total fat: 2 g	Protein: 1 g
Carbohydrate: 8 g	Cholesterol: 0 g	Sodium: 13 mg

FRESH FRUIT SALAD WITH HONEY-MINT DRESSING

6 servings

Late-summer fruits can be lush and ripe, but are often past their peak of flavor. I like my midsummer fruit salads plain, but by Labor Day, fruit salads can use the help of a sauce to enliven the flavors.

Dressing
½ cup vanilla nonfat or low-fat yogurt
1 to 2 tablespoons honey, to taste
1 to 2 tablespoons amaretto liqueur, optional
½ teaspoon vanilla extract
dash nutmeg
2 tablespoons minced fresh mint

Fruits
5 heaping cups fresh fruit, cut into bite-sized pieces
**   (summer fruit varieties are on the wane, but choose**
**   the best possible fruits from among melons, peaches,**
**   nectarines, grapes, and cherries)**

whole mint leaves for garnish

Combine the dressing ingredients in a small bowl and mix until smoothly blended.

Combine the fruits in a mixing bowl. Add the dressing and toss thoroughly. Transfer to a serving bowl and garnish with whole mint leaves. Cover and chill briefly before serving.

Calories: 90	Total fat: 0 g	Protein: 2 g
Carbohydrate: 20 g	Cholesterol: 1 g	Sodium: 16 mg

Gardeners will appreciate the emphasis on common garden produce in this menu. Overripe tomatoes are perfect for the refreshing cold soup; a simple sauté utilizes a variety of squashes; and you'll find a mellow pesto that helps use up all that tender parsley still in the garden.

REAPING THE HARVEST

6 servings

Herbed Sunflower Muffins

Fresh Tomato Soup with Crunchy Vegetables

New Potatoes with Parsley and Almond Pesto

Corn and Snow Pea Salad

Steamed Summer Squashes

Additions to the menu: Peaches and nectarines are still plentiful and lush, just past their peak. Slice some up and serve in parfait glasses layered with vanilla frozen yogurt or, for a vegan menu, with nondairy frozen dessert, topped with sliced or slivered almonds.

Contains egg and dairy products in Herbed Sunflower Muffins only. To adapt menu to vegan, eliminate the muffins and serve breadsticks with the Fresh Tomato Soup.

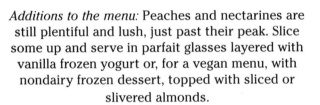

HERBED SUNFLOWER MUFFINS

Makes 1 dozen

Fresh herbs add an exciting savor to breads. These muffins make a perfect team with the cold tomato soup that follows.

1 ½ cups whole wheat pastry flour
½ cup cornmeal
1 teaspoon baking powder
1 teaspoon baking soda
1 teaspoon salt
1 egg, beaten
1 ½ cups plain nonfat yogurt
2 tablespoons honey
⅓ cup mixed minced fresh herbs (choose from chives,
        oregano, dill, parsley, and thyme)
¼ cup toasted sunflower seeds

Preheat the oven to 350 degrees.

Combine the first 5 ingredients in a mixing bowl. In another bowl, beat together the next 3 ingredients. Make a well in the center of the dry ingredients and pour in the wet ingredients. Mix vigorously until completely blended. Stir in the herbs and sunflower seeds.

Divide among 12 oiled or paper-lined muffin tins. Bake for 15 to 20 minutes, or until the tops are golden and a toothpick inserted into the center of a muffin comes out clean.

Per muffin:

Calories: 124	Total fat: 2 g	Protein: 5 g
Carbohydrate: 21 g	Cholesterol: 18 g	Sodium: 209 mg

FRESH TOMATO SOUP WITH CRUNCHY VEGETABLES

6 servings

This soup, if made with late summer's incomparably flavorful tomatoes, is absolutely heavenly. It's a great way to use any tomatoes that have gotten a bit overripe.

2 ½ pounds ripe, red tomatoes
2 tablespoons olive oil
2 cups chopped onion
2 cloves garlic, minced
2 large celery stalks, diced
¼ cup chopped fresh basil
2 tablespoons chopped fresh dill
1 teaspoon dry mustard
1 ½ to 2 cups tomato juice, as needed

1 tablespoon lemon juice
salt and freshly ground pepper to taste

Crunchy vegetable garnish
1 large green bell pepper, finely diced
1 large ear corn, cooked until just done, kernels
    scraped off cob
½ cup crisp cucumber, seeded and finely diced
⅓ cup finely diced radishes
2 tablespoons minced fresh basil

Bring 2 quarts of water to boil in a large soup pot. Place the whole tomatoes in the water and cook for 1 minute. Drain, and when the tomatoes are cool enough to handle, slip the skins off; chop tomatoes, and set aside.

Heat the olive oil and 2 tablespoons water in a large soup pot. Add the onions, garlic, and celery and sauté over moderate heat, stirring frequently, until the onion just begins to turn golden. Add 3 cups of water and bring to a boil, then simmer over moderate heat, covered, until the onions and celery are quite tender, about 15 minutes. Add the tomatoes, basil, dill, and mustard. Simmer for 10 minutes more. Remove from the heat. Stir in the tomato juice and lemon juice and season to taste with salt and pepper (salt carefully—you may not need any at all if the tomato juice is salted). Allow the soup to cool to room temperature, then puree in batches in a food processor or blender until smooth. Chill before serving.

Just before serving, combine all the ingredients for the crunchy vegetable garnish in a small mixing bowl. Ladle the chilled tomato soup into bowls and divide the garnish over the top of each.

Calories: 142	Total fat: 4 g	Protein: 3 g
Carbohydrate: 21 g	Cholesterol: 0 g	Sodium: 246 mg

NEW POTATOES WITH PARSLEY AND ALMOND PESTO

6 servings

While some savor the powerful flavor of the classic basil and walnut or pine nut pesto, others find it overpowering. I like to think of this pesto as a mellower alternative.

24 small new potatoes, scrubbed
1 cup firmly packed fresh parsley leaves
$^1\!/_4$ cup toasted almonds
1 clove garlic, crushed
2 tablespoons extra-virgin olive oil
juice of $^1\!/_2$ lemon
salt and freshly ground pepper to taste

Cook or microwave the new potatoes until tender but firm. Let cool to room temperature, then cut in half.

Place the remaining ingredients in the container of a food processor. Process until ground to a coarse, pastelike texture, adding 1 to 2 tablespoons of water to loosen the mixture. Toss at once with the potatoes. Serve warm or at room temperature.

Calories: 236	Total fat: 7 g	Protein: 3 g
Carbohydrate: 39 g	Cholesterol: 0 g	Sodium: 14 mg

CORN AND SNOW PEA SALAD

6 servings

$^1\!/_4$ pound snow peas
3 cups (about 4 medium ears) cooked fresh corn kernels
1 cup shredded white cabbage
1 medium red bell pepper, cut into thin, l-inch strips
$^1\!/_4$ cup sliced black olives
$^1\!/_4$ cup Garlic Vinaigrette (page 256), or as
    needed to moisten
salt and freshly ground pepper to taste

Trim the snow peas and cut in half crosswise. Steam briefly, just until bright green, then rinse immediately under cool running water until cold and drain well. Combine the snow peas with all the remaining ingredients in a serving container and toss thoroughly.

Refrigerate, covered, for an hour or 2 before serving. Stir once or twice during the time to distribute the vinaigrette. Drain off any excess vinaigrette before serving.

Calories: 147	Total fat: 7 g	Protein: 2 g
Carbohydrate: 18 g	Cholesterol: 0 g	Sodium: 65 mg

- Drying herbs: *Harvest herbs intended for drying before they flower; the flavor is best at that time. Cut long stems just after the sun has dried the morning dew; the plant's essential oils are most concentrated then.*

   Bathe the herbs in water, then let the leaves dry off in a colander or on paper towels. Next, tie several stems together and hang upside down in an airy space away from the sun. An attic is ideal, but any dim, well-ventilated space is fine. The drying process will take several days to a week or more, depending on the herb. When the leaves are completely dry, they will feel crisp and will crumble easily.

   Strip the leaves off the stems and crumble them with clean fingers or crush with a mortar and pestle. Store in tightly lidded jars in your kitchen, away from heat and light.

"Numbers of cooks spoil their garden stuffs by boiling them too much: All kinds of vegetables should have a little crispness; for if you boil them too much, you will deprive them both of their sweetness and beauty."

—John Farley
The London Art of Cookery and Housekeeper's Complete Assistant, 1783

STEAMED SUMMER SQUASHES

6 servings

2 pounds mixed variety of squashes (a combination of zucchini, yellow squash, and pattypan is attractive, but try any multicolored combination you wish)
1 tablespoon reduced-fat margarine
$\frac{1}{4}$ cup finely minced fresh herbs
salt and freshly ground pepper to taste
1 cup lightly steamed squash blossoms, optional

Trim the squashes and slice thinly or cut into small chunks. Place in a large pot with $\frac{1}{2}$ inch of water and steam, covered, stirring frequently, until just crisp-tender. Drain and transfer to a serving container. Toss with the margarine until melted, then toss with the herbs. Season to taste with salt and pepper. Scatter the optional squash blossoms over the top. Serve at once.

Calories: 37   Total fat: 1 g   Protein: 1 g
Carbohydrate: 6 g   Cholesterol: 0 g   Sodium: 17 mg

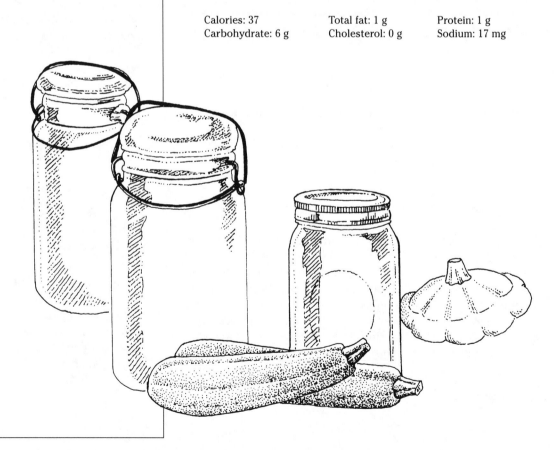

AN ITALIAN INTERLUDE

6 to 8 servings

Cold Angel Hair Pasta with Tomatoes and Basil

Ricotta Dumplings

Eggplant Caponata

Zucchini with Mint

Additions to the menu: Crusty bread or rolls go nicely with the pasta and the caponata. For dessert, serve one of the fruit sherbets on pages 105 to 106, or improvise one of your own, following the basic guidelines and using late summer fruit. Slice some of the fruit from which it was made to go along with it.

Contains egg whites.
Contains dairy products. Can be made dairy-free by following the suggested substitutions in the recipes. Replace Ricotta Dumplings with another protein dish, perhaps Navy Beans and String Beans with Fresh Herbs, page 117.

The first three recipes in this menu were contributed by a young woman originally from Bologna, Italy. The Cold Angel Hair Pasta with Tomatoes and Basil and the Eggplant Caponata are particularly well-loved dishes to serve on the Jewish Sabbath, since they can be made a day ahead and still taste great on the next, when any kind of work or preparation is not allowed. This feature will be appreciated by any busy host or hostess who would like to make most of the meal ahead of time.

COLD ANGEL HAIR PASTA WITH TOMATOES AND BASIL

6 to 8 servings

Teamed with capellini, the classic summer duo, tomatoes and basil, becomes quite a delicacy.

½ pound angel hair pasta (capellini)
1 to 1 ½ pounds ripe tomatoes, diced
½ cup chopped fresh basil
1 medium red onion, halved and thinly sliced
2 to 3 tablespoons capers
2 tablespoons chopped fresh oregano
2 tablespoons extra-virgin olive oil
¼ cup grated fresh Parmesan or pecorino Romano
        cheese, or 3 tablespoons nutritional yeast as
        nondairy substitute
salt and freshly ground pepper to taste

Cook the pasta al dente in plenty of simmering water. Drain and rinse under cool water. Combine with the remaining ingredients in a serving bowl and toss well. This may be made up to an hour ahead of time and refrigerated until needed. Serve chilled or at room temperature.

Calories: 166	Total fat: 5 g	Protein: 6 g
Carbohydrate: 23 g	Cholesterol: 56 g	Sodium: 220 mg

RICOTTA DUMPLINGS

Makes about 20 dumplings

These dumplings make a pleasantly mild contrast to the strong flavors of the capellini and caponata.

½ pound part-skim ricotta cheese
2 tablespoons grated fresh Parmesan cheese
3 egg whites, lightly beaten
¾ cup unbleached white flour
¼ cup cornmeal
salt and freshly ground pepper to taste
dash of nutmeg

reduced-fat margarine for sautéing
chopped fresh parsley
minced fresh oregano
additional grated fresh Parmesan cheese, optional

Combine the first 3 ingredients in a mixing bowl. Work in the flour and cornmeal. Season to taste with salt, pepper, and nutmeg. If time allows, chill the mixture for 30 minutes. With floured hands, roll into l-inch balls.

Bring water to a rolling boil in a large, deep pot. Drop the dumplings in gently. Once they rise to the surface, cook at a gentle, steady simmer for 8 minutes. Remove with a slotted spoon and drain. Let rest for 20 to 30 minutes, or, if making ahead of time, let cool and refrigerate in a covered container.

Before serving, heat just enough margarine to lightly coat the bottom of a nonstick skillet. Sauté the dumplings until golden on all sides. Arrange on a serving plate. Sprinkle with the fresh herbs and with additional Parmesan cheese if desired and serve at once.

Per dumpling:

Calories: 42	Total fat: 1 g	Protein: 3 g
Carbohydrate: 5 g	Cholesterol: 4 g	Sodium: 31 mg

EGGPLANT CAPONATA

6 to 8 servings

A classic, this relish-like eggplant salad is a delightful warm-weather dish.

2 medium eggplants, about ³⁄₄ pound each
2 tablespoons extra-virgin olive oil, divided
1 cup finely chopped onions
1 clove garlic, minced
2 medium celery stalks, diced
1 pound ripe, juicy tomatoes, finely diced
¹⁄₂ cup chopped green olives
¹⁄₄ cup chopped fresh parsley
1 tablespoon chopped fresh oregano, optional
2 tablespoons red wine vinegar
salt and freshly ground pepper to taste
curly parsley for garnish

"To take parsley away from the cook would make it almost impossible for him to exercise his art."

—Louis Bosc d'Antic, 1790

Preheat the oven to 400 degrees.

Place the eggplants on a foil-lined baking sheet and bake until they collapse, about 40 minutes. When cool enough to handle, peel and chop fine.

Heat half of the olive oil in a large skillet. Add the onions and sauté over moderate heat until translucent. Add the garlic and celery and continue to sauté until the onion is lightly browned.

In a mixing bowl, combine the eggplant, the onion mixture, the reserved olive oil, and all the remaining ingredients except the garnish and stir together. Allow to cool to room temperature, then transfer to a serving bowl. Garnish the edges with curly parsley.

Calories: 89	Total fat: 4 g	Protein: 1 g
Carbohydrate: 11 g	Cholesterol: 0 g	Sodium: 110 mg

ZUCCHINI WITH MINT

6 to 8 servings

For this recipe, we travel from northern Italy to Sicily. The contributor remembers her mother making this in late summer, and when I first tried it, I was quite taken with the surprising flavor of zucchini contrasted with mint. It's an unusual and refreshing way to make good use of two abundant garden products of late summer.

2 long, narrow, medium zucchinis, about 1 pound total
$1/4$ cup finely chopped fresh mint, or more to taste
1 scallion, minced
2 tablespoons apple juice
juice of 1 lemon
1 tablespoon honey
salt and freshly ground pepper to taste

Cut the zucchinis into 1/8-inch-thick slices. Combine in a mixing bowl with the mint and scallions and toss together. In a small bowl, combine the apple juice, lemon juice, and honey. Pour over the zucchini mixture and toss well. Cover and refrigerate for an hour before serving. Just before serving, season to taste with salt and pepper.

Calories: 22	Total fat: 0 g	Protein: 0 g
Carbohydrate: 5 g	Cholesterol: 0 g	Sodium: 2 mg

Chapter 9

THE JEWISH NEW YEAR AND HANUKKAH

Next to Passover, no Jewish holidays are more regularly celebrated with family meals by American Jews than the Jewish New Year, or Rosh Hashanah, and Hanukkah, the Festival of Lights, which will be discussed later in this chapter.

The Jewish New Year is traditionally a time of self-reflection and of taking stock. Celebrated in late September or early October, determined by the Hebrew calendar, it is the first of the Days of Awe, or Ten Days of Penitence that culminate with Yom Kippur, the Day of Atonement.

The Jewish New Year is second only to Passover in its emphasis on symbolic foods. Passover was originally a harvest festival, and the foods eaten are those abundant in the early fall. More importantly, many of the foods eaten must be sweet, to symbolize optimism that the year ahead will be a sweet and good one. Both Sephardic and Ashkenazic Jews favor early fall produce with natural sweetness—carrots, apples, beets, pumpkins, leeks, sweet potatoes. Honey, sugar, raisins, prunes, and other dried fruits are used generously to augment the sweetness. Bitter, salty, and sharp-tasting foods are generally avoided.

The Jewish New Year meal is a time to acknowledge the blessings of the home and family. For the occasion, the table is set with the finest linen, a basket of fruits, and candles. And always, the meal opens with a benediction over apples dipped in honey.

Creating a meatless menu from early fall harvest goods, incorporated into classic dishes of Eastern European, or Ashkenazic, Jews, is not a daunting task. The sweetness in the dishes must be treated subtly, so as not to be overwhelming.

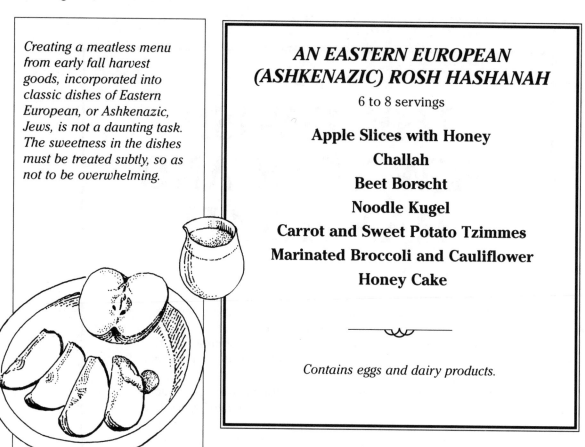

AN EASTERN EUROPEAN (ASHKENAZIC) ROSH HASHANAH

6 to 8 servings

Apple Slices with Honey

Challah

Beet Borscht

Noodle Kugel

Carrot and Sweet Potato Tzimmes

Marinated Broccoli and Cauliflower

Honey Cake

⚜

Contains eggs and dairy products.

APPLE SLICES WITH HONEY

Apple slices dipped in honey are an essential opening to a Rosh Hashanah meal. They symbolize the hope that the year ahead will be a good and sweet one.

4 crisp, sweet apples
honey

Peel and core the apples. Cut each apple into 8 wedges, and arrange on a serving platter.

Pour honey into 1 or 2 small bowls. Guests dip each of their apple slices once into the honey.

Calories: 62	Total fat: 0 g	Protein: 0 g
Carbohydrate: 15 g	Cholesterol: 0 g	Sodium: 1 mg

CHALLAH
(Jewish Egg Bread)

Makes 2 loaves

Challah is eaten at many Jewish holidays, but this moist egg bread is a must for Rosh Hashanah. It's traditional to eat it, not surprisingly, spread with honey. This bread is not usually made with whole wheat, but I have added some to this version for more flavor and body, and it works well.

1 $\frac{1}{2}$ packages active dry yeast
$\frac{1}{4}$ cup canola oil
3 tablespoons honey
3 $\frac{1}{2}$ to 4 cups unbleached white flour
2 cups whole wheat flour
1 $\frac{1}{2}$ teaspoons salt
2 eggs, beaten
egg white for glazing top
poppy or sesame seeds for topping

Combine the yeast with $\frac{1}{2}$ cup of warm water. Let stand for 5 to 10 minutes, or until dissolved. Stir in the oil, honey, and another 1 $\frac{1}{2}$ cups of warm water.

Combine the flours and salt in a large mixing bowl. Make a well in the center and pour in the wet mixture and the beaten eggs. Work together, first with a wooden spoon, then with hands. Add additional flour until the dough loses its stickiness.

Turn the dough out onto a well-floured board. Knead for 8 to 10 minutes. Place in a floured bowl, cover with a tea towel, and put in a warm place to rise until doubled in bulk, about 1 $\frac{1}{2}$ hours.

Punch the dough down and divide into 2 parts. Divide each part into 3 parts. Make long strands, about 1 $\frac{1}{2}$ inches in diameter, from each part. Attach 3 strands at one end by pinching together. Braid the strands and pinch together at the bottom. Place on a lightly floured baking sheet and let rise until doubled in bulk again, about 1 to 1 $\frac{1}{2}$ hours.

Brush the tops of the braids with egg white and sprinkle with sesame or poppy seeds. Bake in a preheated 350-degree oven for about 45 minutes, or until the tops are golden and the loaves feel hollow when tapped. Cool on a rack.

Per $\frac{3}{4}$-inch-thick slice:

Calories: 159	Total fat: 3 g	Protein: 5 g
Carbohydrate: 26 g	Cholesterol: 21 g	Sodium: 168 mg

Make-ahead suggestions for:

An Eastern European Rosh Hashanah

A day ahead:

- *Bake the Challah.*

- *Make the Beet Borscht— especially since it needs time to cool and chill.*

- *Bake the Honey Cake.*

Borscht and bread make your cheeks red.

—Yiddish proverb

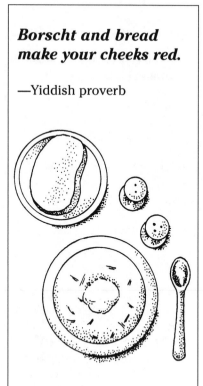

BEET BORSCHT

6 to 8 servings

This refreshing cold soup of Russian origin is appropriately filled with produce favored on this holiday for abundance and subtle sweetness. Grating all the vegetables will be a chore unless you use a food processor.

5 large beets, grated
2 large carrots, grated
1 large sweet apple, grated
1 large onion, grated
juice of 1 lemon, or more to taste
1/4 cup light brown sugar, or to taste
1 teaspoon salt
2 tablespoons minced fresh dill
freshly ground pepper to taste
reduced-fat sour cream, low-fat yogurt,
**   or buttermilk, optional**

Combine the first 7 ingredients in a large soup pot with enough water to cover. Bring to a boil, then lower the heat and simmer, covered, until the vegetables are tender, about 40 to 45 minutes. Stir in the dill and adjust the consistency with more water if the vegetables are too densely packed. Taste and add more lemon and/or sugar to bring the sweet and tangy flavor to your liking. Allow to cool, then refrigerate, covered, until thoroughly chilled. Top each serving with sour cream, yogurt, or a swirl of buttermilk, if desired.

Calories: 57	Total fat: 0 g	Protein: 1 g
Carbohydrate: 14 g	Cholesterol: 0 g	Sodium: 334 mg

NOODLE KUGEL

6 to 8 servings

None other than the classic Jewish comfort food.

1/2 pound medium-width egg noodles, cooked
1 pound part-skim ricotta or farmer cheese
16-ounce can drained, crushed pineapple
2/3 cup dark or golden raisins

1 medium sweet apple, peeled, cored, and grated
2 tablespoons melted reduced-fat margarine
1 cup firmly packed light brown sugar
1 teaspoon vanilla extract
1 teaspoon cinnamon

Preheat the oven to 350 degrees.

Cook the noodles in plenty of simmering water until they are done, then drain.

In the meantime, combine the remaining ingredients in a mixing bowl. Stir in the cooked noodles. Transfer the mixture to an oiled, shallow 9- by 13-inch casserole dish. Bake for 45 to 50 minutes, or until the top begins to brown and look crisp. Let stand 15 minutes before serving.

Calories: 350	Total fat: 6 g	Protein: 10 g
Carbohydrate: 62 g	Cholesterol: 30 g	Sodium: 126 mg

CARROT AND SWEET POTATO TZIMMES

6 to 8 servings

Next to apples and honey, carrots are the most commonly used symbolic food in Eastern European New Year meals. The Yiddish word for carrot also means to increase or multiply, a positive thought with which to begin the year. Here, carrots are appropriately combined with sweet potatoes and prunes in a classic Jewish dish.

1 tablespoon canola oil
1 cup chopped onions
3 large carrots, sliced
3 large sweet potatoes, cooked or microwaved, then peeled and sliced
1 large pear, peeled, cored, and sliced
1/2 cup chopped dried prunes
1/4 cup chopped dried apricots
2/3 cup orange juice
1 1/2 teaspoons cinnamon
1/2 teaspoon ground ginger
1/2 teaspoon salt
1/4 teaspoon nutmeg
1/3 cup finely chopped walnuts for topping, optional

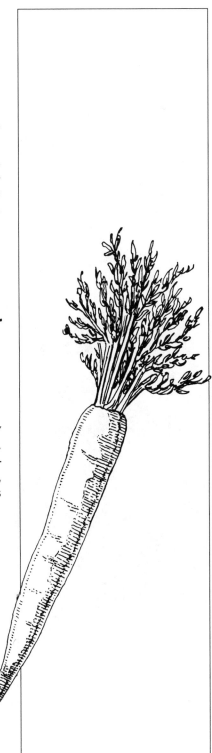

Preheat the oven to 350 degrees.

Heat the oil in a large skillet. Add the onions and sauté over moderate heat until translucent. Add the carrots plus 3 tablespoons of water and continue to sauté until they and the onions are golden. Combine with the remaining ingredients except the walnuts in a mixing bowl and stir until thoroughly mixed. Don't worry if the potato slices break apart.

Oil a large, shallow baking casserole (since the Noodle Kugel is being baked in a rectangular dish, this would be attractive baked in a round one). Bake for 45 to 50 minutes, or until the top begins to turn slightly crusty. Serve hot.

Calories: 170	Total fat: 2 g	Protein: 2 g
Carbohydrate: 36 g	Cholesterol: 0 g	Sodium: 174 mg

MARINATED BROCCOLI AND CAULIFLOWER

6 to 8 servings

This colorful salad is not traditional to this holiday, but provides a nice counterpoint to the sweet dishes without being too pungent. Actually, the red peppers and avocado add a nice sweet touch.

4 heaping cups broccoli, cut into bite-sized pieces and florets
4 heaping cups cauliflower, cut as above
2 medium red bell peppers, cut into narrow strips
2 scallions, minced
3 tablespoons minced fresh parsley

Marinade
2 tablespoons olive oil
juice of 1 large lemon
2 teaspoons honey
1/4 teaspoon salt
freshly ground pepper

1 small avocado, peeled and finely diced

Steam the broccoli and cauliflower until crisp-tender. Rinse until they are cool, then drain thoroughly. Combine in a mixing bowl with the peppers, scallions, and parsley.

In a small bowl, combine the ingredients for the marinade and mix until thoroughly blended. Pour over the vegetables and toss well. Cover and refrigerate for several hours, stirring occasionally. Just before serving, toss in the diced avocado.

Calories: 124	Total fat: 7 g	Protein: 2 g
Carbohydrate: 12 g	Cholesterol: 0 g	Sodium: 330 mg

HONEY CAKE

Makes 2 loaves

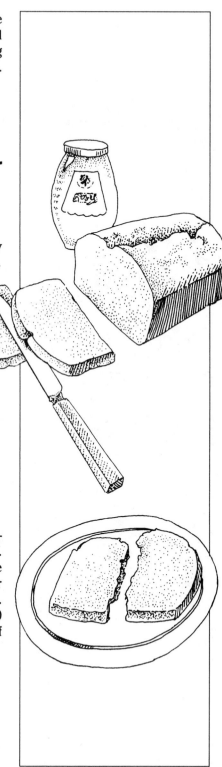

In Jewish tradition, honey cake is served at many happy occasions but is a must for the Ashkenazic Rosh Hashanah.

4 cups whole wheat pastry flour
3 tablespoons baking powder
1 teaspoon baking soda
1/2 teaspoon salt
2 teaspoons cinnamon
1/2 teaspoon ground ginger
1/2 teaspoon ground cloves
3 eggs, beaten
1 cup honey
2 cups applesauce
2 teaspoons vanilla extract
1/2 cup golden raisins
2/3 cup chopped almonds

Preheat the oven to 325 degrees.

Combine the first 7 ingredients in a mixing bowl. In another bowl, combine the eggs, honey, applesauce, and vanilla. Beat together until smooth. Make a well in the center of the dry ingredients and pour in the wet mixture. Beat together until thoroughly combined. Stir in the raisins and almonds. Divide the batter between 2 lightly oiled loaf pans. Bake 50 to 60 minutes, or until a knife inserted in the center of a loaf tests clean.

Per 3/4-inch-thick slice:

Calories: 193	Total fat: 4 g	Protein: 5 g
Carbohydrate: 35 g	Cholesterol: 32 g	Sodium: 68 mg

As in the Eastern European tradition, early fall harvest goods are celebrated and blessed during the Jewish New Year by Sephardic Jews. The produce used, symbolizing fertility and abundance, includes fresh and dried fruits, leeks, squashes, pumpkins, beets, and turnips.

A SEPHARDIC ROSH HASHANAH

6 to 8 servings

Apple Slices with Honey (page 130)
Dried Fruit Soup
Seven-Vegetable Couscous
Leek Croquettes
Beet Salad with Beet Greens
Pumpkin Turnovers

Eggs are used in Leek Croquettes; see alternative preparation described in headnote of this recipe. Menu is dairy-free if optional dairy garnish is eliminated from Dried Fruit Soup.

DRIED FRUIT SOUP

6 to 8 servings

Dried fruits are a favored festive ingredient in Sephardic tradition. Here, several varieties are combined in an unusual and refreshing cold soup.

1 cup dried apples
½ cup dried apricots
½ cup pitted prunes
2 tablespoons raisins
¼ cup dry red wine
1 cinnamon stick
6 whole cloves
1 cup apple juice, plus more as needed
juice of ½ lemon

reduced-fat sour cream, low-fat yogurt, or
    buttermilk, optional
fresh mint leaves

In a deep, heavy saucepan, combine the dried fruits, wine, spices, and just enough water to cover. Bring to a boil, then remove from the heat. Add the apple juice and lemon juice. Let the soup cool. Once cooled, add additional apple juice if the fruits have gotten too crowded, but let the soup stay fairly dense. Chill thoroughly before serving. Serve in small portions, garnishing each serving with a dollop of sour cream or yogurt or a swirl of buttermilk, if desired, and a mint leaf or 2.

Calories: 179	Total fat: 0 g	Protein: 1 g
Carbohydrate: 41 g	Cholesterol: 0 g	Sodium: 12 mg

SEVEN-VEGETABLE COUSCOUS

6 to 8 servings

Since seven is a lucky number in Jewish tradition, Sephardic Jews serve a seven-vegetable soup or stew such as this one for the holiday meal.

1 ¹/₂ cups couscous
1 tablespoon reduced-fat margarine
1 teaspoon turmeric
1 teaspoon salt
1 tablespoon canola oil
2 medium onions, chopped
2 large carrots, sliced
1 cup finely shredded white cabbage
1 medium turnip, peeled and diced
1 medium yellow summer squash, diced
1 ¹/₂ cups canned or cooked chick peas (see Bean
    Basics, page 261)
1 ¹/₂ cups diced ripe tomatoes
1 teaspoon freshly grated ginger
1 teaspoon cinnamon
¹/₂ teaspoon each: ground cumin, coriander, turmeric, salt
¹/₃ cup raisins
¹/₄ cup chopped fresh parsley
¹/₄ cup toasted sliced or slivered almonds

Make-ahead suggestions for:

A Sephardic Rosh Hashanah

A day ahead:

- *Make the Dried Fruit Soup.*

- *Make the Beet Salad with Beet Greens.*

- *Make the Pumpkin Turnovers.*

Of the seven vegetables included in this traditional Rosh Hashanah dish, chick peas are perhaps the most significant. The Hebrew word for these legumes is similar to that for the word meaning "cold"; hence chick peas have come to symbolize the cooling of harsh heavenly judgment. Chick peas, eaten plain or salted, are sometimes a part of Eastern European Rosh Hashanah fare.

Cover the couscous with 3 cups of boiling water in a heatproof bowl. Cover and let stand until the water is absorbed, about 15 minutes. Fluff with a fork, then stir in the margarine, turmeric, and salt. Cover and set aside.

In the meantime, heat the oil in a soup pot. Add the onions and sauté over moderate heat until translucent. Stir in the carrots and cabbage and sauté until crisp-tender, adding small amounts of water as needed to keep the bottom of the pot moist. Add the remaining ingredients except the last 2. Cover and cook over low heat, lifting the lid to stir frequently, for 15 to 20 minutes. Add water in small amounts until the mixture has the consistency of a thick, moist (but not soupy) stew. The vegetables should be tender but still firm.

Before serving, arrange the couscous on the outer perimeter of a large serving platter. Pour the vegetable mixture into the center. Sprinkle with the parsley and almonds. Guests should place a small mound of couscous on their plates and top it with the vegetable mixture.

Calories: 248	Total fat: 6 g	Protein: 7 g
Carbohydrate: 41 g	Cholesterol: 0 g	Sodium: 353 mg

LEEK CROQUETTES

Makes about 2 dozen

Alongside the couscous, these are a delicately flavored accompaniment. If you'd like to keep this meal egg-free, simply prepare and "sweat" the leeks as suggested, then toss them with a bit of margarine, lemon juice to taste, fresh dill, and salt and pepper, rather than making them into croquettes.

**6 large leeks, white and palest green parts only,
　chopped and well rinsed
3 eggs, beaten
$3/4$ cup matzo meal
juice of $1/2$ lemon
1 to 2 tablespoons minced fresh dill
salt and freshly ground pepper to taste
oil for sautéing (about 2 tablespoons)**

Place the leeks in a large skillet with 2 tablespoons of water. Cover and "sweat" them over moderate heat, stirring occasionally, and adding a few drops of water if the skillet gets dry, until they are limp. Combine the leeks in a mixing bowl with the remaining ingredients except the oil, and mix well.

Heat just enough oil to coat the bottom of a large nonstick skillet. When very hot, drop enough of the mixture onto the skillet to form 3-inch croquettes. Cook on both sides over moderately high heat until golden brown. Drain briefly on paper towels, then place in a covered container to keep warm until all are done.

Per croquette:

Calories: 54	Total fat: 2 g	Protein: 2 g
Carbohydrate: 8 g	Cholesterol: 27 g	Sodium: 15 mg

BEET SALAD WITH BEET GREENS

6 to 8 servings

1 large bunch beets, consisting of 4 to 5 good-sized beets with a good quantity of greens
2 scallions, minced
2 tablespoons minced fresh dill
2 tablespoons apple juice or cider
juice of $1/2$ to 1 lemon, to taste
2 teaspoons honey
2 teaspoons poppy seeds, optional
salt and freshly ground pepper to taste

Separate the greens from the beets about 1 inch from where they begin. Rinse the beets, then cook or microwave them until tender. The cooking time will vary widely depending on their size and age. Let the beets cool. In the meantime, wash the greens well and chop them. Steam until bright green and just tender. Place in a colander, rinse briefly with cool water, then squeeze out as much liquid as possible.

When the beets are cool, trim the stem ends, then peel, quarter, and slice them. Combine in a mixing bowl with the greens, scallions, and dill. Combine the apple juice, lemon juice, and honey in a small bowl and stir together. Pour over the beets and toss. Add the optional poppy seeds and season to taste with salt and pepper. Toss well again. Refrigerate for

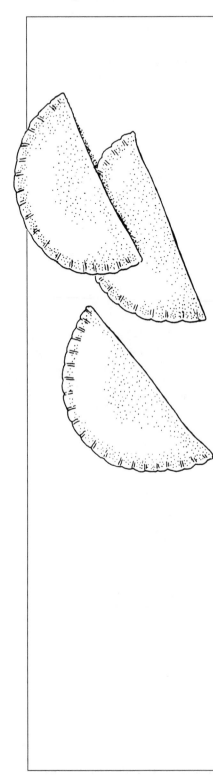

at least an hour before serving, or make a day ahead.

Calories: 46   Total fat: 0 g   Protein: 2 g
Carbohydrate: 10 g   Cholesterol: 0 g   Sodium: 219 mg

PUMPKIN TURNOVERS

Makes about 2 dozen

Desserts made of pumpkin are intrinsic to the Sephardic tradition, in much the same way honey cake is to the Ashkenazic.

Pastry
2 to 2 1/4 cups whole wheat pastry flour
1/2 teaspoon baking powder
1/4 cup granulated sugar
dash of salt
1/3 cup canola oil

Filling
1 cup fresh or canned pureed pumpkin
1/2 cup light brown sugar, or to taste
1 teaspoon cinnamon
1/4 teaspoon each: ground ginger, cloves
dash nutmeg

Preheat the oven to 375 degrees.

Combine the flour, baking powder, sugar, and salt in a mixing bowl. Make a well in the center and pour in the oil and 1/2 cup of water. Work together to form a soft dough, using enough flour so that the dough loses its stickiness. Cover and let rest while preparing the filling.

Combine the ingredients for the filling in a mixing bowl and stir together.

Roll the dough out on a well-floured board to a thickness of 1/16 inch. Cut 3-inch circles. Gather scraps and reroll until the dough is used. Place a heaping teaspoon of the filling on one side of each circle, fold over, and pinch edges shut.

Arrange on a lightly oiled baking sheet and bake 20 minutes, or until the dough is golden. Cool on a rack.

Per turnover:
Calories: 86   Total fat: 3 g   Protein: 1 g
Carbohydrate: 13 g   Cholesterol: 0 g   Sodium: 3 mg

A HANUKKAH OF MIXED TRADITIONS

8 servings

Latkes (Potato Pancakes)
Baked Eggplant and Peppers
Stewed White Beans
Israeli Salad
Cheese Blintzes with Blueberry Sauce

Contains eggs (only in latkes).
Contains dairy products. Can be made
dairy-free by following the suggested
substitutions in the recipes.

Hanukkah, the Festival of Lights, is as eagerly awaited by American Jewish children as Christmas is by Christian children. This December holiday is joyously celebrated with candles, songs, games, and gifts.

Hanukkah commemorates the victory of the Jewish Maccabees over the Syrians many centuries ago. When the Maccabees went to cleanse and rededicate their temple, they found only enough oil to light their menorah, or candelabrum, for one day. The supply, as legend has it, miraculously lasted for eight days. On the first night of the holiday, the head candle plus one of the side candles of the menorah is lit, and on each subsequent night an additional side candle is lit.

Hanukkah hasn't quite the number of symbolic dishes of some other Jewish holidays, but its hallmarks are fried foods, typically potato latkes and deep-fried desserts, and cheese delicacies. I've opted for the latter instead of the fried dessert (usually jelly donuts), since one fried dish seems sufficient in the menu, and latkes are an absolute must for celebrating Hanukkah.

LATKES
(Potato Pancakes)

Makes about 4 dozen

Fried foods are traditionally eaten on Hanukkah to symbolize the sacred oil of the Maccabean temple. Though fried foods are not generally favored by the health-conscious, it's hard to imagine Hanukkah without them. To make them a healthier treat, fry them in a nonstick Silverstone skillet or griddle with a minimal amount of canola oil, and drain them well on paper towels before serving.

6 large potatoes, peeled and finely grated
1 medium onion, finely grated
3 eggs, beaten

Make-ahead suggestions for

A Hanukkah of Mixed Traditions

A day ahead:

- *Make the Stewed White Beans. Cool and store in the refrigerator. The beans can be reheated in the oven while the eggplant casserole bakes.*

- *Make the Blueberry Sauce for Cheese Blintzes.*

½ cup matzo meal
salt and freshly ground pepper to taste
canola oil for frying
applesauce

If grating potatoes in a food processor, run them through the grater twice, otherwise they will be too coarse. Put the grated potatoes in a colander and let drain for 10 minutes, then press down on them with palms to extract excess liquid. Combine in a mixing bowl with the onion, eggs, and matzo meal. Season to taste with salt and pepper.

Heat just enough oil to coat the bottom of a large, non-stick skillet. Drop enough potato batter to form 2 ½- to 3-inch pancakes. Fry on both sides over moderately high heat until golden brown and crisp. Drain briefly on paper towels and place in a covered container to keep warm until serving. Serve warm with applesauce.

Per latke:

Calories: 46	Total fat: 3 g	Protein: 1 g
Carbohydrate: 5 g	Cholesterol: 13 g	Sodium: 5 mg

BAKED EGGPLANT AND PEPPERS

6 to 8 servings

Eggplant and peppers, two well-loved vegetables in both the Eastern European and Sephardic traditions, are combined in a delicious casserole.

1 large or 2 smaller eggplants, 1 ½ pounds total,
    peeled and diced
2 tablespoons olive oil, divided
1 large onion, finely chopped
1 teaspoon dried basil
½ teaspoon ground cumin
¼ cup wheat germ
salt and freshly ground pepper to taste
3 medium green bell peppers, cut into l-inch squares
1 ½ cups diced plum tomatoes
3 tablespoons unbleached white flour
¾ cup low-fat milk or soymilk
1 ½ cups grated part-skim mozzarella cheese or

mozzarella-style soy cheese
dash cayenne pepper

Preheat the oven to 350 degrees.

Place the diced eggplant in a colander and salt it. Let stand for 30 minutes, then rinse thoroughly. Heat half the oil in a large skillet. Add the onion and sauté over moderate heat until it begins to turn golden. Add the eggplant and just enough water to keep the bottom of the skillet moist. Cover and cook, stirring frequently. When the eggplant is about half done, stir in the basil and cumin. Cook until the eggplant is tender, adding small amounts of water as needed while cooking to keep the skillet moist. Stir in the wheat germ and season to taste with salt and pepper.

Lightly oil a large, shallow baking casserole and pat the eggplant mixture into it.

Rinse the skillet and heat the remaining oil. Add the peppers and sauté over high heat, stirring frequently, until they begin to brown. Lower the heat, stir in the tomatoes, and sauté for a minute or 2, just until they begin to soften. Slowly sprinkle in the flour, stirring until it disappears. Then, slowly, stir in the milk and bring to a simmer. Sprinkle in the cheese, a bit at a time, followed by the cayenne. Let the mixture simmer until thickened and the cheese is completely melted. Pour over the eggplant. Bake for 35 to 40 minutes, or until the top is golden brown and bubbly. Let cool for 10 minutes, then scoop out sections with a spatula to serve.

Calories: 183	Total fat: 8 g	Protein: 10 g
Carbohydrate: 16 g	Cholesterol: 15 g	Sodium: 136 mg

STEWED WHITE BEANS

6 to 8 servings

Small white beans cooked in a savory sauce is a common Sephardic dish, served year-round for holidays and everyday meals alike.

1 tablespoon canola oil
1 cup minced onion
½ cup minced celery
14- to 16-ounce can crushed tomatoes
3 tablespoons light brown sugar
1 teaspoon paprika

"Beans are highly nutritious and satisfying; they can also be delicious if and when properly prepared, and they possess over all vegetables the great advantage of being just as good, if not better, when kept waiting, an advantage in the case of people whose disposition or occupation makes it difficult for them to be punctual at mealtime."

—Andre Simon
The Concise Encyclopedia of Gastronomy, 1952

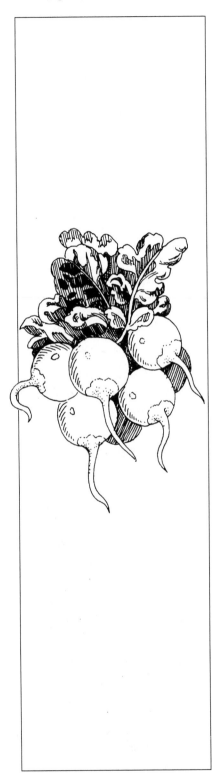

1 teaspoon dried summer savory
2 bay leaves
2 ¼ to 2 ½ cups canned or cooked navy beans
    (see Bean Basics, page 261)
salt and freshly ground pepper

Heat the oil in a deep, heavy saucepan. Add the onion and celery and sauté over moderate heat until they are golden. Stir in the crushed tomatoes, sugar, and seasonings. Bring to a simmer, then stir in the beans. Add a pinch of salt and a grinding of pepper. Simmer, covered, over very low heat, for 45 minutes. Taste to adjust seasonings and serve hot.

Calories: 158	Total fat: 2 g	Protein: 5 g
Carbohydrate: 29 g	Cholesterol: 0 g	Sodium: 35 mg

ISRAELI SALAD

6 to 8 servings

The hallmark of an Israeli salad is that its vegetables are diced very small, resulting in a nice blending of flavors. Let your tomatoes ripen in paper bags in a cool, dark place for 2 to 3 days to develop more flavor.

1 large cucumber, peeled, seeded, and cut into
    ¼-inch dice
4 medium plum tomatoes, or 2 large tomatoes,
    cut into ½-inch dice
2 medium red bell peppers, cut into ¼-inch dice
1 cup finely shredded red cabbage
2 scallions, minced
½ cup finely diced radish
1 medium half-sour pickle, finely diced, or ⅓ cup
    chopped green olives
1 tablespoon olive oil, or as needed
juice of ½ to 1 lemon, to taste
salt and freshly ground pepper to taste

Combine all the vegetables in a salad bowl. Toss together. Use enough olive oil to moisten the vegetables, and add lemon juice to taste. Season to taste with salt and pepper and toss again.

Calories: 43	Total fat: 1 g	Protein: 1 g
Carbohydrate: 5 g	Cholesterol: 0 g	Sodium: 7 mg

CHEESE BLINTZES WITH BLUEBERRY SAUCE

Makes 16 blintzes, 2 per serving

Hanukkah desserts, such as jelly donuts, are traditionally deep-fried, but since this meal includes fried latkes, I decided to opt for the Jewish classic, cheese blintzes. These, too, are appropriate to this holiday, since cheese delicacies are a typical offering. Vegans and those on dairy-free diets are offered an alternative way to prepare this recipe.

2 cups frozen blueberries, thawed
$\frac{1}{4}$ to $\frac{1}{3}$ cup light brown sugar, to taste
dash lemon juice
2 tablespoons cornstarch

Pancake batter
1 $\frac{1}{2}$ cups whole wheat pastry flour
$\frac{1}{2}$ teaspoon salt
3 eggs, beaten
1 cup low-fat milk or soymilk
1 teaspoon canola oil

Filling
1 $\frac{1}{2}$ pounds part-skim ricotta or farmer cheese
(for a dairy-free alternative, substitute
1 $\frac{1}{2}$ pounds soft, well-mashed tofu)
3 tablespoons honey, or to taste
1 teaspoon lemon juice
$\frac{1}{2}$ teaspoon cinnamon

Combine the blueberries, sugar, and lemon juice in a food processor. Pulse on and off until the blueberries are coarsely chopped. Sprinkle in the cornstarch and pulse on and off a few more times. Transfer the mixture to a saucepan and bring to a simmer. Simmer until the mixture has thickened. Remove from the heat and let cool to room temperature. The filling may be done ahead of time and refrigerated. Bring to room temperature before serving.

Combine the flour and salt in a mixing bowl. In another bowl, combine the beaten eggs with 1 $\frac{1}{4}$ cups of water, the milk or soymilk, and oil. Stir until well blended. Make a well in the flour and pour the wet mixture in. Stir vigorously just until smoothly combined—don't overbeat.

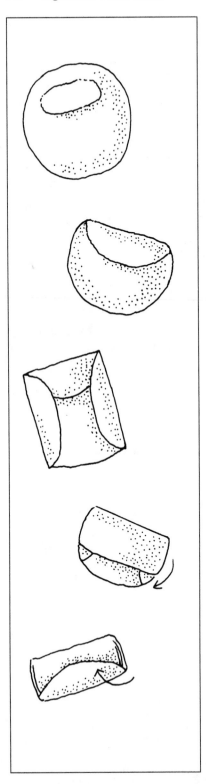

Heat a 6- or 7-inch nonstick skillet. When it is hot enough to make a drop of water sizzle, drop a scant $\frac{1}{4}$ cupful of batter in and swirl it around until it coats the skillet. Cook on both sides until golden. Remove to a plate and repeat until the batter is used up.

Combine the ingredients for the filling in a small mixing bowl. If using farmer cheese and it seems very dry, add a bit of low-fat milk to give it a creamier consistency. Divide the mixture among the pancakes and fold as instructed in the accompanying illustration. Serve at room temperature, passing the sauce around for guests to spoon over their blintzes.

Calories: 160	Total fat: 6 g	Protein: 8 g
Carbohydrate: 21 g	Cholesterol: 54 g	Sodium: 144 mg

Chapter 10

THANKSGIVING

As celebrations go, I'm quite partial to Thanksgiving, though it hasn't the joyous quality of Christmas or Hanukkah, the abandon of New Year's Eve, or the ritual solemnity of certain denominational holidays. Still, it has a unique warmth and coziness about it, and its secular nature makes it a holiday that can be celebrated by all Americans. A day designated for giving thanks for the abundance of the harvest is an idea everyone can appreciate.

As the holiday sets in, so do pleasurable early winter rituals that inspire familiar, nostalgic feelings—building fires in the fireplace, decorating the house with baskets of gourds and pine cones, and stocking the kitchen with late harvest produce so closely associated with the holiday season—Brussels sprouts, winter squashes, sweet potatoes, cranberries.

When Governor William Bradford of Massachusetts proclaimed in 1621 that the Pilgrims set aside a late November day to "render thanksgiving to ye almighty God," he specified "the abundant harvest of Indian corn, wheat, beans, squashes, and garden vegetables"—a perfect basis for a vegetarian feast—even before he mentioned forest game, fish, and crabs. Yet this very food-centered holiday can put vegetarians in a peculiar quandary.

This past year, I made two Thanksgiving dinners; one for family and one for friends, the resulting menus duly reported in this chapter. Both meals emphasized the harvest produce that traditionally marks the start of the holiday season, and were attended by vegetarians and nonvegetarians. My work was cut out for me—I was eager to ensure that neither group left the table disappointed!

A vegetarian menu for Thanksgiving is sure to have its offbeat twists, and this one is no exception. Nevertheless, in devising this menu, I kept in mind that it should please the whole family, including finicky children and adults with more traditional tastes. So, although the presentations may be unusual, the foods used are mostly familiar ones and those most closely associated with the season being celebrated—corn, squashes, sweet potatoes, apples, nuts, and cranberries are here in abundance. To top off the festivities, there's everyone's Thanksgiving favorite, pumpkin pie, with a tasty crumb topping.

A FAMILY THANKSGIVING

8 to 10 servings

Jicama Coleslaw with Citrus Dressing
Maple and Tarragon Sweet Potatoes
Walnut-Apple Stuffing
Corn, Squash, and Rice Loaves
Sweet Cranberry Relish
Pumpkin Streusel Pie

Additions to the menu: Serve Creamy Herbed Cheese Dip (page 239) or Spinach and Cucumber Spread (page 240) with raw vegetables as an appetizer. If desired, serve a purchased whole wheat bread with the meal.

Contains eggs in Corn, Squash, and Rice Loaves. For vegans, make Pueblo Corn Pie (page 165) in addition or as a substitution. Contains dairy products. Can be made dairy-free by following the suggested substitutions in the recipes.

JICAMA COLESLAW WITH CITRUS DRESSING

8 to 10 servings

Jicama, a vegetable quite popular in the Southwest, is becoming increasingly available everywhere else. Though an unusual vegetable, its sweet flavor and crunchy texture have broad appeal. If you can't find jicama, substitute crisp white turnip.

3 cups red cabbage, thinly shredded
3 cups white cabbage, thinly shredded
1 cup peeled, matchstick-cut jicama
2 bunches scallions, sliced

Dressing
$\frac{1}{4}$ cup plain low-fat yogurt
**$\frac{1}{4}$ cup reduced-fat sour cream (for a nondairy
          substitution, replace the 2 ingredients above with
          Tofu Mayonnaise, page 257)**
2 teaspoons prepared mustard
1 teaspoon honey
juice of $\frac{1}{2}$ orange
juice of $\frac{1}{2}$ lime
freshly ground pepper to taste

Combine the cabbages, jicama matchsticks, and scallions in a bowl and toss together. Combine the dressing ingredients in a small bowl and stir until well blended. Pour over the cabbage mixture and toss well. Cover and refrigerate until needed.

Calories: 40	Total fat: 1 g	Protein: 1 g
Carbohydrate: 6 g	Cholesterol: 1 g	Sodium: 46 mg

Thanksgiving was first observed in Plymouth, Massachusetts, in 1621. The celebration of the first harvest lasted three days and included such foods as cornbread, leeks, watercress and other greens, cranberries, and pumpkins. It's well known that no turkey was served at the first Thanksgiving there were other fowl, meats, and seafood.

The first national Thanksgiving was declared by George Washington in the same year as his inauguration, 1789. However, it wasn't until 1863 that Thanksgiving was made an official national holiday by Abraham Lincoln.

Suggested timetable for

A Family Thanksgiving

A day ahead:

- *Prepare the appetizer dip of your choice and store in an airtight container.*

- *Make the Sweet Cranberry Relish.*

- *Prepare the vegetables for Jicama Coleslaw, but don't dress them. Store in a tightly lidded container.*

- *Prepare the bread cubes for Walnut-Apple Stuffing.*

Same day, morning:

- *Make the Pumpkin Streusel Pie and bake it. Let cool, then cover with foil. Let it stand in a fairly cool place; but if your house is warm, refrigerate it and then take it out about 2 hours before serving.*

- *Peel and cut the potatoes for Maple and Tarragon Sweet Potatoes. Sprinkle with water and place in a covered container until later.*

(timetable continues . . .)

MAPLE AND TARRAGON SWEET POTATOES

8 to 10 servings

Maple syrup and tarragon, a sweet herb, are wonderful enhancements for the flavor of sweet potatoes.

4 pounds sweet potatoes, peeled and sliced ¼ inch thick
⅓ cup maple syrup
¼ cup (½ stick) reduced-fat margarine, melted
¼ cup orange juice
¼ teaspoon cinnamon
½ teaspoon salt
2 teaspoons dried tarragon

Preheat the oven to 350 degrees.

Arrange the sweet potato slices in overlapping rows in an oiled shallow 2-quart casserole. In a small bowl, combine the syrup, margarine, juice, cinnamon, and salt. Pour evenly over the potatoes. Sprinkle the tarragon over the top. Cover with lid or foil and bake, covered, for 25 to 30 minutes, or until readily pierced with a fork but still firm. Bake another 20 to 25 minutes, uncovered, or until glazed and golden around the edges.

Calories: 283	Total fat: 2 g	Protein: 2 g
Carbohydrate: 65 g	Cholesterol: 0 g	Sodium: 177 mg

WALNUT-APPLE STUFFING

8 to 10 servings

6 cups firmly packed diced whole-grain bread
1 ½ tablespoons canola oil
1 ½ cups chopped red onion
1 ½ cups peeled, diced tart apple
3 bunches scallions, minced
2 tablespoons chopped fresh parsley
½ teaspoon each: dried thyme, savory
¾ teaspoon seasoned salt, more or less to taste
½ cup finely chopped walnuts
3 tablespoons currants

freshly ground pepper to taste
1 ½ cups apple juice

Preheat the oven to 350 degrees.

Place the diced bread on a baking sheet. Bake 10 to 12 minutes, or until dry and lightly browned.

Heat the oil in a large skillet. Add the red onion and sauté over moderate heat until golden. Add the apple and sauté for another 5 minutes.

In a mixing bowl, combine the bread cubes with the onion and apple mixture. Add all the remaining ingredients except the apple juice and toss together. Sprinkle in the apple juice slowly, stirring at the same time to moisten the ingredients evenly. Transfer the mixture to an oiled shallow 1 ½-quart baking pan. Bake 25 to 30 minutes, or until browned and still slightly moist. Stir once during the baking time.

Calories: 218	Total fat: 8 g	Protein: 5 g
Carbohydrate: 32 g	Cholesterol: 0 g	Sodium: 426 mg

CORN, SQUASH, AND RICE LOAVES

8 to 10 servings

This delicious main dish is a tribute to three abundant American crops.

1 ½ cups raw brown rice
2 tablespoons canola oil
2 cups finely chopped onions
1 medium green or red bell pepper, diced
4 eggs, beaten
½ cup buttermilk or soymilk
2 cups grated reduced-fat cheddar cheese or
    cheddar-style soy cheese
1 ½ cups cooked corn kernels
¼ cup chopped fresh parsley
½ teaspoon each: dried oregano, dill
salt and pepper to taste
2 cups grated zucchini
2 cups grated yellow squash
4 scallions, chopped

- *Trim and prepare the Brussels sprouts or broccoli for Corn, Squash, and Rice Loaves. Place in a large covered pot and leave at room temperature until needed.*

- *Cut the vegetables for the appetizer; cover and store in the refrigerator.*

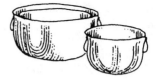

Starting 3 hours before serving:

- *Finish preparing the Maple and Tarragon Sweet Potatoes; cover with foil until ready to bake.*

- *Prepare the Corn, Squash, and Rice Loaves, with the exception of steaming the Brussels sprouts or broccoli. Cover with foil until ready to bake.*

- *Prepare the Walnut-Apple Stuffing. Cover with foil until ready to bake.*

(timetable continues . . .)

Starting about 1 hour before serving:

- *Assemble the appetizer dip and raw vegetables on a serving platter and serve to guests who have already arrived.*

- *Make the Citrus Dressing for the Jicama Coleslaw. Toss together with the slaw and refrigerate until needed.*

- *Begin baking Corn, Squash, and Rice Loaves and Maple and Tarragon Sweet Potatoes.*

Starting 30 minutes before serving:

- *Begin baking Walnut-Apple Stuffing.*

- *Steam the Brussels sprouts or broccoli for Corn, Squash, and Rice Loaves.*

fine dry bread crumbs
4 cups Brussels sprouts or bite-sized broccoli pieces
**   and florets, steamed crisp-tender**
2 teaspoons reduced-fat margarine

Bring 3 ³/₄ cups of water to a boil in a heavy saucepan. Stir in the rice, reduce the heat to a simmer, then cover and cook until the water is absorbed, about 35 minutes. This may be done ahead of time.

Heat the oil in a large skillet. Add the chopped onions and sauté over moderate heat until translucent. Add the diced bell pepper and continue to sauté until the onions are golden. Remove from heat.

In a large bowl, combine the beaten eggs with the buttermilk, cheese, corn kernels, and herbs. Stir in the cooked rice and the onion mixture and mix well. Add salt and pepper to taste.

In the same skillet, combine the grated squashes with just enough water to keep the bottom of the skillet moist. Cover and steam until wilted, about 5 minutes. Stir in the scallions.

Preheat the oven to 350 degrees.

Oil 2 9- by 5- by 3-inch loaf pans, preferably glass. Assemble as follows: Transfer about ¹/₄ of the rice mixture to each of the loaf pans and pat in. Divide the steamed squash evenly between the 2 loaf pans and pat in over the rice mixture. Top each with the remaining rice mixture. Sprinkle the tops with bread crumbs.

Bake for 60 minutes, or until the top and edges are golden and crusty.

In the meantime, if using Brussels sprouts, trim them and cut an X into the base. Cook in 2 inches or so of water in a large, covered saucepan until tender but not overdone, stirring occasionally. If using broccoli, steam until bright green and crisp-tender. Drain and toss the vegetables with the margarine.

Once the loaves are done, cool for 10 minutes before slicing loaves into 8 or 10 slices each, allowing for 2 slices per guest. To serve, arrange the slices in an overlapping circular pattern on a large platter. Place the Brussels sprouts or broccoli in the center.

Calories: 288	Total fat: 11 g	Protein: 14 g
Carbohydrate: 31 g	Cholesterol: 113 g	Sodium: 240 mg

SWEET CRANBERRY RELISH

8 to 10 servings

A sweet-tart relish, this adds a refreshingly tangy note and jewel-like color to the meal.

12 ounces fresh cranberries
1-pound can pineapple chunks with liquid
2 medium apples, peeled, cored, and diced
2 tablespoons agar flakes (see Note, below)
⅓ cup light brown sugar, more or less to taste
½ teaspoon cinnamon

Place the cranberries in the container of a food processor. Pulse on and off until coarsely chopped. Transfer to a mixing bowl.

Drain the liquid from the pineapple chunks into a small saucepan. Transfer the pineapple chunks to the food processor along with the apples. Pulse on and off until coarsely chopped. Add to the cranberries in the mixing bowl.

Combine the agar flakes with the juice in the saucepan. Bring to a simmer, stirring frequently, and cook until the flakes are dissolved, about 5 minutes. Pour into the mixing bowl and mix thoroughly with the fruit. Add enough sugar to create a sweet-tart balance to your taste. Stir in the cinnamon. Pour the mixture into an attractive serving bowl and chill for several hours.

Note: Agar flakes are readily available in most natural food stores as well as Oriental markets. These tiny, flavorless, colorless flakes, derived from a seaweed, are the best vegetable-derived jelling product available.

Calories: 96   Total fat: 0 g   Protein: 0 g
Carbohydrate: 23 g   Cholesterol: 0 g   Sodium: 5 mg

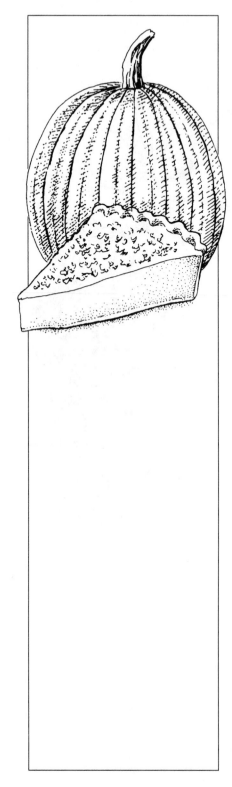

PUMPKIN STREUSEL PIE

Makes 1 9-inch pie, 6 to 8 servings

Guests often bring additional desserts to Thanksgiving dinner, but if you've had no such offers, you might want to double this recipe and make 2 pies.

1 ²/₃ cups pureed pumpkin
1 egg, beaten
¹/₂ to ²/₃ cup light brown sugar, to taste
³/₄ cup applesauce
1 teaspoon cinnamon
¹/₂ teaspoon each: ground ginger, allspice
9-inch pastry crust (page 260)

Streusel topping
¹/₂ cup whole wheat pastry flour
¹/₂ cup wheat germ
¹/₄ cup light brown sugar
¹/₄ teaspoon each: cinnamon and nutmeg
2 tablespoons reduced-fat margarine, melted

Preheat the oven to 350 degrees.

Place the pumpkin, egg, sugar, applesauce, and spices in the container of a food processor or blender. Process until very smoothly pureed. Pour into the pie crust.

In a small bowl, stir the streusel ingredients together and quickly stir in the margarine until all the dry ingredients are lightly coated. Sprinkle evenly over the pumpkin filling. Bake for 45 minutes, or until the crust is golden and the filling is set. Let cool. Serve at room temperature.

Calories: 273	Total fat: 5 g	Protein: 6 g
Carbohydrate: 50 g	Cholesterol: 27 g	Sodium: 235 mg

A HARVEST FEAST FOR FRIENDS

8 servings

Sweet Potato Biscuits

Creamy Mushroom Soup

Jerusalem Artichoke Salad with Greens and Herbs

Cranberry Chutney

Butternut Squash with Whole Wheat, Wild Rice, and Onion Stuffing

Wine and Honey-glazed Brussels Sprouts

Pear and Apple Crumble

———— ∽∾ ————

Additions to the menu: This is a large and hearty meal that can be started with the soup shortly after the guests arrive. However, if you expect early guests or would like to ease into the meal, you may want to have some appetizers on hand that won't add much work to your cooking schedule. Put out a dish of mixed nuts and dried fruits, a bowl of fresh pears, and some good whole-grain crackers.

Contains no eggs or dairy products.

Though Thanksgiving is traditionally a family event, families are rather scattered in today's world, and it's not always possible to gather when we'd like. But rather than miss out on this holiday, why not get a group of good friends together to celebrate the autumn bounty?

The dishes in this menu are geared to more "adult" tastes than those in the previous menu. What that means is that you'll find favorite Thanksgiving foods prepared with a twist—a savory stuffing studded with wild rice and nestled in butternut squash, for instance; Brussels sprouts glazed with wine; a spicy cranberry chutney rather than the usual sweet sauce.

While a veritable cornucopia of late fall produce, this bounteous menu is free of eggs and dairy products. Vegans as well as those on lactose-free and reduced cholesterol diets can sample everything from soup to nuts, literally, without adapting a thing.

Suggested timetable for

A Harvest Feast for Friends

A day ahead:

- *Cook or microwave a sweet potato until well done. When cool enough to handle, peel and mash, then proceed with the recipe for the dough for Sweet Potato Biscuits. Wrap tightly in a plastic bag and refrigerate overnight.*

- *Make the Cranberry Chutney. Cool and refrigerate in a covered container.*

- *Make the stuffing portion of Butternut Squash with Whole Wheat, Wild Rice, and Onion Stuffing. When done, cover, cool to room temperature, and refrigerate overnight.*

The same day, morning:

- *Make the Creamy Mushroom Soup. When done, leave at room temperature, off the heat.*

- *Trim and prepare the Brussels sprouts as directed in the recipe for Wine and Honey-glazed Brussels Sprouts. Place in a deep, heavy saucepan, cover, and leave at room temperature until later.*

(timetable continues . . .)

SWEET POTATO BISCUITS

Makes 16

Delightfully moist and slightly sweet, these biscuits are an American classic. Serve them hot with the soup that follows.

1 ¼ cups whole wheat pastry flour
½ cup unbleached white flour
2 teaspoons baking powder
½ teaspoon salt
3 tablespoons reduced-fat margarine
⅓ cup apple juice
1 cup well-mashed, cooked sweet potato
3 tablespoons honey
⅓ cup finely chopped walnuts or pecans

Preheat the oven to 425 degrees.
In a mixing bowl, sift together the flours, baking powder, and salt. Work the margarine in with a pastry blender or the tines of a fork until the mixture resembles a coarse meal. Add the apple juice, sweet potato, honey, and nuts, and work them in to form a soft dough.

Turn the dough out onto a well-floured board and knead in just enough extra flour to make the dough lose its stickiness. With floured hands, divide the dough into 16 equal parts. Shape into small balls and arrange on a lightly oiled cookie sheet, patting them down a bit to flatten. Bake for 12 to 15 minutes, or until a toothpick inserted into the center of one tests clean. Transfer the biscuits to a plate and serve hot.

Per biscuit:
Calories: 91	Total fat: 2 g	Protein: 2 g
Carbohydrate: 16 g	Cholesterol: 0 g	Sodium: 86 mg

CREAMY MUSHROOM SOUP

8 servings

This flavorful soup gets its creamy thickness from a base of pureed white beans.

2 tablespoons canola oil, divided

1 heaping cup chopped onions
2 medium potatoes, peeled and diced
2 large celery stalks, with leaves, diced
2 cloves garlic, minced
2 vegetable bouillon cubes
$\frac{1}{2}$ teaspoon each: dry mustard, dried basil, and
    dried thyme
$\frac{1}{4}$ cup dry white wine, optional
12 ounces white mushrooms, wiped clean and
    sliced, divided
6 ounces fresh shiitake or other fresh wild mushrooms
2 cups canned or cooked navy beans or cannellini
    (see Bean Basics, page 261)
freshly ground pepper to taste
$\frac{1}{4}$ cup minced fresh parsley

Heat 1 tablespoon of the oil in a large soup pot. Add the onions and sauté over moderate heat until golden. Add the next 4 ingredients plus 6 cups of water and bring to a boil. Add the seasonings and wine; cover and simmer over moderate heat for 15 minutes.

Add half of the sliced white mushrooms (set the rest aside) and simmer another 10 minutes. Remove the soup from the heat and let stand several minutes.

Wipe the shiitake or other mushrooms clean, remove and discard the stems, and slice the caps. Heat the remaining tablespoon of oil in a skillet. Add the reserved white mushrooms and the shiitakes. Sauté, covered, for 10 minutes.

Puree the soup in batches, along with the white beans, in a food processor or blender. Return to the soup pot and stir in the sautéed mushrooms. Grind in pepper to taste. Before serving, bring to a simmer and cook, covered, for at least 10 minutes. Adjust consistency with more water if soup is too thick. Divide among soup bowls and sprinkle each serving with the parsley.

Calories: 159	Total fat: 3 g	Protein: 6 g
Carbohydrate: 25 g	Cholesterol: 0 g	Sodium: 239 mg

Starting 2 $\frac{1}{2}$ hours before serving:

- *Take the chutney out of the refrigerator.*

- *Make the Jerusalem Artichoke Salad. Refrigerate and stir occasionally.*

- *Bake or microwave the butternut squash for Butternut Squash with Whole Wheat, Wild Rice, and Onion Stuffing. When cool enough to handle, stuff as directed in the recipe (if the stuffing seems dry at all, moisten with a bit of additional juice or water). Cover loosely with plastic wrap and set aside until time to bake.*

Starting 1 $\frac{1}{2}$ hours before:

- *Make the Pear and Apple Crumble. Cover with plastic wrap and set aside until time to bake.*

- *Finish making the Wine and Honey-glazed Brussels Sprouts. Cover and keep warm until needed. Heat through if necessary before serving.*

- *Bake the Sweet Potato Biscuits.*

- *Warm the soup.*

(timetable continues . . .)

During the meal:

- *Turn the oven tempera-ture down to 350 degrees. While guests eat the soup and salad, bake the stuffed squash and the dessert.*

- *Warm the Brussels sprouts if necessary.*

JERUSALEM ARTICHOKE SALAD WITH GREENS AND HERBS

8 servings

Jerusalem artichokes are the misnamed underground tubers of a native American sunflower; they have nothing to do with Jerusalem and are not at all related to artichokes. In season in the late fall, they are quite appropriate for a Thanksgiving meal. Those who haven't had them will find them surprising and exotic. Though these brown-skinned, knobby roots are not exactly pretty, their crunchy texture and unusual flavor (a cross between potato, water chestnut, and turnip) are very pleasant. Do make an effort to find them—they are becoming more and more easily available and are sometimes marketed under the name "sunchokes." But if all else fails, substitute the crispest turnips you can find.

1 pound Jerusalem artichokes, scrubbed
1 bunch watercress, most stems removed
2 small red or green bell peppers, stemmed,
      cored, and cut into rings
2 tablespoons minced fresh dill
2 tablespoons minced fresh parsley
1 to 2 scallions, minced

Dressing
juice of 2 limes
1 teaspoon honey
2 tablespoons walnut or hazelnut oil (if unavailable,
      substitute olive oil)

To finish the salad
1 medium head red-leaf lettuce
cherry tomatoes
2 tablespoons toasted sunflower seeds

   Trim the Jerusalem artichokes of any excessively dark or knobby spots and cut into matchstick-shaped pieces. Combine with the next 5 ingredients in a bowl.
   Combine the dressing ingredients in a small bowl and stir. Pour over the salad and toss well. Let the salad marinate, refrigerated, for about 2 hours.
   Before serving, tear the red-leaf lettuce and place in a

serving bowl. Add the salad and toss well. Surround the edges of the salad with cherry tomatoes and sprinkle the sunflower seeds over the top.

Calories: 105	Total fat: 5 g	Protein: 3 g
Carbohydrate: 0 g	Cholesterol: 13 g	Sodium: 29 mg

CRANBERRY CHUTNEY

8 servings

If your only experience with cranberries has been in sweet, jelled sauces, this spicy chutney will provide a welcome change of pace for your grown-up palate!

12 ounces fresh cranberries
1 cup peeled, diced apple
1 cup orange juice
1/2 cup chopped dried apricots
1 teaspoon freshly grated ginger
1 teaspoon ground cinnamon
1/2 teaspoon ground cloves
3 to 4 tablespoons honey, to taste

Place all the ingredients except the honey in a deep, heavy saucepan and bring to a simmer. Cook over low heat with the lid slightly ajar for 20 to 25 minutes, or until the liquid is mostly absorbed. Add honey to taste and simmer uncovered for another 5 to 10 minutes until thick. Let the chutney cool to room temperature, then store in a sterilized jar, tightly covered but not sealed. Refrigerate until needed. Before serving, bring to room temperature.

Calories: 97	Total fat: 0 g	Protein: 1 g
Carbohydrate: 23 g	Cholesterol: 0 g	Sodium: 2 mg

"When pickled or any way, [the Jerusalem artichoke] puts its French brother to shame, in tastiness as well as substance. I cannot understand why I do not meet this excellent vegetable very often."

—J. George Frederick
The Pennsylvania Dutch and Their Cookery, 1935

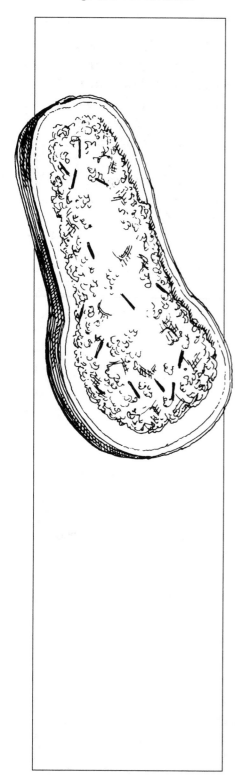

BUTTERNUT SQUASH WITH WHOLE WHEAT, WILD RICE, AND ONION STUFFING

8 servings

Even those of us who have given up turkey welcome a Thanksgiving dish that has been "stuffed." This satisfying dish makes a handsome centerpiece for this meal.

4 medium-small butternut squashes (about 1 pound each)
3/4 cup raw wild rice, rinsed
1 tablespoon canola oil
1 heaping cup chopped red onion
1 clove garlic, minced
2 1/2 cups firmly packed torn whole wheat bread
1 tablespoon sesame seeds
1/2 teaspoon each: dried sage, dried thyme
1 teaspoon seasoned salt, or to taste
1 cup fresh orange juice

Preheat the oven to 375 degrees.

Halve the squashes and scoop out seeds and fibers. Place them cut side up in shallow baking dishes and cover tightly with covers or more foil. Bake for 40 to 50 minutes, or until easily pierced with a knife but still firm.

In the meantime, bring 2 cups of water to a boil in a saucepan. Stir in the wild rice, reduce to a simmer, then cover and cook until the water is absorbed, about 40 minutes.

Heat the oil in a skillet. Add the onion and garlic and sauté until the onion is limp and golden.

In a mixing bowl, combine the cooked wild rice with the sautéed onion and the remaining ingredients. When the squashes are cool enough to handle, scoop out the pulp, leaving firm shells about 1/2 inch thick. Chop the pulp and stir it into the rice mixture. Stuff the squashes, place in foil-lined baking dishes, and cover.

Before serving, place the squashes in a preheated 350-degree oven. Bake for 20 minutes, or until well heated through.

Calories: 189	Total fat: 2 g	Protein: 4 g
Carbohydrate: 37 g	Cholesterol: 1 g	Sodium: 310 mg

VARIATION: To add drama to this presentation, try this recipe with other squash varieties. Hubbard squash, delicata, sweet dumpling, and golden nugget are just a few of the stuffable edible squashes available.

WINE AND HONEY-GLAZED BRUSSELS SPROUTS

8 servings

The slightly sweet glaze gives Brussels sprouts a rich flavor.

2 pounds Brussels sprouts
$1/2$ cup dry red wine
3 tablespoons honey
1 $1/2$ tablespoons soy sauce or tamari
1 $1/2$ teaspoons cornstarch

Trim the stems from the Brussels sprouts and cut an X into the base, about $1/4$ inch deep.

In a small bowl, combine the wine, honey, and soy sauce and stir together. Transfer to a 3-quart saucepan along with $1/2$ cup water and the Brussels sprouts. Stir together, then cook, covered, at a gentle simmer for 15 minutes, stirring occasionally. Uncover and cook, stirring occasionally, for another 10 minutes.

Dissolve the cornstarch in a small amount of water. Stir into the saucepan quickly, then cook for another 5 minutes. Remove from heat and transfer to a covered casserole dish to serve.

Calories: 90	Total fat: 0 g	Protein: 2 g
Carbohydrate: 16 g	Cholesterol: 0 g	Sodium: 215 mg

PEAR AND APPLE CRUMBLE

8 servings

Though pies are a wonderful finish to winter meals, many now wish to avoid them because the pastry crusts harbor a good bit of fat. I think that crumbles and crisps are a fine alternative, especially served warm.

4 medium bosc pears, cored and thinly sliced
3 Granny Smith apples, peeled, cored, and thinly sliced
2 tablespoons light brown sugar
$1/3$ cup finely chopped almonds
$1/2$ teaspoon cinnamon
$1/4$ teaspoon nutmeg
2 tablespoons rum
1 teaspoon vanilla extract

Topping
2 tablespoons reduced-fat margarine, melted
$1/2$ cup whole wheat pastry flour
$1/2$ cup wheat germ
2 tablespoons light brown sugar
$1/4$ teaspoon cinnamon
nondairy frozen dessert (or if dairy is not a concern, vanilla nonfat frozen yogurt), optional

Preheat the oven to 350 degrees.

In a mixing bowl, combine the fruits with the next 6 ingredients and stir together until evenly coated. Pour into a lightly oiled 9- by 13-inch baking pan. In a small bowl, combine the melted margarine with the remaining topping ingredients and toss to coat. Sprinkle evenly over the fruit mixture. Bake for 40 to 45 minutes, or until the fruits are soft and the topping is golden. If desired, serve warm in bowls over nondairy ice cream substitute or frozen yogurt.

Calories: 220	Total fat: 4 g	Protein: 4 g
Carbohydrate: 30 g	Cholesterol: 0 g	Sodium: 28 mg

For those occasions when vegetarians join a traditional Thanksgiving dinner with turkey and all the fixings, here are a few substitute main dishes to choose from, so that we aren't relegated to picking at side dishes. If you're a host, choose one that will be most compatible with the rest of your dinner; the vegetarians can have their main portion from the dish while the meat-eaters will enjoy them as side-portions. If you're going to be a guest at a nonvegetarian Thanksgiving, offer to bring one of these dishes.

SUBSTITUTE MAIN DISHES FOR THANKSGIVING DINNER

Squash, Leek, and Cheddar Soufflé with Greens

Walnut Wedges

Pueblo Corn Pie

SQUASH, LEEK, AND CHEDDAR SOUFFLÉ WITH GREENS

8 servings

A very colorful and elegant winter dish.

2 medium butternut squashes, about 1 $\frac{1}{4}$ pounds each
1 pound Swiss chard or fresh spinach, washed,
  stemmed, and chopped
1 tablespoon olive oil
1 large or 2 medium leeks, white part only, sliced into
  $\frac{1}{4}$-inch rings and well rinsed
2 shallots, minced
2 cloves garlic, minced
$\frac{1}{2}$ cup milk or soymilk
2 eggs, room temperature, separated, plus 1
  additional egg white
1 $\frac{1}{2}$ cups grated reduced-fat cheddar cheese, or
  cheddar-style soy cheese
$\frac{1}{8}$ teaspoon nutmeg
salt and freshly ground pepper to taste

Preheat the oven to 325 degrees.

Cut the squashes in half lengthwise and scoop out the seeds and fibers. Place in shallow foil-lined baking dishes and cover with lid or more foil. Bake for 50 to 60 minutes, or until quite soft when tested with a knife.

Steam the chard or spinach in a large saucepan until wilted. Place in a colander until cool enough to handle.

Heat the oil in a skillet. Add the leeks, shallots, and garlic. Add 2 tablespoons of water and sauté, covered, for 10 minutes, stirring occasionally. Uncover and continue to sauté until the leek rings become slightly touched with gold. Remove from heat.

When the squash is cool enough to handle, scoop out all the pulp and place in a mixing bowl. Mash until smooth, then stir in the milk and lightly beaten egg yolks. Squeeze the moisture out of the chard or spinach and chop finely. Stir into the squash mixture, followed by the grated cheese and seasonings.

Beat the egg whites until they form stiff peaks. Fold into the squash mixture gently. Pour into a shallow, oiled 2-quart

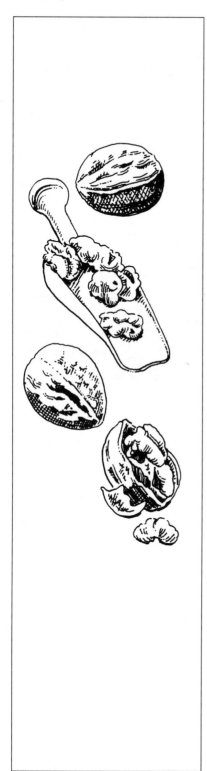

casserole dish (a round one looks very nice). Bake for 45 to 50 minutes, or until the top is golden.

| Calories: 193 | Total fat: 7 g | Protein: 10 g |
| Carbohydrate: 20 g | Cholesterol: 69 g | Sodium: 308 mg |

WALNUT WEDGES

Makes 2 9-inch pies; 16 wedges

A rather rich dish, but a small serving of these savory, high-protein wedges goes a long way.

1 tablespoon canola oil
1 cup finely chopped onion
2 cloves garlic, minced
1 cup mushrooms, finely chopped
1 cup walnut halves
1 cup packed, torn whole-grain bread
3 egg whites
**1 cup well-cooked, leftover grain (such as brown rice,
    quinoa, or bulgur)**
1/4 cup thick tomato sauce
2 tablespoons soy sauce or tamari
1 teaspoon each: paprika, dried oregano, ground cumin
curly parsley for garnish

Preheat the oven to 350 degrees.

Heat the oil in a skillet. Add the onion and sauté until translucent. Add the garlic and continue to sauté until the onion is golden. Add the mushrooms and sauté until they are wilted and juicy. Remove from heat.

Combine the walnuts and bread in the container of a food processor or blender. Process until finely ground.

In a mixing bowl, beat the egg whites lightly and stir in the remaining ingredients except the parsley. Add the onion-mushroom mixture and the walnut mixture. Oil 2 pie tins and divide the mixture between them. Bake for 30 to 35 minutes, or until the outside is nicely browned and crusty. Let stand 10 minutes, then cut each pie into 8 wedges. Arrange in a pie shape on 2 plates, with parsley garnish in the center of each.

Per wedge:

| Calories: 94 | Total fat: 5 g | Protein: 3 g |
| Carbohydrate: 8 g | Cholesterol: 0 g | Sodium: 193 mg |

PUEBLO CORN PIE

6 to 8 servings

This layered casserole is adapted from a Native American recipe.

1 tablespoon olive oil
1 large onion, chopped
2 cloves garlic, minced
1 medium green or red bell pepper, diced
1 ¹/₂ cups cooked fresh or thawed frozen corn kernels
2 ¹/₄ cups canned or cooked pinto beans
   (see Bean Basics, page 261)
2 cups chopped ripe tomatoes, or 14- to 16-ounce can
   diced tomatoes, lightly drained
2 teaspoons chili powder, or to taste
1 teaspoon dried oregano
¹/₂ teaspoon ground cumin
salt to taste

Cornmeal topping
1 ¹/₄ cups cornmeal
¹/₂ teaspoon salt

1 cup grated Monterey Jack cheese, or 1 cup grated
   cheddar-style soy cheese, optional

Heat the oil in a large skillet. Add the onion and sauté until it is translucent. Add the garlic and bell pepper and continue to sauté until the onion is golden brown. Add the corn kernels, pinto beans, tomatoes, and seasonings. Stir well and simmer for 10 to 15 minutes. Season to taste with salt. Remove from the heat.

Bring 5 cups of water to a rolling boil in a heavy saucepan or double boiler. Slowly pour the cornmeal into the water in a thin, steady stream, stirring continuously to avoid lumping. Add the salt and cook over very low heat, covered, for 20 minutes, stirring occasionally.

Preheat the oven to 375 degrees.

Oil a shallow, 1 ¹/₂-quart baking dish and line the bottom with half of the cooked cornmeal. Pour over it the skillet mixture and sprinkle with the optional grated cheese. Top with the remaining cornmeal, patting it in smoothly. Bake for

"This Indian corn was the staff of food, upon which the Indians did ever depend . . . this, with the addition of some peas, beans and such other fruits of the earth as were then in season, was the families' dependence, and the support of their women and children."

—Robert Beverly
The History and Present State of Virginia, 1705

45 to 50 minutes, or until the cornmeal is golden brown and crusty. Let stand for 10 minutes, then cut into squares to serve.

| Calories: 232 | Total fat: 2 g | Protein: 7 g |
| Carbohydrate: 44 g | Cholesterol: 0 g | Sodium: 161 mg |

Vegetarians are very unlikely to eat a stuffing that was cooked inside the turkey. Here are a pair of unusual, savory stuffings that are really more akin to what would be called "dressings" in the southern states, since they are cooked outside the bird.

SUBSTITUTE STUFFINGS

Sauerkraut, Potato, and Apple Stuffing
Skillet Corn Bread Stuffing with Mushrooms and Pine Nuts

SAUERKRAUT, POTATO, AND APPLE STUFFING

8 servings

This recipe is inspired by a Slavic stuffing. The sweetness of the apple contrasted with the tart sauerkraut is what makes it special.

1 tablespoon canola oil
1 cup chopped red onion
3 medium red potatoes (about 1 $\frac{1}{2}$ pounds total), baked, peeled, and sliced
2 large sweet apples, peeled, cored, and thinly sliced
8-ounce can or jar sauerkraut, drained
$\frac{1}{2}$ cup vegetable stock or seasoned broth
$\frac{1}{3}$ cup fresh bread crumbs
1 $\frac{1}{2}$ teaspoons paprika
1 teaspoon poppy seeds
$\frac{1}{2}$ teaspoon dried thyme
freshly ground pepper to taste

Preheat the oven to 350 degrees.

Heat the oil in a skillet. Add the onion and sauté until golden. In a mixing bowl, combine the onion with all the remaining ingredients and mix thoroughly. Pat into a lightly oiled 1 ½-quart casserole dish. Bake for 40 to 45 minutes, or until the top is golden brown. Cover and keep warm until serving. This stuffing may be made ahead of time, then reheated before serving.

Calories: 137	Total fat: 2 g	Protein: 2 g
Carbohydrate: 28 g	Cholesterol: 0 g	Sodium: 203 mg

SKILLET CORN BREAD STUFFING WITH MUSHROOMS AND PINE NUTS

8 servings

For this tasty stuffing, you'll need to bake a simple pan corn bread, which can be done well ahead of time.

Corn bread
1 cup cornmeal
1 teaspoon baking soda
1 teaspoon salt
1 egg, beaten
1 teaspoon honey
1 cup buttermilk

1 tablespoon canola oil
1 cup chopped onion
1 cup chopped celery
6 ounces white mushrooms, chopped
½ teaspoon each: dried sage and thyme
¼ to ½ cup vegetable stock or water
3 tablespoons chopped fresh parsley
seasoned salt to taste
freshly ground pepper
¼ cup toasted pine nuts

Preheat the oven to 400 degrees.

Combine the first 3 ingredients in a mixing bowl. In another bowl, combine the beaten egg with the honey and buttermilk. Pour the wet ingredients into the dry and stir vigorously

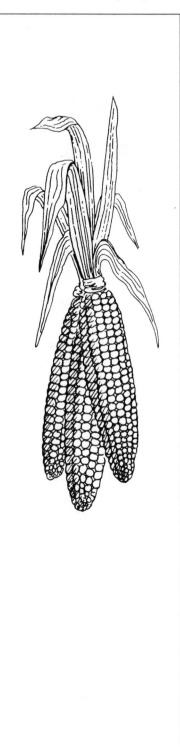

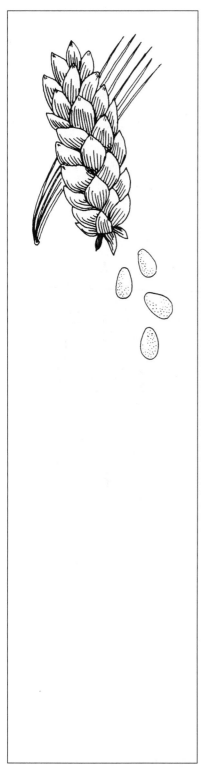

until smooth. Pour the batter into an oiled 9- by 9-inch baking pan and bake for 15 minutes, or until the top is lightly golden. Let the corn bread cool. If this step is done ahead of time, cover the corn bread and refrigerate until needed.

Heat the oil in a large skillet. Add the onion and sauté over moderate heat until translucent. Add the celery and continue to sauté until the onion is golden. Add the mushrooms, cover, and sauté until they are wilted, about 3 to 4 minutes.

In the meantime, remove the corn bread from the pan and crumble it finely with your fingertips. Add it to the skillet along with the sage and thyme and stir until combined with the onion, celery, and mushroom mixture. Add just enough stock or water to make the mixture moist but not soggy. Stir in the parsley, then season to taste with seasoned salt and pepper. Cook, stirring, over low heat for 2 to 3 minutes. Stir in the pine nuts and serve.

| Calories: 142 | Total fat: 5 g | Protein: 5 g |
| Carbohydrate: 19 g | Cholesterol: 28 g | Sodium: 301 mg |

Chapter 11

CHRISTMAS

The flavors and aromas of Christmas imbed themselves forever in memories. The late autumn harvest is still very much with us, to be savored before it dwindles into slim pickings until the first signs of spring arrive; the fragrance of spices wafts through the air as hot beverages, breads, and cookies are prepared for family and guests.

Feasting is a large part of "making great cheer," and the abundance of food and drink poses a challenge to those whose diets are restricted or who are simply loath to go overboard. How does one resist those buttery Christmas cookies, rich eggnog, and caloric meals? And though we are moving away from the meat-centered traditions that hark back to Merry Old England—oysters, the Christmas goose or turkey, roasts of beef or pork, mince pies—vegetarians in particular still must find their own culinary niche during the holiday.

To this end, I have devised three distinct menus, one very American, one based on English customs, and one menu that will probably prove a delightful surprise to vegetarians—a traditionally rooted Italian Christmas Eve meal with the Mediterranean foods and flavors so well loved by those with a meatless orientation.

Continuing the celebration of the harvest that began with Thanksgiving, this menu, which can easily be made dairy-free, is chock-full of the cold-weather produce that is so comforting this time of year. But comforting need not mean bland or winter-dreary, and this meal looks as festive as it tastes. Your taste buds will be perked up by Christmas-spiced flavors, and your eyes will enjoy warm colors—the cheery orange of carrot soup, the deep greens of winter lettuces, the jewel tone of red cabbage, and the bright yellow of corn.

AN AMERICAN COUNTRY CHRISTMAS

8 to 10 servings

Braided Sweet Potato Bread

Spiced Carrot and Orange Soup

Creole Green Salad

Leek and Corn-Stuffed Peppers

Wild Rice Pilaf with Apples and Pecans

Sautéed Red Cabbage

Cocoa Mock-Mince Pie

Additions to the menu: Have a batch of Soy and Honey Nuts and Pretzels (page 237) on hand for nibblers. If you'd like to serve appetizers, Mushrooms Rosemary (page 237) is quite appropriate, since rosemary is one of the classic greens of Christmas. Or choose any of the dips or spreads, pages 239 to 242, to serve with vegetables or crackers.

Contains no eggs.
Can be made dairy-free by following the suggested substitutions in the recipes.

BRAIDED SWEET POTATO BREAD

Makes 2 loaves

A delightful, russet-colored bread with a gentle hint of thyme.

1 package active dry yeast
¼ cup canola oil
1 teaspoon dried thyme
1 ½ cups cooked, well-mashed sweet potato
3 tablespoons honey
1 cup low-fat milk or soymilk
3 cups whole wheat flour
1 cup unbleached white flour
½ cup cornmeal
1 ½ teaspoons salt
milk or soymilk to brush tops of loaves

Combine the yeast with ¼ cup lukewarm water in a medium-sized mixing bowl and let stand for 10 minutes, or until dissolved. Stir in the oil and thyme, then the mashed sweet potato, honey, and milk or soymilk. Stir gently until the mixture is smooth.

In another bowl, combine the flours, cornmeal, and salt. Make a well in the center and pour in the wet mixture. Work together, using a spoon at first, then hands, until thoroughly combined into a dough. Turn out onto a floured board and knead for 8 to 10 minutes, adding additional flour until the dough loses its stickiness. Place in a clean bowl and cover with a tea towel. Let rise in a warm place for 1 ½ hours, or until doubled in bulk.

Punch the dough down and turn back out onto the board. Divide into 6 equal pieces. With hands, roll each piece into a long coil, about 1 inch in diameter. To make each loaf, braid 3 coils and pinch the ends together. Place the loaves on a floured baking sheet, cover with the tea towel, and let rise until doubled in bulk, about 1 hour. Brush the tops of the loaves with milk or soymilk. Bake in a preheated 350-degree oven for 40 to 50 minutes, or until the tops are golden and the loaves feel hollow when tapped.

Per ³/4-inch-thick slice:

Calories: 143	Total fat: 3 g	Protein: 4 g
Carbohydrate: 24 g	Cholesterol: 1 g	Sodium: 169 mg

"At Christmas play and make good cheer, For Christmas comes but once a year."

—Thomas Tusser
A Hundred Points of Good Husbandry, 1557

Suggested timetable for

An American Country Christmas

A day ahead:

- *Make the Braided Sweet Potato Bread. Let cool, then store at room temperature wrapped in foil, then plastic.*

- *Make the French Dressing for Creole Green Salad and refrigerate.*

- *Cook the wild and brown rice for Wild Rice Pilaf with Apples and Pecans. Let cool and refrigerate, covered.*

- *Make the dough for the Pastry Crust for Cocoa Mock-Mince Pie. Wrap it tightly in plastic wrap and store in the refrigerator.*

Same day, morning:

- *Make the Cocoa Mock-Mince Pie and bake it.*

- *Make the Spiced Carrot and Orange Soup. Let it stand off the heat, covered, until needed.*

- *Cook the corn for Leek and Corn-Stuffed Peppers.*

(timetable continues . . .)

SPICED CARROT AND ORANGE SOUP

8 to 10 servings

A warming soup with the cheering color of carrots and the zesty flavor of citrus.

2 pounds carrots, thinly sliced
2 tablespoons fragrant nut oil or canola oil
2 cups chopped onions
2 large celery stalks, diced
1 1/2 cups fresh orange juice
1/4 cup dry white wine
1 teaspoon each: ground cumin, coriander, ginger
1/2 teaspoon ground nutmeg
1 cup low-fat milk or soymilk, or as needed
salt and freshly ground pepper to taste
3 tablespoons minced fresh parsley
3 tablespoons finely minced scallion

Reserve and set aside about 1/2 pound of the carrots.

Heat the oil in a large soup pot. Add the onions and celery and sauté over moderate heat, stirring frequently, until golden. Add the carrots (except for the reserved batch), along with 4 cups of water, the juice, wine, and spices. Bring to a boil, then cover and simmer over moderate heat until the vegetables are quite tender, about 30 minutes. Transfer in batches to the container of a food processor or blender and puree until quite smooth.

Return to low heat and stir in enough milk or soymilk to give the soup a medium-thick consistency. Season to taste with salt and pepper. Let the soup stand off the heat for several hours before serving.

Just before serving, steam the reserved carrots until crisp-tender and stir into the soup along with the parsley and scallion. Taste to correct consistency and seasonings before serving.

Calories: 124	Total fat: 3 g	Protein: 2 g
Carbohydrate: 19 g	Cholesterol: 1 g	Sodium: 91 mg

CREOLE GREEN SALAD

8 to 10 servings

2 cups stemmed, torn spinach leaves
2 cups watercress leaves
2 cups torn chicory leaves
2 cups endive leaves (if large, cut in half)
1 small onion, minced, or 3 bunches scallions, minced
1 large celery stalk, finely diced
1 pint cherry tomatoes, hulled and halved
French Dressing (page 257), as needed

Combine the greens, onion or scallions, celery, and tomatoes in a large salad bowl. Toss together. Add enough dressing to lightly coat and toss again; or pass the dressing around separately so that guests may dress their own salad.

Calories: 50	Total fat: 2 g	Protein: 1 g
Carbohydrate: 5 g	Cholesterol: 0 g	Sodium: 40 mg

LEEK AND CORN-STUFFED PEPPERS

8 to 10 servings

Fresh southern corn is widely sold this time of year, and it is usually quite good. Use it if you can, leaving frozen corn only as a last resort. This dish makes an attractive centerpiece for this dinner, encircling the wild rice pilaf that follows.

10 medium green or red bell peppers, or a combination
2 tablespoons olive oil
4 large leeks, white and palest green parts only,
    chopped and well rinsed
2 tablespoons minced shallots
2 cloves garlic, minced
4 cups cooked corn kernels, preferably fresh
1/4 cup fine bread crumbs
1/4 cup minced fresh parsley
1 teaspoon dried summer savory
1 teaspoon ground coriander
salt and freshly ground pepper to taste

Starting 3 hours before serving:

- *Assemble the Leek and Corn-Stuffed Peppers.*

- *Shred the cabbage for Sautéed Red Cabbage.*

- *Make the Creole Green Salad, but don't dress it. Cover and refrigerate.*

Starting 1 1/2 hours before serving:

- *Serve appetizers suggested in Additions to the menu, page 170, if desired, to any guests who have arrived.*

- *Make the Wild Rice Pilaf with Apples and Pecans. Cover and leave off the heat until needed.*

(timetable continues . . .)

Starting 1 hour before serving:

- *Bake the Leek and Corn-Stuffed Peppers.*

- *Finish making the Sautéed Red Cabbage.*

- *Finish making the soup and heat through. Warm the Braided Sweet Potato Bread, wrapped in foil, in the oven.*

- *Dress the salad if desired, or leave dressing separate so that guests may dress their own.*

During the meal:

- *While soup and bread are being eaten, gently heat any dishes that need heating through, such as Sautéed Red Cabbage and Wild Rice Pilaf with Apples and Pecans. After the soup dishes have been cleared, arrange the Leek and Corn-Stuffed Peppers and the wild rice dish as described in the recipe.*

wheat germ for topping
paprika for topping

Preheat the oven to 350 degrees.

Carefully cut away the top stems of the peppers and remove the seeds. Cut a very thin slice from the bottoms so that the peppers can stand. Arrange, standing snugly against one another for support, in 1 or 2 very deep casserole dishes or a roasting pan.

Heat the oil with 2 tablespoons of water in a large skillet. Add the leeks, shallots, and garlic. Sauté over medium heat, covered, lifting the lid to stir occasionally, until the leeks are tender. Stir in the remaining ingredients except the toppings. Cook, stirring, another 5 minutes.

Distribute the stuffing among the peppers. Top each with a sprinkling of wheat germ, followed by a dusting of paprika. Cover the casserole or roasting pan and bake for 40 to 50 minutes, or until the peppers are tender but still firm enough to stand. Arrange in a circle on a large platter surrounding the pilaf, following. Serve at once.

Calories: 146	Total fat: 2 g	Protein: 3 g
Carbohydrate: 26 g	Cholesterol: 0 g	Sodium: 24 mg

WILD RICE PILAF WITH APPLES AND PECANS

8 to 10 servings

Wild rice, apples, and pecans just seem to belong together. The texture will invigorate your palate.

$2/3$ cup wild rice, rinsed
$2/3$ cup long-grain brown rice, rinsed
1 teaspoon seasoned salt
2 tablespoons reduced-fat margarine
1 cup chopped red onion
$1/2$ cup finely diced celery
2 medium tart apples, such as Granny Smith, peeled, cored, and diced
$1/3$ cup orange juice (from 1 large orange)
2 scallions, green parts only, thinly sliced
$1/4$ cup currants
dash each: cinnamon, nutmeg

freshly ground pepper to taste
2 tablespoons minced fresh parsley
½ cup finely chopped pecans

Bring 3 ¾ cups of water to a boil in a heavy saucepan. Stir in the wild and brown rice and the seasoned salt, return to a boil, then lower the heat and simmer, covered, until the water is absorbed, about 40 minutes.

Heat the margarine in a very large skillet. Add the onion and celery and sauté until the onion is golden. Add the apples and sauté another 5 minutes. Stir in the cooked rice mixture along with the juice, scallions, currants, and spices. Season to taste with pepper.

Sauté over low heat, stirring frequently, another 5 minutes. This may be done somewhat ahead of time to this point, then left covered off the heat until needed. Just before serving, heat through, adding a bit more liquid if the mixture needs it, then stir in the parsley and pecans. Mound in the center of a large serving platter and surround with the stuffed peppers, above.

Calories: 169	Total fat: 4 g	Protein: 3 g
Carbohydrate: 28 g	Cholesterol: 0 g	Sodium: 309 mg

SAUTÉED RED CABBAGE

8 to 10 servings

1 tablespoon canola oil
1 large red onion, quartered and sliced
6 cups thinly shredded red cabbage
¼ cup dry red wine
3 to 4 tablespoons cider vinegar or red wine vinegar,
    to taste
3 tablespoons honey
3 tablespoons poppy seeds
salt and freshly ground pepper to taste

Heat the oil in a large skillet or 3-quart saucepan. Add the onion and sauté until golden. Add the cabbage, wine, and vinegar. Cover and sauté until crisp-tender, about 12 minutes, lifting the lid to stir occasionally. Stir in the honey and poppy seeds and sauté over very low heat, stirring occasionally, another 8 to 10 minutes. Season to taste with salt

and pepper, then transfer to a serving container to serve.

Calories: 78   Total fat: 2 g   Protein: 1 g
Carbohydrate: 10 g   Cholesterol: 0 g   Sodium: 8 mg

COCOA MOCK-MINCE PIE

Makes 1 9-inch pie, 8 servings

Mince pies are a long-standing Christmas tradition, but of course the standard versions use mincemeat or suet. Nineteenth-century American housewives began making mock-mince pies, and they're so good that I suspect no one ever missed the meat. My version has an additional twist— a bit of cocoa for a deep, rich flavor. If none of your guests have offered to bring additional desserts, you might want to double this recipe.

¼ cup dry, unsweetened cocoa
1 teaspoon instant coffee
¼ cup light brown sugar
2 tablespoons molasses
½ cup currants
½ cup golden raisins
**2 medium Granny Smith apples, peeled, cored, and
    finely chopped**
¾ cup fine fresh bread crumbs
¼ cup finely chopped walnuts or pecans
1 teaspoon vanilla extract
1 teaspoon cinnamon
½ teaspoon allspice
¼ teaspoon each: ground ginger and nutmeg
1 recipe Basic Pastry Crust (page 260)

Topping
1 tablespoon reduced-fat margarine
¼ cup fine fresh bread crumbs
2 tablespoons light brown sugar
¼ teaspoon cinnamon

Preheat the oven to 350 degrees.
Combine the first 4 ingredients in a large saucepan with ½ cup of water. Bring to a simmer and stir until smoothly dissolved and combined. Add the currants, raisins, and apples

and simmer over low heat, covered, for 10 minutes. Remove from the heat.

In a mixing bowl, combine the bread crumbs, nuts, vanilla, and spices. Pour in the mixture from the saucepan and stir until thoroughly combined. Pour into the pastry crust.

Melt the margarine in the same saucepan used previously. Remove from the heat and stir in the bread crumbs, sugar, and cinnamon. Sprinkle over the top of the pie. Bake for 35 minutes, or until the crust is golden.

Let cool and serve just warm or at room temperature.

Calories: 284	Total fat: 7 g	Protein: 5 g
Carbohydrate: 52 g	Cholesterol: 1 g	Sodium: 295 mg

AN ENGLISH CHRISTMAS

8 servings

Cauliflower-Cheddar Soup

Yorkshire Pudding

Lentil and Mushroom Loaf with Savory Potato Filling

Sage and Onion Stuffing

Brussels Sprouts with Chestnuts

Cranberry Sauce

Trifle

Additions to the menu: Have some appetizers on hand, if you like. Try Creamy Horseradish Dip in Rye "Bowl," page 241, serving it with the vegetables recommended in the recipe and also some sesame breadsticks. You might also like to add Sweet and Sour Quick-Pickled Vegetables (page 238).

Contains egg and dairy products.

I adapted many of the dishes in this English-style menu from recipes passed down to their contributor, a young Englishwoman, from her grandmother, who lived in Liverpool. My interpretations of these recipes are lighter, that is, lower in fat, than the originals. However, I've attempted to retain their hearty and homey qualities. After all, that's what English cookery is all about.

Suggested timetable for

An English Christmas

A day ahead:

- *Cook the lentils and bake or microwave the potatoes for Lentil and Mushroom Loaf with Savory Potato Filling. Let them cool and store separately, refrigerated.*

- *Bake the chestnuts for Brussels Sprouts with Chestnuts. When cool enough to handle, peel them. Store at room temperature in a covered container.*

- *Make the cake base for Trifle. Bake it, let cool, and store, covered, in the refrigerator.*

- *Make the Cranberry Sauce. Let cool and refrigerate, covered.*

(timetable continues . . .)

CAULIFLOWER-CHEDDAR SOUP

8 to 10 servings

For anyone coming in from the cold, this is a soothing treat.

2 tablespoons canola oil
1 cup finely chopped onions
2 medium celery stalks, diced
4 medium potatoes, peeled and cut into ½-inch dice
1 medium head cauliflower, finely chopped
Light Vegetable Stock (page 260) or water
1 teaspoon curry powder
1 teaspoon dry mustard
1 to 1 ½ cups low-fat milk, or soymilk, or as needed
**2 cups loosely packed grated reduced-fat cheddar cheese
    or cheddar-style soy cheese**
1 ½ cups thawed frozen peas
2 tablespoons minced fresh dill, or 2 teaspoons dried dill
¼ teaspoon dried rosemary
salt and freshly ground pepper to taste

Heat the oil in a large soup pot. Add the onions and celery and sauté over moderate heat until the onions are golden. Add the potatoes, cauliflower, and enough water or stock to barely cover. Stir in the curry and mustard. Bring to a boil, then cover and simmer until all the vegetables are tender, about 20 to 25 minutes. Remove from the heat.

With a slotted spoon, transfer half of the solid ingredients to the container of a food processor. Process until smoothly pureed. Stir back into the soup pot with the remaining soup. Add just enough milk to achieve a slightly thick consistency. Return to low heat and bring to a gentle simmer. Sprinkle the cheese in a bit at a time, stirring in each batch until melted (soy cheese will not melt as completely as dairy cheese). Stir in the peas and dill and simmer over low heat for 10 minutes, stirring occasionally.

Adjust the consistency with more milk if necessary and season to taste with salt and pepper. Let stand several hours, then heat through before serving.

Calories: 214	Total fat: 8 g	Protein: 11 g
Carbohydrate: 22 g	Cholesterol: 19 g	Sodium: 216 mg

YORKSHIRE PUDDING

8 to 10 servings

Yorkshire pudding is a simple, quick pan bread traditionally made for Christmas to catch the drippings from roast beef. For this meal, use it to accompany the Cauliflower-Cheddar Soup.

1 cup unbleached white flour
1 cup whole wheat pastry flour
1 teaspoon salt
2 eggs, beaten
1 cup low-fat milk or soymilk
2 tablespoons reduced-fat margarine, melted

Preheat the oven to 425 degrees.

In a mixing bowl, combine the flours and salt. Make a well in the center and add the eggs. Stir together briefly, then add the milk and 1 cup of very cold water, a bit at a time. Stir until the batter is smooth, but don't overbeat.

Swirl the melted margarine around a shallow, 9- by 13-inch baking pan. Pour out any excess and reserve. Pour the batter into the pan and pour any remaining margarine over the top. Bake for 20 minutes, or until golden on top and a knife inserted into the center tests clean. Let cool somewhat, then cut into squares to serve.

Calories: 127	Total fat: 3 g	Protein: 5 g
Carbohydrate: 20 g	Cholesterol: 48 g	Sodium: 287 mg

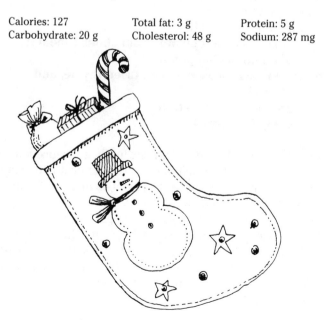

Same day, morning:

- *Make the eggless custard for Trifle. When cooled, assemble the Trifle and refrigerate it.*

- *Make the Cauliflower-Cheddar Soup. Let stand at room temperature until needed.*

- *Trim the Brussels sprouts as directed for Brussels Sprouts with Chestnuts. Place them in a covered saucepan until later.*

Starting 3 hours before serving:

- *Assemble the Lentil and Mushroom Loaf with Savory Potato Filling. Set aside at room temperature, covered, until later.*

- *Assemble the Sage and Onion Stuffing. Set aside at room temperature, covered, until later.*

Starting 1 ½ hours before serving:

- *Serve appetizers, if desired, to any guests already present.*

- *Make the Yorkshire Pudding. Bake it, then turn the oven temperature down to 350 degrees.*

Starting 1 hour before serving:

- *Bake the Lentil and Mushroom Loaf with Savory Potato Filling.*

- *Bake the Sage and Onion Stuffing.*

- *Finish making the Brussels Sprouts with Chestnuts.*

- *Heat the soup.*

LENTIL AND MUSHROOM LOAF WITH SAVORY POTATO FILLING

8 to 10 servings

Meat pies are a long tradition for English Christmases, so I wanted to devise something not necessarily imitative of meat but with a sort of stick-to-the-ribs quality characteristic of English foods. This flavorful loaf contains the pleasant surprise of a nicely seasoned potato filling in the center.

1 cup raw lentils
1 tablespoon canola oil
2 cloves garlic, minced
6 ounces white mushrooms
5 ounces (½ package) thawed frozen spinach
1 tablespoon soy sauce or tamari
2 tablespoons wheat germ
freshly ground pepper to taste
dash nutmeg
1 cup firmly packed grated Stilton or Gruyère cheese
**   (or substitute mozzarella-style soy cheese)**

Filling
1 tablespoon canola oil
1 cup chopped onion
¼ cup dry bread crumbs
1 cup coarsely mashed potato (from about 1 medium
**   cooked and peeled potato)**
½ teaspoon each: seasoned salt, dried thyme, and
**   dried basil**
freshly ground pepper to taste
curly parsley for garnish

Rinse and sort the lentils. Combine in a heavy saucepan with 4 cups water. Bring to a boil, then lower the heat and simmer, covered, until the lentils are tender, about 45 minutes. Drain.

Preheat the oven to 350 degrees.

Heat the oil in a large skillet. Add the garlic and mushrooms and sauté over medium heat, stirring, until the mushrooms are wilted. Stir in the spinach, lentils, soy sauce, and wheat germ. Grind in some pepper and add the nutmeg. Cook, stirring, until the mixture is heated through, then stir in the cheese.

Lightly oil a 9- by 5- by 3-inch loaf pan, preferably glass. Pour in about $2/3$ of the lentil mixture. Press some of the mixture up the sides of the pan to create a shell about $1/2$ inch thick. Transfer the remaining lentil mixture to a small bowl and reserve until needed.

Rinse the skillet and heat the oil. Add the onion and sauté until golden brown. Add the remaining filling ingredients and sauté, stirring occasionally, for 5 minutes. Transfer into the shell created by the lentil mixture, then cover the top with the reserved lentil mixture. Bake for 40 to 45 minutes, or until the top is crusty.

Remove from the oven and let the loaf stand for 15 minutes. Slide a spatula or knife around the edges to loosen it. Cut slices and arrange them on an oblong dish. Garnish with parsley and serve.

Calories: 197	Total fat: 7 g	Protein: 10 g
Carbohydrate: 20 g	Cholesterol: 14 g	Sodium: 311 mg

SAGE AND ONION STUFFING

8 to 10 servings

Using an infusion of sage rather than the strong-flavored leaves themselves gives this stuffing that wonderful herbal flavor without overpowering it.

3 tablespoons fresh sage leaves, or 1 tablespoon dried
2 tablespoons canola oil
$1/2$ pound onions, finely chopped
4 cups fine fresh bread crumbs
1 medium Granny Smith apple, peeled, cored, and
    finely diced
juice of $1/2$ lemon
1 teaspoon grated lemon rind
2 eggs, beaten
salt and freshly ground pepper

Preheat the oven to 350 degrees.

Combine the sage leaves with 1 cup of boiling water. Steep for at least 15 minutes, then strain. Discard the sage and reserve the water. Heat the oil in a large skillet. Add the onions and sauté over medium heat, stirring frequently, until they are lightly browned. In a mixing bowl, combine the

CHRISTMAS BEVERAGES

Each of these recipes makes 22 to 24 ³/₄-cup servings.

Wassail Bowl

Wassail (from the Anglo-Saxon, meaning "be of good health") is the most famous of English Christmas beverages. The contributor of this recipe related that this is a rustic version, or as she put it, "rough," of this classic punch, hence the dark beer or ale and chunks of apple.

In a large pot, combine 3 quarts dark beer or ale, 1 pint dry sherry, 1 cup packed light brown sugar (or to taste), 1 stick cinnamon, grated fresh or ground nutmeg and ginger to taste, 2 lemons, cut into chunks, and 2 cored apples, cut into chunks. Bring to a simmer and cook just long enough for the sugar to dissolve. Serve hot, ladled straight from the pot.

onions with the bread crumbs and the remaining ingredients. Sprinkle in the sage stock until the ingredients are evenly moistened. Transfer to an oiled, shallow 1 ½-quart casserole dish (a round glass one works well). Bake for 35 to 40 minutes, or until the outside is golden brown and crusty.

Calories: 116	Total fat: 5 g	Protein: 3 g
Carbohydrate: 14 g	Cholesterol: 49 g	Sodium: 119 mg

BRUSSELS SPROUTS WITH CHESTNUTS

8 to 10 servings

1 pound chestnuts
1 ½ pounds Brussels sprouts
2 cups Light Vegetable Stock (page 260), or 2 cups water
    plus 1 vegetable bouillon cube
2 tablespoons reduced-fat margarine
2 to 3 tablespoons minced fresh parsley
salt and freshly ground pepper to taste

Preheat the oven to 375 degrees.

Cut an X into the domed side of each chestnut. Arrange on a large baking sheet. Cover with foil. Bake for 45 minutes. Remove the foil and let the chestnuts cool until they can be handled. While still warm, peel them and chop them into quarters.

Trim the Brussels sprouts and cut an X into the base, about ¼ inch deep. Combine them in a large, heavy saucepan with the stock or water plus bouillon cube and bring to a simmer. Cover and simmer until they are tender but not overdone. Drain any excess liquid, then toss with the margarine and add the chestnuts. Sprinkle in the parsley and season with salt and pepper to taste. Transfer to a covered serving container.

Calories: 159	Total fat: 1 g	Protein: 3 g
Carbohydrate: 33 g	Cholesterol: 0 g	Sodium: 39 mg

CRANBERRY SAUCE

8 to 10 servings

A simple recipe for traditional cranberry sauce—its English character comes from the port or sherry.

12-ounce bag fresh cranberries
$\frac{1}{2}$ cup firmly packed light brown sugar, or to taste
$\frac{1}{4}$ cup port or sherry, more or less to taste

Combine the ingredients in a large saucepan. Cook over low heat, covered, until the cranberries have burst and the mixture thickens, about 20 to 25 minutes. Let cool, then refrigerate until needed. Serve cold or at room temperature.

Calories: 74	Total fat: 0 g	Protein: 0 g
Carbohydrate: 16 g	Cholesterol: 0 g	Sodium: 6 mg

TRIFLE

8 to 10 servings

After steamed puddings, trifle is the most traditional of English Christmas desserts. I must admit that I have "trifled" with the standard recipe, since I wanted to eliminate the heavy, eggy quality of traditional versions. The cake base uses only egg whites, while the custard eliminates eggs completely.

Cake base
3 egg whites
$\frac{1}{2}$ cup granulated sugar
$\frac{1}{4}$ cup low-fat milk
2 teaspoons lemon juice
1 cup whole wheat pastry flour
1 teaspoon baking powder
$\frac{1}{4}$ teaspoon salt

Eggless custard
$\frac{1}{3}$ cup cornstarch
$\frac{1}{2}$ cup granulated sugar
2 cups whole milk

Spiced Fruit Punch

In a large pot, combine 1 quart each of orange juice and pineapple juice, a 1-liter bottle port or sherry, 1 pint dry white wine, sugar to taste, 2 3-inch strips lemon peel, and a stick of cinnamon. Bring to a simmer and simmer gently for 3 to 4 minutes, stirring occasionally. Remove from the heat and let cool to room temperature. Put 2 sliced oranges in a punch bowl and pour the punch over them. Serve with ice on the side for whoever wishes it.

Sparkling Fruit Punch

Squeeze 2 limes and slice 1 lime; squeeze 2 small oranges and slice 1 small orange. Place in a punch bowl and combine with 3 quarts cranberry juice, a 750-ml. bottle of champagne (or, substitute sparkling water for a nonalcoholic punch), and 3 to 6 tablespoons of light brown sugar to taste. Allow time for the sugar to dissolve, and give the punch a stir. Serve with ice on the side for whoever wishes it.

"Trifle: that time-honoured, excellent dish, so dear to the hearts of our elderly cousins and our maiden aunts."

—Col. A. Kenney-Herbert
Wyvern's Sweet Dishes,
1881

2 teaspoons vanilla extract
2 teaspoons lemon juice

good-quality raspberry preserves
$\frac{1}{3}$ cup sweet sherry or port
1 medium pear, cored and thinly sliced
$\frac{1}{4}$ cup sliced almonds

Preheat the oven to 350 degrees.

Beat the egg whites until stiff with an electric mixer. Fold in the sugar, milk, and lemon juice and beat again. Combine the flour, baking powder, and salt in a small mixing bowl. Sprinkle into the egg white mixture, a bit at a time, beating in each time with the mixer until velvety smooth. Pour into a lightly oiled, 9- by 13-inch baking pan. Bake for 25 minutes, or until the top is golden and a knife inserted into the center tests clean. This cake may be made well ahead of time; let it cool completely, then store in an airtight container or proceed with the remaining steps.

For the custard, combine the cornstarch and sugar in a heavy saucepan. Pour in enough milk to dissolve them. Whisk in the remaining milk. Place over moderate heat and bring to a simmer, whisking almost continuously, so that the cornstarch does not lump on the bottom. Let the mixture simmer gently, whisking frequently, until thick. Remove from the heat. Stir in the vanilla and lemon juice. Let the custard cool to room temperature.

Before assembling the trifle, cut the cake base into 4 to 6 sections, then carefully split the sections in half through the center so that they are half the thickness. Spread the bottom halves with the raspberry preserves, then cover with the tops. Cut the sandwiched cake into approximately 1- by 2-inch fingers.

Assemble the trifle in a trifle dish or a 10-inch round, preferably clear-glass casserole dish at least 3 to 4 inches deep: half the cake fingers, sprinkled with half of the sherry or port, half of the custard, the pear slices, the remaining cake fingers, the remaining sherry or port, the remaining custard. Sprinkle the top with the sliced almonds and decorate with small dots of raspberry preserves, either in an irregular or regular pattern. Chill thoroughly before serving.

Calories: 247	Total fat: 4 g	Protein: 6 g
Carbohydrate: 43 g	Cholesterol: 8 g	Sodium: 108 mg

CHRISTMAS EVE IN SOUTHERN ITALY

8 to 10 servings

Antipasto

Artichoke Pie

Double-crust Layered Pizza

Spaghetti Aglia Olio with Sun-dried Tomatoes and Pine Nuts

Sautéed Broccoli Rabe

Italian Chocolate Nut Cookies

———— ༽⚬༼ ————

Contains eggs and dairy products.

I liked the idea of including a rather unexpected menu and found a gem in this one from southern Italy. Andy Frisari, owner and chef at Café Veronica in Manhattan's garment district, and his brother Vincent, who works alongside him, shared their memories and recipes from their boyhoods in the Bari region of southern Italy.

Christmas Eve dinner, as they recalled, was a meal composed of vegetable dishes, pastas, and fish—but no meat. Here are some of the tasty meatless offerings that appeared on their family table.

ANTIPASTO

8 to 10 servings

2 heaping cups cauliflower, cut into bite-sized pieces
2 large celery stalks, trimmed, cut in half lengthwise, then into 2-inch lengths
2 medium sweet red bell peppers, cut into long julienne strips
1 medium zucchini, about $\frac{1}{2}$ pound, quartered lengthwise, then cut into approximately 1 $\frac{1}{2}$-inch pieces
Nutty Vinaigrette or Basic Vinaigrette (page 256)
$\frac{1}{2}$ cup cured black olives
$\frac{1}{2}$ pound creamy goat cheese, chilled and cut into $\frac{1}{2}$-inch dice
curly parsley for garnish

Suggested timetable for

Christmas Eve in Southern Italy

Same day, morning:

- *Prepare and marinate the vegetables for the Antipasto.*

- *Assemble the Artichoke Pie, cover, and refrigerate until later.*

- *Make the fillings for Double-crust Layered Pizza. Cover and store them separately, refrigerated.*

- *Make and bake the Italian Chocolate Nut Cookies.*

Starting 2 ½ hours before serving:

- *Make the pizza dough.*

- *Prepare the broccoli rabe or broccoli for Sautéed Broccoli Rabe. Place in a covered container and leave at room temperature until needed.*

- *Arrange the vegetables and cheeses for the Antipasto on a large serving platter. Cover securely with plastic wrap and refrigerate.*

(timetable continues . . .)

Steam the cauliflower until just crisp-tender. Rinse under cold running water until cool. Drain well. Group the vegetables in a shallow container and pour the vinaigrette over them. Let stand, covered, for several hours, stirring occasionally to distribute the vinaigrette.

Before serving, drain excess vinaigrette from the vegetables. Arrange attractively on a large platter along with the olives and cheeses and garnish with parsley. Serve along with the Artichoke Pie (recipe follows) as a first course.

Calories: 131	Total fat: 10 g	Protein: 4 g
Carbohydrate: 4 g	Cholesterol: 22 g	Sodium: 360 mg

ARTICHOKE PIE

8 to 10 servings

The Frisaris recall that this delicate pie was a frequent component of their mother's antipasto plate.

1 tablespoon olive oil
½ cup chopped onion
2 to 3 cloves garlic, minced
3 eggs, beaten
10-ounce package frozen artichoke hearts, thawed and coarsely chopped
2 tablespoons minced fresh parsley
1 teaspoon dried basil
¼ cup grated fresh Parmesan cheese
¼ cup low-fat milk
salt and freshly ground pepper to taste
fine dry bread crumbs or wheat germ

Preheat the oven to 350 degrees.

Heat the oil in a small skillet. Add the onion and sauté over moderate heat until translucent. Add the garlic and continue to sauté until the onion is golden.

In a mixing bowl, combine the beaten eggs with the onion mixture and all the remaining ingredients except the crumbs or wheat germ. Stir well to combine.

Oil a 9- or 10-inch glass pie dish or tart pan. Line the bottom with a sprinkling of crumbs or wheat germ. Pour in the artichoke mixture and top with another sprinkling of crumbs or wheat germ. If desired, sprinkle additional parsley over the top, as well. Bake for 25 to 30 minutes, or until set and lightly golden on top. Let cool to warm or room temperature. Cut into thin wedges to serve.

Calories: 68	Total fat: 3 g	Protein: 4 g
Carbohydrate: 4 g	Cholesterol: 73 g	Sodium: 83 mg

DOUBLE-CRUST LAYERED PIZZA

8 to 10 servings

The original recipe given to me was for *fritella*, deep-fried pizza-dough pockets stuffed with ricotta and vegetables. The stuffing is delicious, but after making the individual pockets I found the procedure rather labor-intensive in conjunction with preparing the rest of this meal. I also find deep-frying difficult, as many home cooks do. I adapted the recipe to make a double-crust pizza using the same tasty filling. A lot less work for the cook, but the results are just as elegant and delicious.

Pizza dough
2 envelopes active dry yeast
2 tablespoons canola oil
2 tablespoons granulated sugar
3 cups whole wheat flour
2 cups unbleached white flour
1 teaspoon salt
cornmeal

Combine the yeast with 2 cups of warm water. Let stand 10 minutes to dissolve. Stir in the oil and sugar.

In a large mixing bowl, combine the flours and salt. Make a well in the center, and pour in the liquid mixture. Work together, first with a wooden spoon, then with hands, to form a dough. Turn out onto a well-floured board and knead, adding flour until the dough loses its stickiness, for 8 minutes. Place the dough in a floured bowl, covered with a tea towel, in a warm place. Let rise until doubled in bulk, 1 to 1 ½ hours.

Punch the dough down and form into 2 rounds. Roll out and stretch on a well-floured board to fit 2 12- or 14-inch round pizza pans. Lightly oil the pans and sprinkle them with cornmeal.

Starting 1 ½ hours before serving:

- *Bake the Artichoke Pie.*

- *Assemble the Double-crust Layered Pizza.*

- *Make the Spaghetti Aglia Olio.*

- *Make the Sautéed Broccoli Rabe.*

During the meal:

- *While serving the Antipasto, bake the pizza.*

- *Heat the Spaghetti Aglia Olio and the Sautéed Broccoli Rabe, if needed.*

First layer of filling
1 pound part-skim ricotta cheese
10-ounce package frozen chopped spinach, thawed
and squeezed
$1/4$ cup grated fresh Parmesan cheese
2 tablespoons chopped fresh parsley
1 teaspoon dried oregano
dash nutmeg
salt and freshly ground pepper to taste

Second layer of filling
2 cloves garlic, minced
14-ounce can diced tomatoes, drained
$1/4$ cup chopped black olives
dash cayenne or hot pepper flakes
salt and freshly ground pepper to taste

Prepare the dough as directed in the recipe. Place 1 circle of dough as directed on a 12- to 14-inch round pizza pan, and reserve the other.

Preheat the oven to 425 degrees.

Combine the ingredients for the first layer of filling in a mixing bowl and stir until thoroughly combined. Combine the ingredients for the second layer in another bowl and stir together.

Spread the first layer of filling over the pizza dough on the pan. Arrange the second layer of filling over it. Top with the second circle of dough. Pinch the outer edges shut.

Bake for 12 to 15 minutes, or until the dough is golden. Let the pizza stand for 10 minutes, then cut into narrow wedges to serve.

Calories: 369
Carbohydrate: 55 g
Total fat: 9 g
Cholesterol: 17 g
Protein: 16 g
Sodium: 405 mg

SPAGHETTI AGLIA OLIO WITH SUN-DRIED TOMATOES AND PINE NUTS

8 to 10 servings

$1/4$ cup extra-virgin olive oil, divided
8 to 10 cloves garlic, finely minced
3 tablespoons toasted pine nuts
1 pound spaghetti, broken in half
2 to 4 ounces finely chopped oil-cured sun-dried
      tomatoes, to taste
$2/3$ cup finely chopped fresh parsley
$1/4$ cup grated fresh Parmesan cheese
salt and freshly ground pepper to taste

Heat 1 tablespoon of the olive oil in a small skillet and reserve the rest. Add the garlic and sauté over moderate heat, stirring frequently, for about 1 minute, or until golden. Remove from heat. Toast the pine nuts in a small, dry skillet, tossing frequently, until golden.

Cook the pasta al dente in plenty of rapidly simmering water. Drain and transfer to a serving bowl. Add the garlic, tomatoes, parsley, pine nuts, Parmesan cheese, and remaining olive oil. Toss together. Season to taste with salt and pepper (taste first—you may not need salt because of the Parmesan cheese).

Calories: 167	Total fat: 7 g	Protein: 5 g
Carbohydrate: 19 g	Cholesterol: 2 g	Sodium: 48 mg

SAUTÉED BROCCOLI RABE

8 to 10 servings

According to the Frisaris, this dish is quite typical for Christmas Eve dinner, but bear in mind that while many people consider broccoli rabe a delicacy, others may be put off by the bitter flavor. If you're unsure of your guests' tastes, substitute ordinary broccoli.

2 tablespoons olive oil
2 to 3 cloves garlic, minced
$1/4$ cup dry white wine

"He who enters paradise through a door is not a Neapolitan. We make our entrance into that heavenly abode by delicately parting a curtain of spaghetti. As soon as we get weaned from our mother's breast we are fed a fragment of spaghetti . . . what better inheritance can I leave my sons than spaghetti?"

—Giuseppe Marotta, quoted in *Spaghetti Dinner* by Giuseppe Pressolini, 1955

1 ½ pounds broccoli rabe or broccoli, trimmed and cut into large bite-sized pieces
salt and freshly ground pepper to taste

Heat the oil in an extra-large skillet or a wok. Add the garlic and sauté over moderate heat for 1 minute, or until golden. Add the wine. Stir the broccoli rabe or broccoli in quickly. Sauté, covered, lifting the lid to stir frequently, until bright green and tender but still firm. Season to taste with salt and pepper.

Calories: 56   Total fat: 1 g   Protein: 1 g
Carbohydrate: 4 g   Cholesterol: 0 g   Sodium: 21 mg

ITALIAN CHOCOLATE NUT COOKIES

Makes about 4 dozen

½ **cup (1 stick) reduced-fat margarine, cut into several pieces**
²⁄₃ **cup dry unsweetened cocoa**
2 cups firmly packed light brown sugar
2 ½ cups whole wheat pastry flour
1 ½ teaspoons baking powder
2 teaspoons cinnamon
1 teaspoon ground cloves or allspice
²⁄₃ **cup finely chopped almonds**
1 cup raisins or currants

Preheat the oven to 350 degrees.

Combine the first 3 ingredients in a saucepan with ½ cup of water. Heat slowly, stirring, until the mixture resembles a smooth syrup. Remove from heat and let cool to room temperature.

In a large mixing bowl, combine the flour with the baking powder and spices. Make a well in the center and pour in the chocolate syrup. Work together, first with a spoon, then with clean hands, to make a stiff batter. Add the almonds and raisins or currants and work in.

Form into balls no larger than 1 inch and arrange on cookie sheets. Bake for 12 to 15 minutes, or until a toothpick inserted into the center of a cookie tests clean.

Per cookie:
Calories: 88   Total fat: 2 g   Protein: 1 g
Carbohydrate: 16 g   Cholesterol: 0 g   Sodium: 21 mg

WHOLE-GRAIN QUICK BREADS FOR THE HOLIDAYS

Cranberry-Pecan Bread

Russian Honey and Dried Fruit Bread

Maple Date-Hazelnut Bread

Pumpkin Muffins

It's nice to have easy-to-make quick breads on hand for drop-in holiday company; a fresh loaf also makes a nice gift to bring when you are invited to others' homes for holiday meals or visits

CRANBERRY-PECAN BREAD

Makes 1 loaf; recipe doubles easily for 2 loaves

1 cup whole wheat pastry flour
$\frac{1}{2}$ cup unbleached white flour
$\frac{1}{2}$ cup amaranth or quinoa flour (if unavailable, substitute an additional $\frac{1}{2}$ cup whole wheat pastry flour)
1 teaspoon baking powder
1 teaspoon baking soda
$\frac{1}{2}$ teaspoon salt
1 teaspoon allspice
1 egg, or 2 egg whites beaten
$\frac{3}{4}$ cup firmly packed dark brown sugar
1 cup vanilla nonfat yogurt
1 teaspoon grated lemon rind
1 teaspoon vanilla extract
1 cup chopped cranberries
$\frac{1}{4}$ cup chopped pitted prunes
$\frac{1}{4}$ cup finely chopped pecans

Preheat the oven to 350 degrees.

Combine the first 7 ingredients in a mixing bowl and stir together. In another bowl, combine the next 5 ingredients and stir until thoroughly combined. Make a well in the center of the flour mixture. Pour in the wet mixture and stir together vigorously until thoroughly combined. Stir in the cranberries, prunes, and pecans. Pour the mixture into an oiled 9- by 5- by

3-inch loaf pan. Bake for 50 minutes, or until a knife inserted into the center tests clean. Cool on a rack, then cover tightly with foil to store.

Per ³/4-inch-thick slice:

Calories: 198	Total fat: 2 g	Protein: 5 g
Carbohydrate: 38 g	Cholesterol: 22 g	Sodium: 142 mg

RUSSIAN HONEY AND DRIED FRUIT BREAD

Makes 1 loaf; recipe doubles easily for 2 loaves

²/3 **cup honey**
¹/2 **teaspoon cinnamon**
¹/4 **teaspoon each: ground cloves, ground nutmeg**
¹/2 **teaspoon baking soda**
2 eggs, separated
³/4 **cup vanilla nonfat yogurt**
¹/2 **cup raisins**
¹/4 **cup chopped pitted dates**
¹/4 **cup chopped apricots**
¹/4 **cup finely chopped walnuts**
1 ³/4 cups whole wheat pastry flour
1 ¹/2 teaspoons baking powder
¹/2 **teaspoon salt**

Preheat the oven to 325 degrees.

In a small saucepan, heat the honey, bringing it just to the boiling point. Remove from heat and stir in the spices and baking soda.

In a mixing bowl, combine the egg yolks and yogurt and beat together until smooth. Add the honey mixture and mix in thoroughly, then stir in the dried fruits and nuts.

In a large mixing bowl, combine the flour, baking powder, and salt. Make a well in the center and pour in the honey-nut mixture. Stir together vigorously until thoroughly combined. Beat the egg whites until stiff, then fold into the batter. Pour into an oiled 9- by 5- by 3-inch loaf pan. Bake for 55 minutes, or until a knife inserted into the center tests clean. Cool on a rack, then cover tightly with foil to store.

Per ³/4-inch-thick slice:

Calories: 225	Total fat: 4 g	Protein: 6 g
Carbohydrate: 43 g	Cholesterol: 43 g	Sodium: 140 mg

MAPLE DATE-HAZELNUT BREAD

Makes 1 loaf; recipe doubles easily for 2 loaves

2 cups whole wheat pastry flour
1 ½ teaspoons baking powder
1 teaspoon cinnamon
½ teaspoon allspice
¼ teaspoon each: ground nutmeg, ground cloves,
    and salt
2 eggs, beaten
2 tablespoons canola oil
½ cup pure maple syrup
½ cup applesauce
1 teaspoon grated lemon rind
1 cup chopped pitted dates
¼ cup currants
¼ cup finely chopped hazelnuts

Preheat the oven to 350 degrees.

In a mixing bowl, combine the flour with the baking powder, spices, and salt. In another bowl, beat the eggs together with the oil, syrup, applesauce, and lemon rind. Make a well in the center of the flour mixture and pour in the wet mixture. Stir vigorously until thoroughly combined. Stir in the dates, currants, and hazelnuts. Pour into an oiled 9- by 5- by 3-inch loaf pan. Bake 45 to 50 minutes, or until a knife inserted into the center tests clean. Cool on a rack, then cover tightly with foil to store.

Per ³/₄-inch-thick slice:

Calories: 248	Total fat: 6 g	Protein: 5 g
Carbohydrate: 42 g	Cholesterol: 43 g	Sodium: 72 mg

Holly: *Holly is a Christmas symbol for its appearance— the red berries stand for the blood shed by Christ, and the pointed leaves recall His crown of thorns.*

Mistletoe: *Historically, mistletoe was thought to have curative powers, to make poison harmless, to promote fertility, to ward off evil spirits, and to protect the home from foul weather. But more significantly, the plant early became a symbol of peacemaking, leading to the custom of hanging it in doorways to encourage reconciliation among enemies. This later evolved to the custom of kissing beneath it.*

PUMPKIN MUFFINS

Makes 1 dozen

2 cups whole wheat pastry flour
$1/4$ cup wheat germ
1 teaspoon ground ginger
$1/2$ teaspoon allspice
2 teaspoons baking powder
$1/4$ teaspoon salt
1 egg, beaten
1 cup fresh or canned pumpkin puree
$1/2$ cup applesauce
$1/3$ cup firmly packed brown sugar
$1/2$ cup apple juice
$2/3$ cup raisins or currants
$1/4$ cup toasted sunflower seeds

Preheat the oven to 350 degrees.

Combine the first 6 ingredients in a mixing bowl. In another bowl, beat the eggs together with the pumpkin, applesauce, brown sugar, and apple juice until smooth. Make a well in the center of the flour mixture and pour in the wet ingredients. Stir together vigorously until thoroughly combined. Stir in the raisins or currants and the seeds.

Divide the mixture among 12 oiled or paper-lined muffin tins. Bake for 20 to 25 minutes, or until a toothpick inserted in the center of a muffin tests clean. Cool on a rack, then remove muffins from the tin and store in an airtight container.

Per muffin:
   Calories: 163   Total fat: 2 g   Protein: 5 g
   Carbohydrate: 30 g   Cholesterol: 18 g   Sodium: 58 mg

Chapter 12

INFORMAL BUFFETS

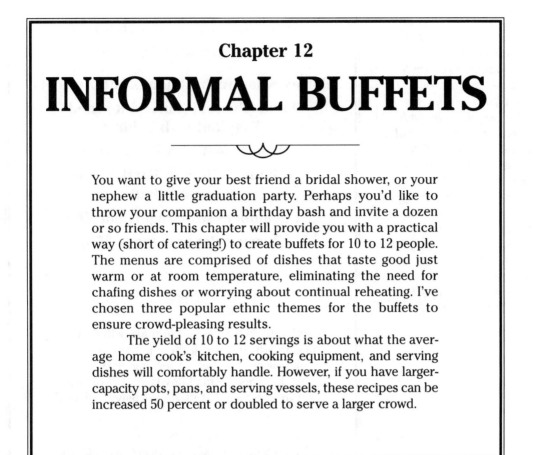

You want to give your best friend a bridal shower, or your nephew a little graduation party. Perhaps you'd like to throw your companion a birthday bash and invite a dozen or so friends. This chapter will provide you with a practical way (short of catering!) to create buffets for 10 to 12 people. The menus are comprised of dishes that taste good just warm or at room temperature, eliminating the need for chafing dishes or worrying about continual reheating. I've chosen three popular ethnic themes for the buffets to ensure crowd-pleasing results.

The yield of 10 to 12 servings is about what the average home cook's kitchen, cooking equipment, and serving dishes will comfortably handle. However, if you have larger-capacity pots, pans, and serving vessels, these recipes can be increased 50 percent or doubled to serve a larger crowd.

Middle Eastern fare such as that in this menu is already familiar enough to the American palate to stir anticipation, yet is still exotic enough to cause excitement. I love the use of grains and chick peas, the strong herbal and garlicky notes, and the refreshing use of yogurt. Of the three theme buffets given here, I would say that this is the easiest to prepare, since there is little cooking to do, apart from cooking the grains and roasting the eggplant and peppers. And since all the dishes are cold, it's a perfect one for summer entertaining.

MIDDLE EASTERN BUFFET

10 to 12 servings

Barley Salad with Almonds and Apricots

Baba Ghanouj (Pureed Roasted Eggplant with Tahini)

Hummus (Chick Pea Puree)

Tabouleh (Bulgur, Parsley, and Tomato Salad)

Cucumbers with Yogurt and Dill

Roasted Peppers (page 258)

―――――⟶ꞈ⟵―――――

Additions to the menu: Purchase whole wheat pita breads and warm them in the oven or in a microwave just before serving. Serve cured black olives in small bowls, and, if desired, serve purchased stuffed vine leaves, as well.

Contains no eggs.
Contains dairy products (yogurt only). Can be made dairy-free by substituting soy yogurt.

BARLEY SALAD WITH ALMONDS AND APRICOTS

10 to 12 servings

Note that I call for "pot" barley, a less refined form of barley than the common pearled barley sold in supermarkets. Sold in natural food stores, it's not only more nutritious, but cooks to a less sticky consistency. Do use ordinary barley if you can't find pot barley.

1 ½ cups pot barley (or substitute regular pearl barley)
1 tablespoon canola oil
1 large onion, quartered and thinly sliced
³⁄₄ cup moist dried apricots, sliced
½ cup slivered or sliced almonds
2 tablespoons minced fresh parsley

Dressing
1 cup plain low-fat yogurt or soy yogurt
2 tablespoons honey
juice of ½ to 1 lemon, to taste
½ teaspoon each: cinnamon, turmeric, salt
dash of nutmeg

Rinse the barley in a fine sieve. Bring 4 ½ cups of water to a boil in a heavy saucepan. Stir in the barley, return to a boil, then reduce heat and simmer, covered, until the water is absorbed, about 45 to 50 minutes. Let the barley cool to room temperature.

Heat the oil in a small skillet. Add the onion and sauté over moderate heat until golden brown. In a serving dish, combine the barley, onion, apricots, almonds, and parsley, and toss together.

In a small mixing bowl, combine the dressing ingredients. Pour over the barley mixture and toss well to combine. Serve at room temperature.

Calories: 166	Total fat: 5 g	Protein: 4 g
Carbohydrate: 26 g	Cholesterol: 1 g	Sodium: 21 mg

Make-ahead suggestions for

Middle Eastern Buffet

A day ahead:

- *Cook the barley for the Barley Salad with Almonds and Apricots.*

- *Make the Baba Ghanouj. Allow time to bring it to room temperature before serving.*

- *Cook the bulgur for Tabouleh.*

- *Make the Roasted Peppers. Allow time to bring them to room temperature before serving.*

BABA GHANOUJ
(Pureed Roasted Eggplant with Tahini)

10 to 12 servings

An eggplant lover's delight, this is meant to be scooped up on wedges of pita bread.

3 medium eggplants, about 3 pounds total
1 tablespoon olive oil
1 heaping cup chopped onion
3 to 4 cloves garlic, minced
$\frac{1}{4}$ cup tahini (sesame paste)
juice of 1 lemon, or more to taste
$\frac{1}{2}$ teaspoon ground cumin
salt and freshly ground pepper to taste

Preheat the oven broiler. Arrange the whole eggplants on a foil-lined baking sheet. Set under the broiler until the skin is charred and the eggplants have collapsed, turning the eggplants with tongs once or twice. This will take from about 20 to 40 minutes, depending on how hot your broiler runs and the size of the eggplants. Remove and let cool. When cool enough to handle, slip off the skins and stems.

Heat the oil in a skillet. Add the onion and sauté over moderate heat until translucent. Add the garlic and continue to sauté until the onion is golden brown.

Combine the eggplant, the onion and garlic mixture, and the remaining ingredients in a food processor. Process until the mixture is a slightly chunky puree. Transfer to a serving container and serve at room temperature.

Calories: 86   Total fat: 4 g   Protein: 2 g
Carbohydrate: 11 g   Cholesterol: 0 g   Sodium: 7 mg

HUMMUS
(Chick Pea Puree)

10 to 12 servings

Like the previous recipe, this classic dip should be scooped up on wedges of pita bread.

2 ½ cups canned or well-cooked chick peas
   (see Bean Basics, page 261)
⅓ cup tahini (sesame paste)
2 cloves garlic, crushed
juice of 1 lemon
1 teaspoon ground cumin
salt and freshly ground pepper to taste
paprika for garnish

   Combine all the ingredients except the paprika in a food processor. Add ⅓ cup water and process until smoothly pureed. Transfer to a serving bowl. Sprinkle with paprika. Serve at room temperature.

Calories: 106	Total fat: 5 g	Protein: 4 g
Carbohydrate: 13 g	Cholesterol: 0 g	Sodium: 4 mg

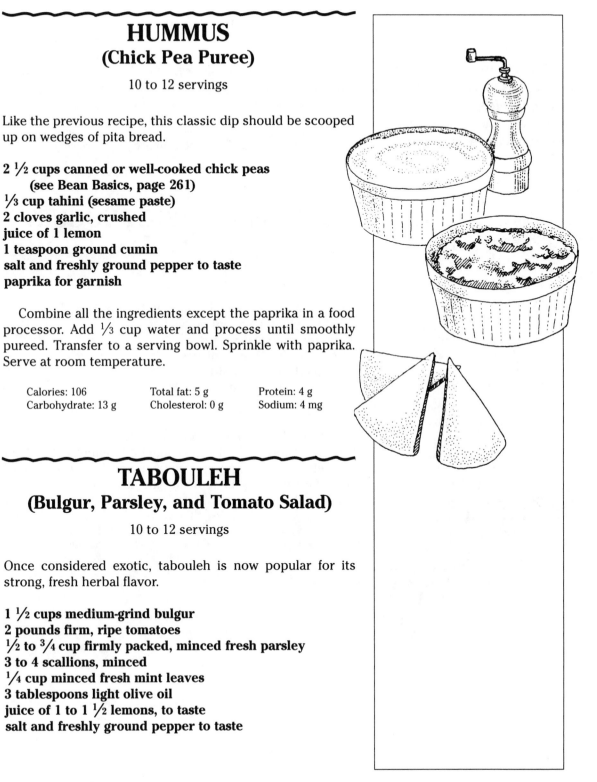

TABOULEH
(Bulgur, Parsley, and Tomato Salad)

10 to 12 servings

Once considered exotic, tabouleh is now popular for its strong, fresh herbal flavor.

1 ½ cups medium-grind bulgur
2 pounds firm, ripe tomatoes
½ to ¾ cup firmly packed, minced fresh parsley
3 to 4 scallions, minced
¼ cup minced fresh mint leaves
3 tablespoons light olive oil
juice of 1 to 1 ½ lemons, to taste
salt and freshly ground pepper to taste

*"Strange to see how
a good dinner and
feasting reconciles
everybody."*

—Samuel Pepys
Diary, 1665

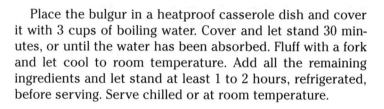

Place the bulgur in a heatproof casserole dish and cover it with 3 cups of boiling water. Cover and let stand 30 minutes, or until the water has been absorbed. Fluff with a fork and let cool to room temperature. Add all the remaining ingredients and let stand at least 1 to 2 hours, refrigerated, before serving. Serve chilled or at room temperature.

Calories: 134	Total fat: 4 g	Protein: 4 g
Carbohydrate: 21 g	Cholesterol: 0 g	Sodium: 10 mg

CUCUMBERS WITH YOGURT AND DILL

10 to 12 servings

6 medium Kirby cucumbers, scrubbed, or 3 medium-large firm cucumbers, peeled
1 cup plain low-fat yogurt
³/₄ cup thinly sliced radishes
¹/₄ cup minced fresh dill
1 tablespoon minced fresh mint
freshly ground pepper to taste

Thinly slice the cucumbers and place them in a colander. Salt them lightly and let them stand for 30 minutes. Pat them dry between paper towels. Combine them in a serving bowl with the remaining ingredients and toss well to combine. Serve chilled.

Calories: 26	Total fat: 0 g	Protein: 2 g
Carbohydrate: 4 g	Cholesterol: 1 g	Sodium: 19 mg

SOUTHWESTERN BUFFET

10 to 12 servings

Tomato Salsa
Tomatillo Relish
Guacamole
Zucchini Chilaquiles
Wheat Tortilla Pizzas
Black Bean and Corn Salad
Piquant Rice Salad

Additions to the menu: You'll need lots of good-quality (preferably low-fat) tortilla chips for scooping up the salsa, relish, and guacamole.

Contains no eggs.
Contains dairy products. Can be made dairy-free by following the suggested substitutions in the recipes.

Southwestern cuisine has been hot, so to speak, for the last several years. I'm quite partial to the earthy combinations of "peasant foods"— tortillas, rice, and beans, enveloped in spicy flavors. This menu consists of easy-to-make classics like salsa and guacamole, plus some of my own interpretive uses of the basic components of this style of cookery. For instance, "drunken" (beer-stewed) pinto beans as a topping for wheat tortillas, to create pizza-like wedges.

TOMATO SALSA

Makes about 3 cups

2 ½ cups diced ripe tomatoes
1 or 2 scallions, chopped
4-ounce can mild green chiles, drained
1 or 2 jalapeño peppers, chopped, to taste
2 tablespoons chopped fresh cilantro or parsley
juice of ½ large lemon, or more to taste
1 teaspoon ground cumin
½ teaspoon salt

Make-ahead suggestions for

Southwestern Buffet

A day ahead:

- *Make Tomato Salsa.*

- *Make Tomatillo Relish.*

- *Make pinto bean topping for Wheat Tortilla Pizzas.*

- *If cooking black beans for Black Bean and Corn Salad from scratch, start them today.*

- *Cook the rice for Piquant Rice Salad.*

Combine the ingredients in the container of a food processor. Pulse on and off until the mixture is a coarse puree. Store in an airtight container, refrigerated, until needed. Transfer to a shallow serving bowl to serve.

Per $1/4$-cup serving:

Calories: 16	Total fat: 0 g	Protein: 0 g
Carbohydrate: 3 g	Cholesterol: 0 g	Sodium: 243 mg

TOMATILLO RELISH

Makes about 2 cups

Tomatillos resemble small green tomatoes and are members of the berry family. Their flavor is very distinct, though not hot. Tomatillos are available in cans from Spanish and Mexican groceries and gourmet specialty shops.

2 13-ounce cans tomatillos
1 clove garlic, minced
1 small onion, minced
$1/2$ medium green or red bell pepper, minced
1 to 2 jalapeño peppers, to taste, minced
2 to 3 tablespoons minced cilantro or fresh parsley
juice of $1/2$ to 1 lime, to taste
$1/2$ teaspoon salt, or to taste
freshly ground pepper

Combine all the ingredients in a mixing bowl and stir together. Cover and refrigerate for at least an hour before serving to allow the flavors to blend. Transfer to a shallow serving bowl to serve.

Calories: 32	Total fat: 0 g	Protein: 1 g
Carbohydrate: 6 g	Cholesterol: 0 g	Sodium: 63 mg

GUACAMOLE

Makes about 3 cups

A Southwestern buffet just wouldn't be complete without guacamole. A friend who grew up in San Antonio taught me to make it with roasted peppers and tomatoes, which give it an extra-special flavor.

2 medium firm, ripe tomatoes
1 medium green bell pepper
3 large, very ripe avocados
juice of 1 lemon
1 scallion, minced
1 to 2 cloves garlic, crushed, optional
1 teaspoon ground cumin
salt and freshly ground pepper to taste

Roast the tomatoes and green pepper under a broiler. Turn on all sides until the skins are quite blistered. Place in a paper bag, shut it, and let steam for 30 minutes. Remove and slip off the skins. Discard the seeds from the tomatoes and the seeds and fibers from the pepper. Chop both fine. Cool to room temperature.

Just before serving, peel the avocados and mash them in a mixing bowl. Stir in the lemon juice immediately to prevent discoloration. Stir in the tomatoes and pepper and the remaining ingredients. Transfer to a shallow serving bowl to serve.

Calories: 94	Total fat: 6 g	Protein: 1 g
Carbohydrate: 8 g	Cholesterol: 0 g	Sodium: 6 mg

ZUCCHINI CHILAQUILES

Makes 10 to 12 servings

Chilaquiles is a casserole that, according to tradition, was designed to use up scraps of slightly stale tortillas. I think it's a delicious way to bring together the flavors of enchiladas without having to roll them up individually. The result is somewhat akin to a lasagna with the flavor of the Southwest.

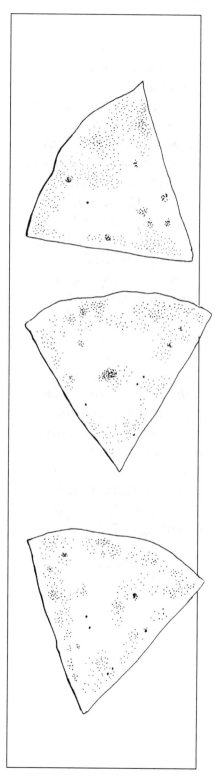

"Let the number of guests not exceed twelve . . . so chosen that their occupations are varied, their tastes similar . . . the dining room brilliantly lighted, the cloth white, the temperature between 60 and 68 degrees; the men witty and not pedantic, the women amiable and not too coquettish; the dishes exquisite but few, the wines vintage, the eating unhurried . . . the coffee hot . . . the tea not too strong, the toast artistically buttered . . . the signal to leave not before eleven and everyone to bed at midnight."

—Jean-Anthèlme
   Brillat-Savarin
   La Physiologie du Goût,
   1825

12 corn tortillas
1 tablespoon olive oil
1 large onion, chopped
3 cloves garlic, minced
1 medium green bell pepper, finely diced
2 medium zucchini, about ³⁄₄ pound total, grated
28-ounce can crushed tomatoes
4-ounce can mild green chiles, drained and chopped
2 to 3 tablespoons chopped fresh cilantro or parsley
1 teaspoon dried oregano
1 teaspoon ground cumin
1 ¹⁄₂ cups grated Monterey Jack cheese or
    cheddar-style soy cheese

Preheat the oven to 350 degrees.

Pile the tortillas on a baking sheet and bake for about 15 minutes, or until they are dry and rather crisp. When they are cool enough to handle, crumble them into large bits.

In the meantime, heat the oil in a large skillet. Add the onion and sauté over medium heat until it is translucent. Add the garlic and bell pepper and continue to sauté until the onion is golden. Stir in the grated zucchini, cover, and sauté until it is wilted. Stir in the crushed tomatoes, chiles, cilantro or parsley, oregano, and cumin. Bring to a simmer and remove from the heat.

Lightly oil a shallow rectangular 2-quart casserole dish. Arrange half the tortillas on the bottom, followed by half the zucchini and tomato mixture, then half the cheese. Repeat. Bake for 20 to 25 minutes, or until the cheese is bubbly. Cool for 15 minutes, then cut into 2-inch squares, and serve.

Calories: 190	Total fat: 7 g	Protein: 8 g
Carbohydrate: 24 g	Cholesterol: 14 g	Sodium: 119 mg

WHEAT TORTILLA PIZZAS

10 to 12 servings

Pinto beans cooked in beer make a terrific topping for these easy tortilla pizzas. Use fresh cilantro if you can; it adds an unusual and distinctive flavor.

Topping
1 tablespoon olive oil
2 cups finely chopped ripe tomatoes
2 scallions, minced
4 cups canned or cooked pinto beans, coarsely mashed
     (see Bean Basics, page 261)
½ cup beer
1 jalapeño pepper, seeded and minced, or 4-ounce can
     mild green chiles, drained and chopped
¼ cup fresh cilantro (substitute fresh parsley only if
          cilantro is unavailable)
½ teaspoon ground cumin
salt to taste

6 burrito-sized (10-inch) flour tortillas
1 ½ cups reduced-fat cheddar or cheddar-style
     soy cheese
thinly sliced scallions for garnish

Preheat the oven to 350 degrees.

Heat the oil in a large skillet. Add the tomatoes and sauté for 2 minutes, until they soften. Add the remaining topping ingredients and stir together. Bring to a simmer, then lower the heat and cook, covered, for 25 to 30 minutes. The mixture should be moist but not soupy. If there is excess liquid, cook, uncovered, until thickened. Remove from the heat and cover tightly.

Arrange 3 of the tortillas on 1 or 2 nonstick baking sheets. Sprinkle evenly with the cheese, then top each with the remaining tortillas so that the cheese is sandwiched between. Bake for 10 minutes, or until the cheese is melted. Remove from the oven and place each tortilla sandwich on a flat plate. Distribute the topping over them and garnish each with a sprinkling of scallion. Cut each "pizza" into X wedges with a sharp knife. Serve warm.

| Calories: 232 | Total fat: 7 g | Protein: 11 g |
| Carbohydrate: 30 g | Cholesterol: 11 g | Sodium: 378 mg |

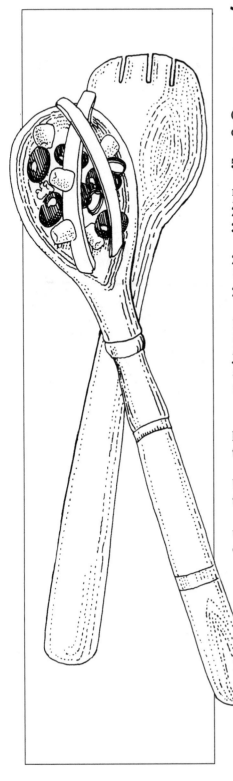

BLACK BEAN AND CORN SALAD

10 to 12 servings

Corn and multicolored peppers look enticing against the dark backdrop of the black beans.

**5 cups canned or cooked black beans
    (see Bean Basics, page 261)**
½ cup Garlic Vinaigrette (page 256)
2 cups cooked corn kernels, preferably fresh
**3 large bell peppers, preferably one each green,
    red, and yellow, cut into narrow strips**
2 to 3 scallions, thinly sliced
¼ cup chopped fresh parsley
**2 tablespoons minced fresh oregano, or 1 ½
    teaspoons dried**
1 teaspoon ground cumin
½ teaspoon ground coriander
juice of ½ lemon
salt and freshly ground pepper to taste
round or triangular tortilla chips for garnish

Marinate the beans in Garlic Vinaigrette for at least 2 hours, then drain excess. Reserve vinaigrette for dressing the salad.

Combine all the ingredients except garnish in a mixing bowl and toss together thoroughly. Use enough vinaigrette to coat and flavor the ingredients but not drench them.

This can be made several hours ahead and refrigerated until needed. Transfer to a large serving bowl and tuck tortilla chips around the edges for garnish.

Calories: 185   Total fat: 6 g   Protein: 7 g
Carbohydrate: 26 g   Cholesterol: 0 g   Sodium: 16 mg

PIQUANT RICE SALAD

10 to 12 servings

2 cups raw medium- or long-grain brown rice, rinsed
1 10-ounce package frozen green peas, thawed
12-ounce jar marinated artichoke hearts, with liquid,
    chopped
12-ounce jar roasted red peppers, with liquid,
    cut into strips
1 medium red onion, halved and thinly sliced
²/₃ cup sliced black olives
¼ cup chopped fresh parsley
1 jalapeño pepper, seeded and minced, optional

Dressing
2 tablespoons olive oil
juice of 1 ½ limes
2 teaspoons honey
1 teaspoon salt, or to taste
freshly ground pepper to taste

cherry tomatoes for garnish
curly parsley for garnish

Bring 5 cups of water to a boil in a heavy saucepan. Stir in the rice, return to a boil, then cover and simmer over medium heat until the water is absorbed, about 35 minutes. Let cool to room temperature.

Combine the rice with the remaining salad ingredients in a mixing bowl and toss together. Combine the dressing ingredients in a small bowl and stir together. Pour over the salad and toss well. Let the salad stand for 1 hour before serving to allow the flavors to blend.

Transfer to a serving bowl and surround the edges with cherry tomatoes alternating with sprigs of curly parsley.

Calories: 189	Total fat: 5 g	Protein: 4 g
Carbohydrate: 33 g	Cholesterol: 0 g	Sodium: 271 mg

The familiar flavors of Chinese-style food come together in a colorful buffet. The dishes here are designed to be served at room temperature so that crisp-tender textures and bright colors won't fade as the food stands.

ORIENTAL BUFFET

10 to 12 servings

Cold Sesame Noodles

Sweet and Sour Vegetables

Rice with Peas and Scallions

Spicy String Beans with Walnuts

Tofu in Black Bean Sauce

Bean Sprout Salad with Snow Peas and Red Cabbage

———— ꙮ ————

Contains no eggs or dairy products.

COLD SESAME NOODLES

10 to 12 servings

6 large or 8 medium dried shiitake mushrooms

Sauce
1 tablespoon dark sesame oil
1 cup chopped onion
1 to 2 cloves garlic, minced
1/2 cup reduced-fat peanut butter
1/4 cup sesame tahini
2 tablespoons lemon or lime juice
2 to 3 tablespoons soy sauce or tamari, to taste
1 to 2 teaspoons chili powder, to taste
dash cayenne pepper

1 pound whole wheat udon noodles (see Note), cut in half
2 scallions, thinly sliced

1 large red bell pepper, cut into very thin, l-inch strips
2 tablespoons sesame seeds

Soak the mushrooms in ½ cup of hot water for 15 minutes. Reserve the liquid. Remove and discard the tough stems, squeeze excess liquid from the caps, and cut them into strips. Set aside.

Heat the oil in a small skillet. Add the onion and sauté over medium heat until translucent. Add the garlic and continue to sauté until the onion is golden. Transfer to the container of a food processor along with the reserved soaking liquid and the remaining sauce ingredients and process until velvety smooth. Add up to ¼ cup of water if the sauce seems too thick.

Cook the noodles al dente in plenty of simmering water. Drain and rinse until cool. Combine in a mixing bowl with the mushrooms, sauce, and remaining ingredients. Toss well. Let stand at room temperature for no more than an hour before serving, then transfer to a serving bowl.

Note: Whole wheat udon noodles are available at most natural food stores. If unavailable, substitute the equivalent amount of ordinary or whole wheat linguini.

Calories: 200	Total fat: 9 g	Protein: 7 g
Carbohydrate: 21 g	Cholesterol: 0 g	Sodium: 284 mg

SWEET AND SOUR VEGETABLES

10 to 12 servings

I devised this stir-fry so that it can remain at room temperature for some time without losing color and texture.

1 tablespoon canola oil
2 teaspoons dark sesame oil or unrefined peanut oil
1 large red onion, quartered and sliced
3 tablespoons dry sherry
2 large carrots, sliced diagonally
1 medium red or green bell pepper, cut julienne
2 large stalks bok choy, sliced diagonally
1 cup thinly sliced white mushrooms
2 medium tomatoes, diced

Make-ahead suggestions for

Oriental Buffet

A day ahead:

- *Make the Cold Sesame Noodles. Allow time to bring to room temperature before serving. Add a bit of water and toss if the sauce has gotten too thick.*

- *Cook the rice for Rice with Peas and Scallions.*

- *Trim the string beans for Spicy String Beans with Walnuts.*

- *Make the Black Bean Sauce for Tofu in Black Bean Sauce.*

- *Trim the snow peas for Bean Sprout Salad with Snow Peas and Red Cabbage.*

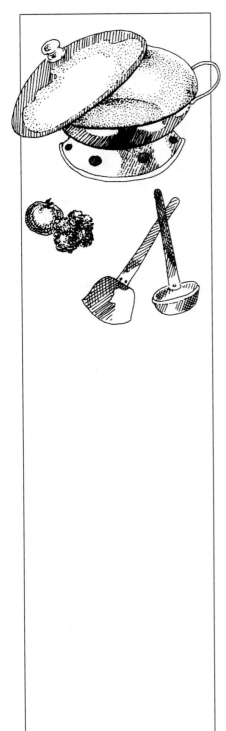

1-pound can pineapple chunks, drained, liquid reserved
1-pound can baby corn, drained, liquid reserved
6-ounce can sliced water chestnuts, drained

Sauce
½ cup liquid from pineapple
3 tablespoons cornstarch
½ cup liquid from baby corn
3 tablespoons rice vinegar
3 tablespoons soy sauce or tamari, or to taste
2 tablespoons honey
1 teaspoon grated fresh ginger

1 large bunch broccoli, cut into bite-sized pieces and florets

Heat the oils in a wok. Add the onion and stir-fry over medium-high heat until translucent. Add the sherry, carrots, pepper, and bok choy and stir-fry until just barely crisp-tender. Stir in the mushrooms and tomatoes and stir-fry for another minute or so, until they are wilted. Remove from the heat and stir in all the canned ingredients.

In the meantime, combine the pineapple liquid with the cornstarch and stir until it dissolves. Combine with the remaining sauce ingredients in a saucepan and heat slowly to a simmer. Cook until the mixture thickens. Let cool until just warm. Stir into the vegetable mixture.

Just before serving, steam the broccoli until very bright green and crisp-tender. Drain and rinse until almost cool. Stir into the vegetable mixture. Taste and adjust sweet and sour flavors if necessary. Serve warm or at room temperature.

Calories: 126	Total fat: 2 g	Protein: 2 g
Carbohydrate: 22 g	Cholesterol: 0 g	Sodium: 301 mg

RICE WITH PEAS AND SCALLIONS

10 to 12 servings

1 ½ cups long-grain brown rice
1 ½ tablespoons canola oil
1 tablespoon unrefined peanut oil or dark sesame oil
5 scallions, white and green parts, thinly sliced
3 tablespoons soy sauce or tamari, or to taste
2 tablespoons rice vinegar or white wine vinegar
freshly ground black pepper
2 cups frozen green peas, thawed

Bring 4 cups of water to a boil in a heavy saucepan. Stir in the rice, return to a boil, then lower the heat and simmer, covered, until the water is absorbed, about 35 minutes.

Heat half the oil in a large skillet. Add the scallions and sauté very briefly over medium heat, just until they've lost their raw quality. Add the remaining oil along with the soy sauce and vinegar. Add the rice and sauté, stirring, until the ingredients are well combined. Grind in lots of black pepper. Remove from the heat and let cool to room temperature.

Before serving, stir in the peas and taste to correct the seasonings. Serve warm or at room temperature.

Calories: 139	Total fat: 3 g	Protein: 4 g
Carbohydrate: 23 g	Cholesterol: 0 g	Sodium: 245 mg

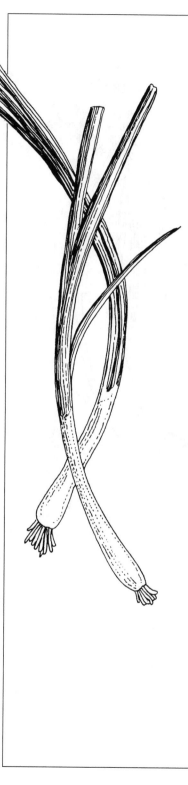

SPICY STRING BEANS WITH WALNUTS

10 to 12 servings

Crunchy string beans taste wonderful in a rich, nutty coating of walnuts and sesame oil.

2 tablespoons dark sesame oil
1 ½ pounds string beans, trimmed
5 to 6 cloves garlic, minced
1 ½ to 2 teaspoons grated fresh ginger
2 to 3 tablespoons soy sauce or tamari, to taste

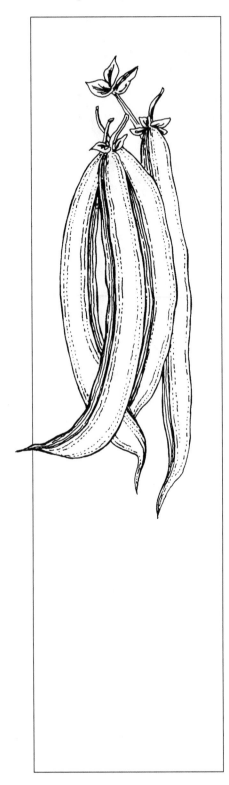

1 tablespoon good-quality chili powder, or to taste
$\frac{1}{2}$ cup finely chopped walnuts

Heat the oil plus 2 tablespoons of water in an extra-large skillet or wok. Stir in the string beans and stir-fry until bright green. Add the garlic, ginger, soy sauce, and chili powder and continue to stir-fry until the string beans are crisp-tender. Stir in the walnuts and remove from the heat. Serve warm or at room temperature.

Calories: 80	Total fat: 6 g	Protein: 2 g
Carbohydrate: 6 g	Cholesterol: 0 g	Sodium: 233 mg

TOFU IN BLACK BEAN SAUCE

10 to 12 servings

3 pounds firm tofu

Black bean sauce
1 tablespoon dark sesame oil
1 medium onion, minced
3 to 4 cloves garlic, minced
3 tablespoons cornstarch
**$\frac{1}{3}$ cup fermented black beans (see Note), rinsed
    and chopped**
3 tablespoons soy sauce or tamari
$\frac{1}{4}$ cup dry sherry
2 teaspoons dry mustard
1 teaspoon five-spice powder, optional
2 tablespoons minced fresh cilantro
sliced scallions for garnish
sesame seeds for garnish

Cut the tofu into approximately $\frac{1}{2}$-inch thicknesses. Place on a clean absorbent towel or several thicknesses of paper towel and cover with another towel or more paper towels. Place a cutting board on top. Press for 30 to 45 minutes. Cut the tofu into $\frac{1}{2}$-inch dice.

Heat the oil in a large, deep saucepan. Add the onion and garlic and sauté over medium heat until they are golden. Dissolve the cornstarch in about $\frac{1}{4}$ cup of cold water. Pour into the saucepan and stir in the black beans, soy sauce, sherry, mustard, and optional five-spice powder, along with

1 $\frac{1}{4}$ cups of water. Bring to a simmer and cook until thickened, about 10 minutes. Stir in the diced tofu and simmer over very low heat, with a cover left slightly ajar, for 15 minutes. Stir in the optional cilantro.

Serve just warm, garnished with scallions and sesame seeds sprinkled over the top.

Note: Fermented black beans, which are made from soy beans, are available in Oriental food stores and natural food stores. They most often come in small glass jars.

Calories: 139	Total fat: 6 g	Protein: 10 g
Carbohydrate: 8 g	Cholesterol: 0 g	Sodium: 284 mg

BEAN SPROUT SALAD WITH SNOW PEAS AND RED CABBAGE

10 to 12 servings

Always pleasing to guests, this colorful, crisp salad has become one of my standards.

$\frac{3}{4}$ cup mung bean sprouts
$\frac{1}{2}$ pound snow peas, trimmed
3 cups loosely packed shredded red cabbage
2 scallions, minced

Dressing
2 tablespoons sesame oil
2 tablespoons soy sauce or tamari
3 tablespoons rice vinegar or white wine vinegar
1 tablespoon honey
2 teaspoons sesame seeds
$\frac{1}{2}$ teaspoon chili powder

Steam the sprouts and snow peas together until they are just crisp-tender. Rinse immediately under cool water until they are cool and drain well. Combine with the cabbage and scallions in a salad bowl and toss.

Combine the dressing ingredients in a small bowl and stir together. Pour over the salad and toss well. Let the salad

"For the dinner to be really good the host must feel a glow of inward joy during the whole week which precedes it. He must await with impatience the day of the party. He must ask himself every day what he can do to improve it. . . . Whatever such a host offers his guests, I am sure that it will be good, because he will have enjoyed the anticipation of it for a week beforehand and he will feel the same joy for a week afterwards in his pleasure at having charmed his guests."

—Edouard de Pomaine
Cooking with Pomaine,
1962

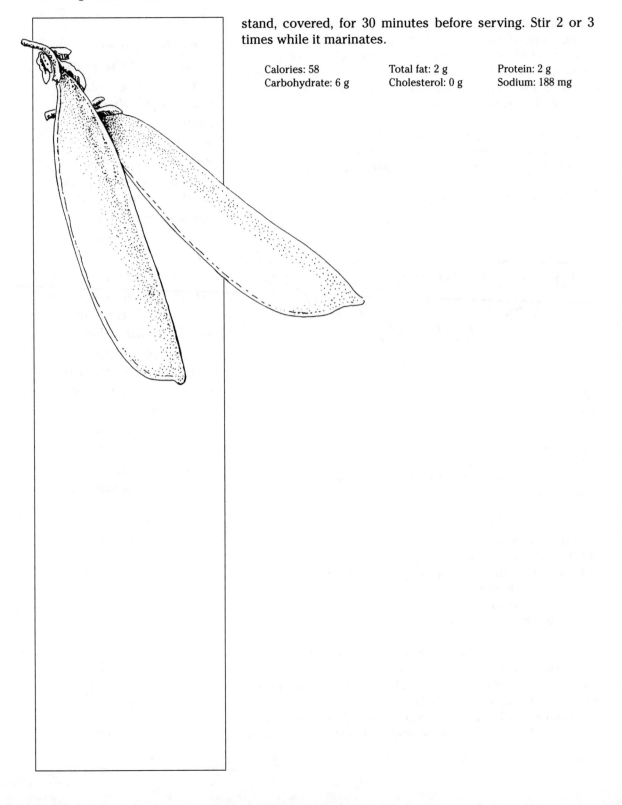

stand, covered, for 30 minutes before serving. Stir 2 or 3 times while it marinates.

Calories: 58   Total fat: 2 g   Protein: 2 g
Carbohydrate: 6 g   Cholesterol: 0 g   Sodium: 188 mg

Chapter 13

SMALL CELEBRATIONS

This chapter is designed to help hosts fill in some common gaps in entertaining ideas. Included are a handful of intimate lunch and dinner menus appropriate for casually celebrating any number of "big" little occasions (birthdays, promotions, anniversaries), yet elegant enough to serve as business meals. Also included here are breakfast goodies for overnight guests; easy quick breads and scones for casual afternoon teas; and a baker's dozen of appetizers that can accompany many of the menus throughout these chapters or be used on their own when a tasty nibble is needed to serve with drinks.

Here we need hardly think in terms of "vegetarian"— nonvegetarians, after all, rarely clamor for meat at breakfast and certainly not at tea. And even meat eaters won't feel deprived when served with colorful lunches of light, seasonally balanced fare.

These are just the sorts of occasions I find cropping up fairly often. In the past, however, these left me desperate for ideas at the last minute—especially when guests arrived on short notice, or when I felt like inviting someone over spontaneously. Now that I've devised the kinds of recipes and menus I need to have on hand for these occasions, many of them have already become solid standards for me. I hope you'll find them equally useful.

AN AUTUMN LUNCH

4 servings

Stuffed Avocados
Stewed Bell Peppers
Skillet Potato Pie
Herbed Cream Cheese (page 259), or Herb
"Butter" (page 258)

Additions to the menu: Serve assorted fresh
whole-grain rolls or a fresh whole-grain bread.
You might also like to serve some sliced, crisp
cucumbers alongside the Stewed Bell Peppers
and Skillet Potato Pie. For dessert, serve
fresh fruit in season, plus, if desired,
purchased cookies.

Contains no eggs.
Can be made dairy-free by choosing Herb
"Butter" and following the suggested
substitutions in the recipes.

STUFFED AVOCADOS

4 servings

Individual avocado cups, studded with corn and crisp vegetables, are an elegant and easy alternative to an ordinary salad.

Stuffing
$3/4$ cup cooked corn kernels
1 medium celery stalk, finely diced
$1/2$ medium green or red bell pepper, minced

2 small, ripe plum tomatoes
1 tablespoon minced fresh dill, or 1 teaspoon dried dill
juice of $\frac{1}{2}$ lemon
salt and freshly ground pepper to taste
2 medium firm, ripe avocados

curly parsley for garnish

Combine all the stuffing ingredients in a mixing bowl. This may be done an hour or 2 ahead of time. Cover and refrigerate until needed. Just before serving, cut the avocados in half lengthwise. Carefully separate the halves and remove the pits. Scoop out some of the pulp, leaving sturdy shells about $\frac{1}{4}$ inch thick. Chop the avocado flesh and stir into the stuffing mixture. Divide the mixture among the 4 avocado shells. Arrange on small plates garnished with curly parsley and serve at once.

Calories: 211	Total fat: 12 g	Protein: 3 g
Carbohydrate: 21 g	Cholesterol: 0 g	Sodium: 23 mg

STEWED BELL PEPPERS

4 servings

A lovely way to combine the colorful peppers of early fall, this is also delicious over pasta or in omelets.

1 tablespoon olive oil
1 large onion, quartered and thinly sliced
3 each medium green and red bell peppers, or 2 each
       green, red, and yellow bell peppers, 6 in all,
       cut julienne
2 to 3 cloves garlic, minced
$\frac{1}{2}$ pound ripe, juicy tomatoes, finely diced
2 to 3 tablespoons minced fresh or canned mild
       green chiles
1 tablespoon minced fresh oregano, or l/2 teaspoon dried
2 to 3 tablespoons minced fresh parsley or cilantro
$\frac{1}{2}$ teaspoon granulated sugar
salt and freshly ground pepper to taste

Heat the oil in a large skillet. Add the onion and sauté over moderate heat until golden. Stir in the peppers and garlic and

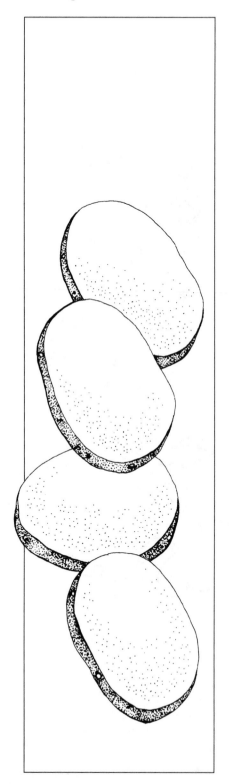

cover. Cook 10 minutes, lifting the lid to stir occasionally. Add the tomatoes and green chiles. Cover and cook over low heat for 10 minutes. Add the herbs and season to taste with salt and pepper. Cook for another 10 minutes or so, uncovered, or until the liquid thickens. Serve hot over Skillet Potato Pie, following.

Calories: 89	Total fat: 4 g	Protein: 2 g
Carbohydrate: 11 g	Cholesterol: 0 g	Sodium: 10 mg

SKILLET POTATO PIE

4 servings

Wedges of crisp potatoes make a tasty bed for the stewed pepper sauce.

1 ½ pounds red-skinned potatoes, scrubbed, cooked or
    microwaved, and sliced ¼ inch thick
½ cup buttermilk or soymilk
1 to 2 scallions, minced
salt and freshly ground pepper to taste
oil for frying

Place the potato slices in a mixing bowl. Mash lightly with a fork or masher, just until the slices are broken up into several pieces. Stir in the buttermilk and scallions and season to taste with salt and pepper.

Spray the bottom of a nonstick 9- or 10-inch skillet with cooking oil spray. When the skillet is hot enough to make a drop of water sizzle, pour in the potato mixture and pat in evenly. Turn the heat to moderate and cook until the bottom of the pie is crisp and nicely browned. Slide out onto a plate and cut into 4 wedges. To serve, place a wedge of the potato pie on each guest's plate. Top with a generous portion of the stewed peppers and serve at once.

Calories: 160	Total fat: 0 g	Protein: 3 g
Carbohydrate: 36 g	Cholesterol: 1 g	Sodium: 24 mg

A SPRING SOUP AND SALAD LUNCH

4 servings

Potato, Leek, and Watercress Soup
Asparagus in Mustard Vinaigrette
Melon Cups with Strawberries and Kirsch

———— ⟆ ————

Addition to the menu: A fresh rye bread
complements both the soup and salad nicely.

Contains no eggs.
Can be made dairy-free by following the
suggested substitutions in the recipes.

POTATO, LEEK, AND WATERCRESS SOUP

6 servings

Leek and potato soup is often thought of as a comforting winter classic, but here, the peppery, bright green watercress adds a touch of spring. Though this lunch is designed for four, this soup will actually yield 6 servings or so; but you won't mind having leftovers. If you can make this soup the night before it's needed, so much the better, as the flavors improve from standing overnight.

1 ½ **tablespoons canola oil**
3 **large leeks, white and palest green parts only,**
    chopped and rinsed well
1 **large onion, finely chopped**
2 **pounds potatoes, peeled and diced**
1 **bay leaf**

"Potato: bland, amiable and homely, an honest vegetable, giving honor where honor is due—in an honest soup."

—Della Lutes
The Country Kitchen,
1938

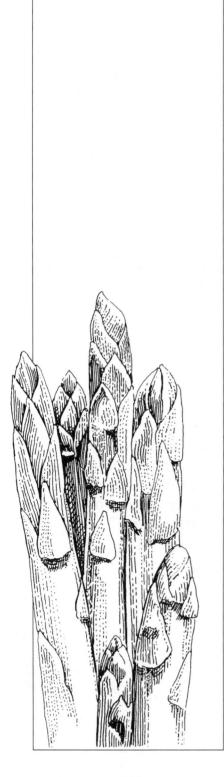

Light Vegetable Stock (page 260) or water
1 cup packed chopped watercress
1 to 1 ½ cups low-fat milk or soymilk
salt and freshly ground pepper to taste
2 tablespoons chopped fresh parsley

Heat the oil in a large soup pot. Add the leeks and onions and sauté over moderate heat, covered, until the onion begins to turn golden. Lift the lid occasionally to stir. Add the potatoes, bay leaf, and just enough stock or water to cover. Bring to a boil, then simmer, covered, until the potatoes are tender, about 15 to 20 minutes.

Mash some of the potatoes against the side of the pot with the side of a spoon. Add the watercress and milk or soymilk and simmer over very low heat for 20 minutes. Season to taste with salt and pepper. Allow to stand off the heat for an hour or 2 before serving, or let cool and refrigerate overnight. Heat through before serving. Stir in the parsley. Adjust the consistency with more milk or soymilk, then adjust the seasonings.

Calories: 273	Total fat: 4 g	Protein: 5 g
Carbohydrate: 53 g	Cholesterol: 2 g	Sodium: 432 mg

ASPARAGUS IN MUSTARD VINAIGRETTE

4 servings

Slender stalks of asparagus are a delightful sign of spring, and benefit nicely from the tang of a mustard dressing.

1 to 1 ¼ pounds slender asparagus
Grainy Mustard Vinaigrette (page 256)
3 firm, ripe plum tomatoes, finely diced
2 tablespoons minced fresh dill
salt and freshly ground pepper to taste
Boston or red-leaf lettuce
2 tablespoons toasted pine nuts

Trim the tough ends from the asparagus. If the asparagus is very young and tender, you need not scrape the stalks, but otherwise, scrape the bottom half of the stalks. Cut the stalks in half and steam just until bright green and crisp-tender. Rinse immediately under cool water and drain well. Place in a shallow container and cover with Grainy Mustard Vinaigrette. Allow to marinate for an hour, then drain off most of the vinaigrette, returning it to its container for reuse.

Toss the asparagus with the tomatoes and dill in a mixing bowl. Season to taste with salt and pepper. To arrange, line 4 plates with lettuce leaves. Divide the asparagus mixture among the 4 plates. Top with the pine nuts and serve.

| Calories: 120 | Total fat: 7 g | Protein: 3 g |
| Carbohydrate: 9 g | Cholesterol: 0 g | Sodium: 63 mg |

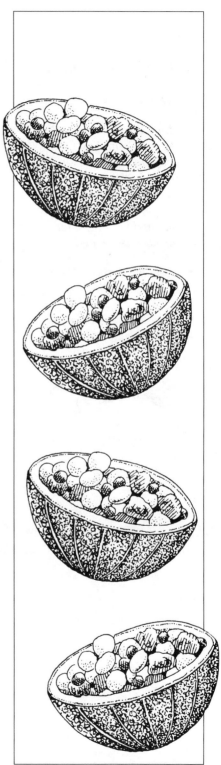

MELON CUPS WITH STRAWBERRIES AND KIRSCH

4 servings

The attractive presentation of this fruity dessert makes it quite special.

2 ripe cantaloupes, halved and seeded
1 cup strawberries, hulled, halved if small,
    quartered if large
$3/4$ cup blueberries, if available, or small red or green
    seedless grapes
$1/4$ cup kirsch (cherry liqueur), more or less to taste
mint leaves for garnish, if available

Scoop the flesh out of the cantaloupes, using the small end of a melon baller; leave a shell about $1/4$ inch thick. Combine the melon balls with the remaining fruit and kirsch in a shallow bowl and let stand, refrigerated, for 30 minutes to an hour, stirring occasionally. Cover and refrigerate the melon shells until needed.

Before serving, cut a thin slice from the bottom of each melon shell so that it will stand securely. Divide the fruit mixture among the shells. Garnish with mint leaves and serve.

| Calories: 139 | Total fat: 0 g | Protein: 2 g |
| Carbohydrate: 26 g | Cholesterol: 0 g | Sodium: 26 mg |

Make-ahead suggestions for

An Early Harvest Supper

A day ahead:

- *Make the Roasted Bell Pepper Soup. Store the soup and garnish separately in the refrigerator. Bring the garnish to room temperature before serving, and heat the soup through as needed.*

- *Cook the corn for Corn and Ricotta Pie.*

- *Bake the spaghetti squash for Spaghetti Squash with Peas and Almonds.*

AN EARLY HARVEST SUPPER

6 servings

Roasted Bell Pepper Soup
Greens with Goat Cheese and Grapes
Corn and Ricotta Pie
Spaghetti Squash with Peas and Almonds
Fresh Apple Cake

Contains eggs and dairy products.

ROASTED BELL PEPPER SOUP

6 servings

The phrase "beautiful soup" suits this one well, with its colorful garnish against a rich red background.

6 large red bell peppers
1 large green bell pepper
1 large yellow bell pepper
2 tablespoons olive oil
2 cups chopped red onion
2 cloves garlic, minced
¼ cup dry red wine
1 teaspoon chili powder, or to taste
1 to 2 tablespoons lemon juice, to taste
⅓ cup mixed minced fresh herbs of your choice
salt and freshly ground pepper to taste

Preheat the oven's broiler.
Broil the whole peppers, turning with tongs, until the

skins on all sides are charred and puckered. Remove and divide among 2 paper bags. Shut tightly and allow to stand for at least 30 minutes. Slip the skins off, then remove and discard the stems, seeds, and fibers. Chop the red peppers coarsely and set aside. Cut the yellow and green peppers into narrow 1-inch strips, and set aside separately from the red pepper.

Heat the oil in a large soup pot. Add the onion and sauté until translucent. Add the garlic and continue to sauté until the onion is soft and just beginning to turn golden. Transfer the onion mixture to the container of a food processor and add the red bell peppers and 1 cup water. Puree until quite smooth. Return to the soup pot along with 3 cups of water, or enough to give the soup a moderately thick consistency. Add the wine and chili powder. Bring to a simmer and simmer gently over moderately low heat for 15 minutes.

Remove from the heat, then stir in the lemon juice and herbs. Season to taste with salt and pepper. If time allows, let the soup stand for an hour or 2 before serving, or make a day ahead, then heat through as needed. Garnish each serving with the reserved green and yellow pepper strips.

Calories: 96	Total fat: 5 g	Protein: 1 g
Carbohydrate: 9 g	Cholesterol: 0 g	Sodium: 5 mg

GREENS WITH GOAT CHEESE AND GRAPES

6 servings

The pungent cheese, contrasted with the sweetness of grapes, offers the palate a pleasant surprise.

1 cup watercress leaves
1 cup red cabbage, thinly shredded
1 cup seedless red or green grapes
3 to 4 tablespoons crumbled goat cheese, to taste
8 leaves red-leaf lettuce, torn

Dressing
3 tablespoons reduced-fat mayonnaise or soy mayonnaise
juice of ½ lime
½ teaspoon honey

"To remember a successful salad is generally to remember a successful dinner; at all events, the perfect dinner necessarily includes the perfect salad."

—George Ellwanger
Pleasures of the Table, 1903

Combine the salad ingredients and toss together. In a small bowl, combine the dressing ingredients and stir together. Pour over the salad just before serving and toss well.

Calories: 52	Total fat: 4 g	Protein: 1 g
Carbohydrate: 3 g	Cholesterol: 8 g	Sodium: 115 mg

CORN AND RICOTTA PIE

6 servings

Fresh corn will soon be gone, not to reappear in your market until the November or December crop comes in from the south. Take advantage of it while you can!

2 teaspoons olive oil
2 cloves garlic, minced
3 cups cooked fresh corn kernels (from about 4
**   medium ears)**
1 to 2 tablespoons minced oil-cured sun-dried tomatoes,
**   to taste**
2 eggs plus 2 egg whites, beaten
salt and freshly ground pepper to taste

Ricotta mixture
1 cup part-skim ricotta cheese
1/2 cup shredded part-skim mozzarella cheese
2 tablespoons low-fat milk

1/2 cup fine bread crumbs
2 tablespoons minced fresh parsley

Preheat the oven to 350 degrees.

Heat the olive oil in a small skillet. Add the garlic and sauté over low heat until it just begins to turn golden. Set aside.

Combine the corn kernels with the sun-dried tomatoes in a food processor. Pulse on and off until the corn kernels are coarsely pureed. In a mixing bowl, combine the beaten eggs with the garlic and corn puree. Season to taste with salt and pepper.

In another bowl, combine the ricotta, mozzarella, and milk. Stir together thoroughly.

Oil a 1/2-quart round casserole dish. Layer as follows: half of the bread crumbs, half of the corn mixture, all of the cheese mixture, the remaining corn mixture, and the remaining bread crumbs. Sprinkle with the parsley. Bake for 30 to 35 minutes, or until firm to the touch. Let stand for 10 minutes, then cut into wedges to serve.

| Calories: 236 | Total fat: 8 g | Protein: 14 g |
| Carbohydrate: 26 g | Cholesterol: 90 g | Sodium: 207 mg |

SPAGHETTI SQUASH WITH PEAS AND ALMONDS

6 servings

Though spaghetti squash is commonly available, many still haven't tried it. I enjoy introducing guests to it and have won over even those who profess not to like winter squashes. A hint of curry adds an interesting flavor twist to this amusing vegetable.

1 large spaghetti squash
1 tablespoon reduced-fat margarine
1 medium red onion, halved and sliced
14- to 16-ounce can diced tomatoes, undrained
1/2 teaspoon grated fresh ginger
1/2 teaspoon dried basil
dash nutmeg
1 teaspoon good-quality curry powder
salt and freshly ground pepper to taste
1 1/2 cups thawed frozen green peas
3 tablespoons chopped fresh parsley
1/3 cup slivered toasted almonds

Preheat the oven to 375 degrees.

Cut the squash in half lengthwise; remove the stem and seeds. Place, cut side up, in a casserole dish with 1/2 inch of water. Cover tightly with foil and bake for 40 to 50 minutes, or until easily pierced with a fork. Or follow manufacturer's recommendations for baking in a microwave. When cool enough to handle, scrape the squashes lengthwise with a fork to remove the spaghettilike strands of flesh.

Heat the margarine in a large skillet. Add the onion and sauté over moderate heat until golden. Add the tomatoes, ginger, basil, nutmeg, and curry powder, then stir in the

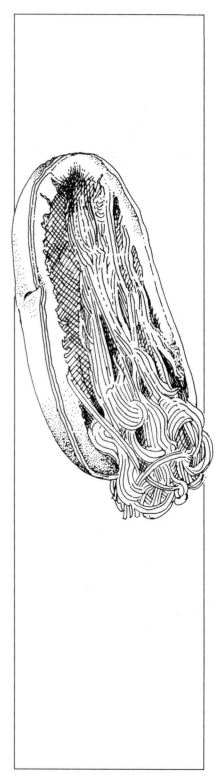

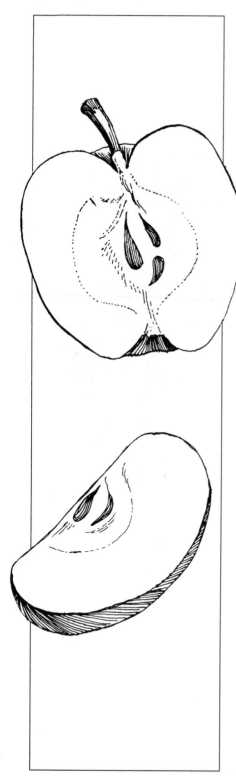

squash. Simmer over low heat, covered, for 10 minutes, stirring occasionally. Season to taste with salt and pepper. This dish may be made ahead of time up to this point.

Just before serving, add the peas and parsley and heat through. Take care not to overcook, so that the peas don't lose their bright color. Transfer to a serving container and scatter the almonds over the top. Serve at once.

Calories: 138	Total fat: 4 g	Protein: 5 g
Carbohydrate: 18 g	Cholesterol: 0 g	Sodium: 25 mg

FRESH APPLE CAKE

12 servings

It may seem odd to use the word "fresh" in the title of this recipe, since most apple desserts use fresh apples. Somehow, though, this cake highlights the fresh flavor of apples better than almost any apple dessert I've had. It's one of those foolproof recipes that I rely on quite often when I want an easy and tasty homemade dessert for guests.

2 cups whole wheat pastry flour
1 teaspoon baking powder
1 teaspoon baking soda
1 teaspoon cinnamon
1/2 teaspoon salt
1/2 cup vanilla low-fat yogurt
3/4 cup undiluted apple juice concentrate
1/3 cup light brown sugar
1 egg or 2 egg whites, beaten
2 tablespoons canola oil
1 teaspoon vanilla extract
2 1/2 cups peeled, tart apple, cut into 1/2-inch dice
1/2 cup chopped walnuts

Preheat the oven to 350 degrees.

Combine the first 5 ingredients in a mixing bowl. In another bowl, combine the yogurt, juice, sugar, egg, oil, and vanilla and stir vigorously to combine. Make a well in the center of the dry ingredients and pour in the wet mixture. Stir together until thoroughly combined, then stir in the apples and walnuts.

Pour into an oiled 9- by 13-inch baking pan. Bake for 30 to

35 minutes, or until golden and a knife inserted into the center tests clean.

Calories: 197	Total fat: 6 g	Protein: 4 g
Carbohydrate: 31 g	Cholesterol: 18 g	Sodium: 109 mg

AN INTIMATE SPRING SUPPER

6 servings

Chick Pea Salad with Zucchini and Fresh Mozzarella

Fresh Pasta with Asparagus and Sun-dried Tomatoes

Sautéed Fennel, Leeks, and Mushrooms

Strawberry-Rhubarb Pandowdy

———⚜———

Addition to the menu: The salad and pasta demand a really crusty, fresh loaf of Italian bread.

Contains egg whites (in dessert only).
Can be made dairy-free by following the suggested substitutions in the recipes.

CHICK PEA SALAD WITH ZUCCHINI AND FRESH MOZZARELLA

6 servings

Serve this hearty salad on its own as a first course. I've recommended replacing the fresh mozzarella with tofu for those on a dairy-free diet.

2 cups cooked chick peas
4 ounces fresh mozzarella, finely diced (for a dairy-free alternative, use an equal amount of diced, very fresh tofu)
6- or 8-ounce jar roasted peppers, cut into strips, with liquid
1 small zucchini, very thinly sliced
1 tablespoon olive oil
2 to 3 tablespoons wine vinegar, to taste
2 tablespoons chopped fresh parsley
1/2 teaspoon dried oregano
salt and freshly ground pepper to taste

Combine all the ingredients in a serving bowl and mix well. Let stand at room temperature for 30 minutes to an hour before serving.

Calories: 182	Total fat: 7 g	Protein: 9 g
Carbohydrate: 19 g	Cholesterol: 15 g	Sodium: 86 mg

FRESH PASTA WITH ASPARAGUS AND SUN-DRIED TOMATOES

6 servings

Look for fresh pasta in Italian groceries and gourmet food shops. I like its delicacy in this dish, teamed with the equally delicate asparagus of spring. However, if fresh pasta is unavailable, this won't suffer from the substitution of good-quality dry fettucine.

Sauce
1 tablespoon olive oil
3 cloves garlic, minced
2 tablespoons minced shallots
14- to 16-ounce can diced tomatoes, undrained
$\frac{1}{2}$ cup thick tomato sauce or tomato puree
$\frac{1}{4}$ cup finely chopped oil-cured sun-dried tomatoes
$\frac{1}{2}$ teaspoon dried basil
$\frac{1}{4}$ teaspoon hot red pepper flakes, or a few grains cayenne pepper

$\frac{1}{2}$ pound asparagus, trimmed, scraped if necessary, and cut into l-inch pieces
$\frac{3}{4}$ pound fresh fettucine
salt and freshly ground pepper to taste
grated fresh Parmesan cheese, optional

Heat the oil in a large, heavy saucepan. Add the garlic and shallots and sauté over moderate heat until they just begin to turn golden. Add the remaining sauce ingredients and simmer over low heat for 20 minutes. This may be done ahead of time; cover and let stand off the heat until needed.

Just before serving, steam the asparagus until bright green and crisp-tender. Gently heat the sauce. Cook the pasta al dente in plenty of simmering water, then drain. In a serving bowl, combine the pasta, asparagus, and sauce and toss well. Season to taste with salt and pepper. Serve at once, with grated Parmesan if desired.

Calories: 230	Total fat: 5 g	Protein: 10 g
Carbohydrate: 37 g	Cholesterol: 93 g	Sodium: 182 mg

"The fennel is beyond every other vegetable, delicious. It greatly resembles the largest size celery, perfectly white, and there is no vegetable that equals it in flavour . . . indeed I prefer it to every other vegetable, or to any fruit."

—Thomas Jefferson
(1783-1826)
Garden Books

SAUTÉED FENNEL, LEEKS, AND MUSHROOMS

6 servings

Though anise-flavored fennel is one of the vegetables I enjoy most, I reserve its use primarily for special occasions. Along with leeks and mushrooms, it makes a nice accompaniment to the pasta.

1 tablespoon reduced-fat margarine
2 tablespoons dry white wine
2 large leeks, white and palest green parts only,
    chopped and rinsed well
1 large fennel bulb, quartered and sliced
1 cup small white mushrooms, sliced
1 scallion, minced
2 tablespoons minced fresh parsley
2 tablespoons finely crushed walnuts
salt and freshly ground pepper to taste

Heat the margarine and wine in a large skillet. Add the leeks and fennel and sauté over moderate heat, stirring frequently, until golden. Add tiny amounts of water if needed to keep the skillet moist. Add the mushrooms and wine and continue to sauté until the mushrooms are just wilted. Stir in the scallion, parsley, and walnuts. Season to taste with salt and pepper and serve.

Calories: 64	Total fat: 2 g	Protein: 1 g
Carbohydrate: 8 g	Cholesterol: 0 g	Sodium: 52 mg

STRAWBERRY-RHUBARB PANDOWDY

6 servings

Pandowdy is an old American term for a baked dessert of fruit, most often apples, covered with a lightly sweetened batter. It makes for a simple, homey dessert. Before I improvised this recipe, I'd never seen this presentation for that classic spring duo, strawberries and rhubarb. It's a nice alternative to baking them, as is usually done, in a pastry crust.

1 ½ pounds rhubarb stalks
1 pint strawberries, hulled and chopped
½ to ⅔ cup light brown sugar, to taste
1 teaspoon cinnamon
dash each: ground nutmeg, cloves

Batter
1 cup whole wheat pastry flour
1 teaspoon baking powder
½ teaspoon baking soda
¼ teaspoon salt
2 egg whites, lightly beaten
¼ cup light brown sugar
⅔ cup vanilla nonfat yogurt

Preheat the oven to 350 degrees.

Trim the rhubarb and cut into l-inch slices. Place in a saucepan and cover with water. Bring to a simmer and cook until soft, about 10 to 15 minutes. Let drain for several minutes in a colander. In a mixing bowl, combine with the strawberries, sugar, and spices and stir well to combine. Pour into a lightly oiled, 9- by 9-inch baking pan.

Combine the flour, baking powder, baking soda, and salt in a mixing bowl. In another bowl, combine the egg whites, sugar, and yogurt and stir together until thoroughly blended. Make a well in the center of the dry ingredients and pour the wet mixture into it. Stir vigorously until smooth. Pour over the strawberry-rhubarb mixture. Bake for 35 to 40 minutes, or until the top is golden brown. Serve warm or at room temperature.

Calories: 235	Total fat: 0 g	Protein: 6 g
Carbohydrate: 51 g	Cholesterol: 1 g	Sodium: 145 mg

"The first rhubarb of the season is to the digestive tract of the winter-logged inner man what a good hot bath with plenty of healing soap is to the outer after a bout with a plough and harrow. Even the tongue and teeth have a scrubbed feeling after a dish of early rhubarb."

—Della Lutes
The Country Kitchen, 1938

Having a cache of tasty appetizer ideas on hand that don't involve meat, seafood, and heavy, sour cream-based dips is a boon not only to vegetarians but to all those who wish to keep their premeal munchies on the lighter side. Most of the appetizers given here are quite simple to prepare, too. If I'm preparing a meal for guests, even a relatively simple one, I have little desire to add to the work load by preparing elaborate appetizers. Some of the ideas here will be useful for those times when you wish to serve a light nibble with drinks rather than a full meal.

APPETIZERS

Baked Garlic with Brie

Baked Cottage Cheese Diamonds

Mung Bean Sprout and Mushroom Spring Rolls

Cabbage Spring Rolls

Hazelnut-Stuffed Mushrooms

Mushrooms Rosemary

Soy and Honey Nuts and Pretzels

Sweet and Sour Quick-pickled Vegetables

Dips and Spreads

Three-Cheese Spread

Creamy Herbed Cheese Dip

Spinach and Cucumber Spread

Creamy Horseradish Dip in Rye "Bowl"

Herb and Curry Dip

White Bean and Sun-dried Tomato Pâté

BAKED GARLIC WITH BRIE

8 to 10 servings

Garlic aficionados will love this, and those shy of the pungent taste of raw garlic will be pleasantly surprised by the absence of its usual bite. In its place is a mild, nutty flavor that leaves none of that characteristic aftertaste.

2 whole bulbs garlic
8 ounces Brie, at room temperature
cocktail bread, crispbread, or narrow crusty French
    bread, sliced ½ inch thick
6-ounce jar roasted red peppers, well drained, cut into
    small, narrow strips

    Remove some of the papery outer layers from the garlic, but leave the bulbs intact. Place on a baking sheet and bake in a 350-degree oven or 400-degree toaster oven for 40 to 45 minutes, or until the cloves are soft. Test with a toothpick or a sharp skewer.

    To serve, gently separate the cloves and arrange them on a serving plate. Place the Brie on a larger plate, surrounded by the bread of your choice. Place the red pepper strips in a small bowl and provide a small fork. Each guest should spread a little Brie on a piece of bread with a spreading knife, squeeze a garlic clove directly onto it, then top it with a strip or 2 of red pepper. You could prepare a few at first as examples.

Calories: 151	Total fat: 7 g	Protein: 8 g
Carbohydrate: 13 g	Cholesterol: 25 g	Sodium: 270 mg

BAKED COTTAGE CHEESE DIAMONDS

6 to 8 servings

2 cups low-fat small-curd cottage cheese
½ cup grated Swiss cheese
2 eggs, beaten
1 small onion, finely grated
⅓ cup fine dry bread crumbs

1 teaspoon mixed dried herbs of your choice
salt and freshly ground pepper to taste

Preheat the oven to 350 degrees.

Combine all the ingredients in a mixing bowl and stir together thoroughly. Pour into a lightly oiled 9- by 9-inch baking dish. Bake for 40 minutes, or until the top is golden brown. Let stand 10 to 15 minutes, then cut into small diamond shapes. Arrange on a platter and serve warm or at room temperature.

Calories: 121	Total fat: 4 g	Protein: 13 g
Carbohydrate: 6 g	Cholesterol: 72 g	Sodium: 287 mg

MUNG BEAN SPROUT AND MUSHROOM SPRING ROLLS

Makes 1 dozen, or 6 servings

These spring rolls and the ones in the recipe that follows, along with the sweet dipping sauce, make a festive opening for an Oriental meal. Vegetarians in particular will appreciate them, since the spring rolls or egg rolls served in restaurants are seldom available without meat or seafood inside. These are also a lot less oily than the deep-fried version!

Dipping sauce
½ cup orange or apricot preserves, or marmalade
2 tablespoons orange juice
1 tablespoon rice vinegar or white wine vinegar
½ teaspoon freshly grated ginger
1 teaspoon soy sauce or tamari
dash cayenne pepper

1 tablespoon canola oil
1 teaspoon dark sesame oil
1 large onion, quartered and thinly sliced
½ pound mung bean sprouts
1 cup small white mushrooms, sliced
1 to 2 tablespoons soy sauce or tamari, to taste
freshly ground pepper to taste
1 dozen egg roll wrappers

Combine all the ingredients for the dipping sauce in a

small mixing bowl and stir until thoroughly combined. Transfer to a small serving bowl and set aside.

Heat the oils in a large skillet. Add the onion and sauté over moderate heat until lightly browned. Add the sprouts and mushrooms. Sauté, covered, lifting the lid to stir occasionally, until the sprouts are wilted but not overdone. Season to taste with soy sauce and pepper. Remove from the heat.

Divide the mixture among 12 egg roll wrappers, folding and rolling them according to the illustrations at left and right.

Spray the bottom of a large, nonstick skillet with cooking oil spray. Cook the spring rolls over moderately high heat on both sides until golden brown and crisp. Serve at once.

Calories: 117	Total fat: 3 g	Protein: 2 g
Carbohydrate: 20 g	Cholesterol: 0 g	Sodium: 156 mg

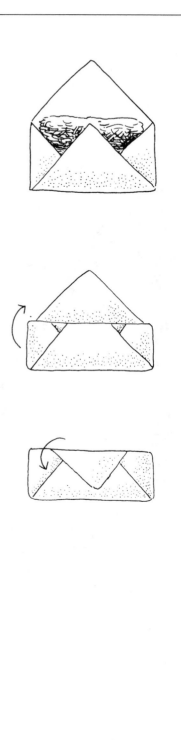

CABBAGE SPRING ROLLS

Makes 1 dozen, or 6 servings

1 recipe Dipping Sauce (see previous recipe, page 234)
1 tablespoon canola oil
1 tablespoon dark sesame oil
2 cups thinly sliced onion
4 cups thinly shredded cabbage
1 cup finely diced celery
1 to 2 tablespoons soy sauce or tamari, to taste
freshly ground pepper to taste
12 egg roll wrappers

Prepare the dipping sauce as described in the previous recipe and set aside.

Heat the oils in a large skillet. Add the onion and sauté over moderate heat until translucent. Add the cabbage and diced celery and sauté until the onion and cabbage are lightly browned. Season to taste with soy sauce and pepper.

Divide the mixture among 12 egg roll wrappers, folding and rolling according to the illustration on pages 234 to 235.

Spray the bottom of a large, nonstick skillet with cooking oil spray. Cook the spring rolls over moderately high heat on both sides until golden brown and crisp. Serve at once.

Calories: 128	Total fat: 3 g	Protein: 2 g
Carbohydrate: 23 g	Cholesterol: 0 g	Sodium: 168 mg

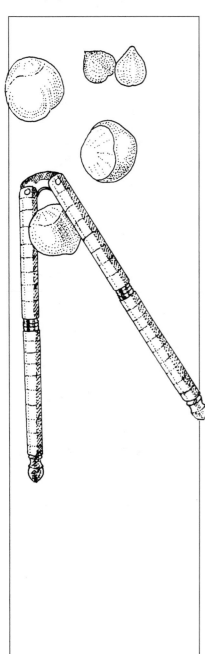

HAZELNUT-STUFFED MUSHROOMS

Makes 2 dozen, or 8 to 12 servings

I remember reading an aphorism once, attributed to whom I can't recall, that stated, "Life is too short to stuff mushrooms." One can make an argument for that viewpoint, perhaps, but honestly, stuffing a couple dozen mushrooms is not really a lot of work and it produces a perennially pleasing appetizer.

24 large white mushrooms
1 tablespoon reduced-fat margarine
1/3 cup finely ground hazelnuts
2 tablespoons wheat germ
2 teaspoons grated fresh Parmesan cheese, optional
1 tablespoon finely minced chives or scallion
1 tablespoon finely minced fresh parsley
1/2 teaspoon teriyaki sauce, or to taste
1/4 teaspoon garlic powder
salt and freshly ground pepper to taste
curly parsley for garnish

Preheat the oven to 350 degrees.

Wipe the mushrooms clean and carefully remove the stems. Arrange the caps, cut side up, on a lightly oiled baking sheet. Trim stems of their rough bottoms and chop them very fine.

Heat the margarine in a small skillet and sauté the chopped stems over medium-low heat until they have lost their raw quality. Remove from the heat and stir in the remaining ingredients except garnish.

Stuff the mushroom caps with the mixture from the skillet. Cover the baking sheet loosely with foil. Bake, covered, for 10 minutes, then uncover and bake for another 5 minutes. Transfer to a platter and garnish with curly parsley. Serve warm.

| Calories: 54 | Total fat: 3 g | Protein: 2 g |
| Carbohydrate: 3 g | Cholesterol: 0 g | Sodium: 31 mg |

MUSHROOMS ROSEMARY

8 servings

Another delicious mushroom appetizer that can also be used as a first course.

1 ½ pounds large fresh mushrooms
2 ½ tablespoons reduced-fat margarine, cut into
    thin slices
1 small onion, finely chopped
1 to 2 cloves garlic, minced
1 teaspoon teriyaki sauce, or more to taste
1 tablespoon fresh rosemary, or 1 teaspoon dried
    rosemary
salt and freshly ground pepper to taste
rosemary and parsley sprigs for garnish

Preheat the oven to 350 degrees.

Cut the stems off the mushrooms. Arrange the caps, smooth side up, in a lightly oiled oblong baking dish. Arrange the sliced margarine over the mushrooms, then sprinkle with the remaining ingredients except garnish and season with a bit of salt and pepper. Bake, uncovered, for 40 minutes. Serve warm with cocktail breads or warm pita wedges on a platter garnished with rosemary and parsley sprigs.

Calories: 41	Total fat: 1 g	Protein: 1 g
Carbohydrate: 5 g	Cholesterol: 0 g	Sodium: 62 mg

SOY AND HONEY NUTS
AND PRETZELS

Makes 4 cups

This tasty snack is particularly nice to have on hand for guests to munch on during the winter holidays.

2 tablespoons soy sauce or tamari
3 tablespoons honey
½ teaspoon cinnamon
¼ teaspoon ground ginger
2 cups shelled nuts (a mixture of peanuts, cashews,
    and almonds is very good)

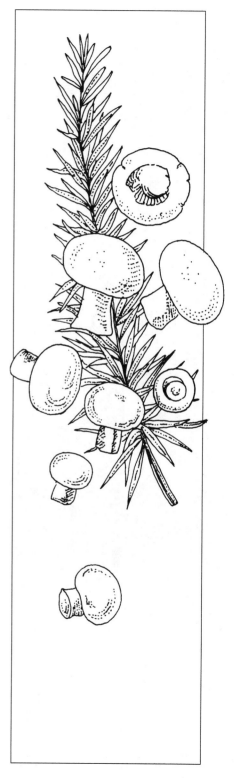

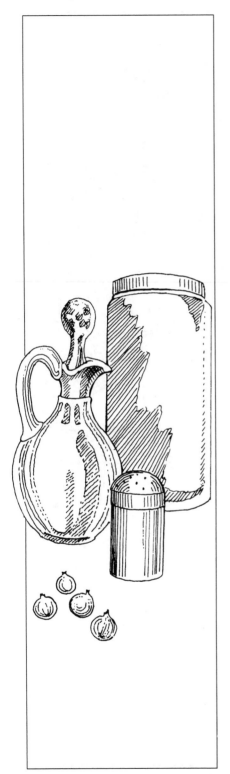

2 cups small, salt-free pretzels

Preheat the oven to 300 degrees.
Combine the first 4 ingredients in a large mixing bowl. Stir in the nuts and toss to coat them evenly. Spread on a non-stick baking sheet and bake for 15 to 20 minutes, stirring occasionally, or until the coating is fairly dry. Let cool, then break apart any nuts that have clumped together. Mix in the pretzels and store in jars until needed.

Per $\frac{1}{4}$-cup serving:
   Calories: 146   Total fat: 9 g   Protein: 4 g
   Carbohydrate: 12 g   Cholesterol: 0 g   Sodium: 129 mg

SWEET AND SOUR QUICK-PICKLED VEGETABLES

Makes 5 cups

This keeps well for at least 2 weeks in the refrigerator, and so it is nice to keep on hand for spontaneous company during both the summer and the winter holidays. And the yield is generous enough for you to pack a pint jar to give as a gift when visiting others.

1 cup baby carrots, scraped
1 heaping cup bite-sized cauliflower florets
1 cup string beans, trimmed, cut into 1-inch lengths
1 small zucchini, sliced into $\frac{1}{4}$-inch-thick rounds
1-pound jar pearl onions, drained, liquid reserved

Marinade
liquid from pearl onions, plus enough water to make
   1 $\frac{1}{2}$ cups
$\frac{1}{2}$ cup cider vinegar
$\frac{1}{2}$ cup apple juice
1 teaspoon salt
freshly ground pepper to taste
$\frac{1}{2}$ teaspoon each: dried dill, oregano

Steam the carrots, cauliflower, and string beans briefly until just crisp-tender. Rinse under cold water until they are completely cool. Combine with the zucchini and pearl onions in a mixing bowl and stir together.

Stir the marinade ingredients together in a mixing bowl until thoroughly combined. Divide the marinade between 2 1-quart jars. Divide the vegetables between the jars. Cover and refrigerate for at least 24 hours before serving.

Per $\frac{1}{2}$-cup serving:

Calories: 32	Total fat: 0 g	Protein: 1 g
Carbohydrate: 7 g	Cholesterol: 0 g	Sodium: 394 mg

THREE-CHEESE SPREAD

Makes 2 3-inch balls

Rich and pungent, this spread goes a long way and is perfect for serving with whole-grain crackers and celery sticks. Keep one for your own get-togethers, and wrap the second in plastic wrap and give it as a gift.

8 ounces reduced-fat cream cheese
4 ounces creamy goat cheese
1 to 2 ounces blue cheese, to taste
1 teaspoon dried chives
$\frac{1}{4}$ teaspoon each: dried thyme, dill
$\frac{1}{4}$ cup coarsely ground almonds

Combine the cheeses and dried herbs in the container of a food processor or blender. Process until thoroughly blended. Scrape the sides down as necessary. With a plastic spatula, transfer the mixture into a container. Cover and chill for at least an hour. Divide the mixture into 2 equal parts and roll into balls. Spread the ground almonds on a small plate. Roll each ball in the almonds until completely coated. Wrap each ball in plastic wrap and refrigerate until needed.

Per 1-tablespoon serving:

Calories: 41	Total fat: 3 g	Protein: 2 g
Carbohydrate: 1 g	Cholesterol: 10 g	Sodium: 87 mg

CREAMY HERBED CHEESE DIP

Makes about 2 cups

Crudités and a creamy dip have become quite a common-

"Cheese, as a food, is as wholesome as its use is widespread; as an item in a coursed dinner there is nothing known to the world of gastronomy which can so quickly rectify the palate . . . like the tang of a true cheese."

—Frederick W. Hackwood
Good Cheer, 1911

place appetizer or buffet dish, doubtless because everyone enjoys the combination so much! To serve, place the dip in a bowl in the center of a large platter colorfully arranged with bite-sized pieces of seasonal vegetables. Think also of including baby vegetables if available, such as baby zucchini and carrots. And feel free, especially in the summer, to add any other herbs you'd like, and in any amount to suit your taste.

4 ounces low-fat cream cheese
1 cup low-fat cottage cheese
½ cup buttermilk
½ green bell pepper, cut into chunks
2 tablespoons parsley leaves
2 scallions, coarsely chopped
2 tablespoons minced fresh dill, or 2 teaspoons dried dill
½ teaspoon each: dry mustard, salt

Combine all the ingredients in the container of a food processor or blender. Process until smoothly pureed. Transfer to a covered container and refrigerate until needed.

Per 2-tablespoon serving:
Calories: 34	Total fat: 2 g	Protein: 3 g
Carbohydrate: 1 g	Cholesterol: 7 g	Sodium: 146 mg

VARIATION:

Creamy Herbed Goat Cheese Dip: Substitute 4 ounces of goat cheese for the cream cheese for a more pungent flavor.

SPINACH AND CUCUMBER SPREAD

Makes about 2 cups

Delicious served with crispbreads and whole-grain crackers, this spread will be especially appreciated by those who eat no dairy products.

½ cup finely chopped, seeded cucumber
10 ounces silken tofu (if unavailable, substitute soft tofu)
10-ounce package frozen spinach, thawed, moisture completely squeezed out

juice of $\frac{1}{2}$ lemon
1 bunch finely minced scallion
1 tablespoon minced fresh dill, or 1 teaspoon dried dill
1 teaspoon seasoned salt, more or less to taste
$\frac{1}{4}$ teaspoon dried basil
freshly ground pepper to taste

Spread the chopped cucumber over 2 or 3 layers of paper towel. Cover with another 2 layers, then place a cutting board or some other weight on top. Let stand for 30 minutes or so.

Combine the remaining ingredients in the container of a food processor or blender. Process until the spinach and tofu are well incorporated. Transfer to a serving bowl and stir in the cucumber. Cover and refrigerate until needed.

Per 2-tablespoon serving:
Calories: 20   Total fat: 1 g   Protein: 2 g
Carbohydrate: 2 g   Cholesterol: 0 g   Sodium: 89 mg

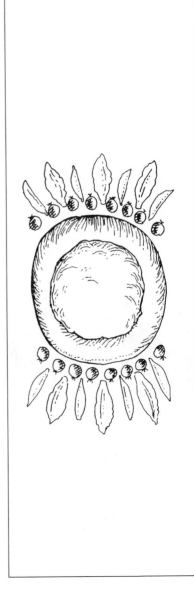

CREAMY HORSERADISH DIP IN RYE "BOWL"

Makes about 1 $\frac{1}{2}$ cups

This dip tastes rich and creamy, though it is made from low-fat cottage cheese. I suggest placing the hollowed-out rye bread, filled with the dip, in the center of a large platter, and arranging around it endive leaves, cherry tomatoes, and very briefly steamed snow peas.

1 $\frac{1}{2}$ cups low-fat cottage cheese
2 to 3 tablespoons prepared horseradish, more or
    less to taste
1 $\frac{1}{2}$ tablespoons grainy mustard
2 to 3 tablespoons chopped fresh herbs of your choice
1 small, round rye or pumpernickel bread, about 6 to 7
    inches in diameter

Place the first 4 ingredients in the container of a food processor or blender and process until the cottage cheese is completely smooth.

Cut a slice off the top of the bread and hollow out enough of the inside of the bread to hold the dip. Fill with the dip and serve as suggested above, or with raw vegetables of your choice.

Per 2-tablespoon serving:

Calories: 64	Total fat: 1 g	Protein: 5 g
Carbohydrate: 9 g	Cholesterol: 1 g	Sodium: 248 mg

HERB AND CURRY DIP

Makes about 1 ½ cups

A great way to utilize the herbal harvest of late summer: serve this strong dip with crisp vegetable crudités—carrots, bell peppers, cauliflower, broccoli.

1 cup firmly packed fresh parsley leaves
2 to 3 tablespoons minced fresh chives
2 to 3 tablespoons chopped fresh chervil
1 tablespoon minced shallot
1 tablespoon diced orange peel
2 teaspoons good-quality curry powder, more or less to taste
½ teaspoon salt
1 cup plain low-fat yogurt

Place all the ingredients in a food processor or blender. Process until all that remains of the herbs are small flakes. Transfer to a covered container and refrigerate until needed.

Per 2-tablespoon serving:

Calories: 16	Total fat: 0 g	Protein: 1 g
Carbohydrate: 2 g	Cholesterol: 1 g	Sodium: 106 mg

WHITE BEAN AND SUN-DRIED TOMATO PÂTÉ

Makes about 2 cups

Though this makes a classy appetizer, served with whole-grain crackers or crispbreads, I like to pack it for picnics to use as a spread for fresh French or rye bread.

1 tablespoon olive oil

1 large onion, chopped
2 cloves garlic, minced
1 $\frac{1}{2}$ cups well-cooked cannellini or navy beans
$\frac{1}{4}$ cup oil-cured sun-dried tomatoes
juice of $\frac{1}{2}$ lemon
1 sprig parsley
$\frac{1}{4}$ teaspoon each: dried thyme, summer savory
salt and freshly ground pepper to taste

Heat the oil in a skillet. Add the onion and sauté over moderate heat until translucent. Add the garlic and continue to sauté until the onion is just beginning to brown. Combine the onion mixture with all the remaining ingredients except the salt and pepper in the container of a food processor and process until completely smooth. Drizzle in 2 tablespoons of water or so, to loosen the consistency. Stop and scrape down the sides as needed.

Season to taste with salt and pepper. Pat into an attractive shallow crock to serve.

Per 2-tablespoon serving:
Calories: 41	Total fat: 1 g	Protein: 1 g
Carbohydrate: 6 g	Cholesterol: 0 g	Sodium: 2 mg

AFTERNOON TEA: SCONES AND QUICK BREADS

Currant Scones
Strawberry Oat Bran Scones
Chocolate Chip Pear Bread
Almond Banana Bread

CURRANT SCONES

Makes 8 large wedges

Currant scones are a classic accompaniment to afternoon tea, traditionally served split and buttered. Fresh out of the

Can you think of anything cozier than an afternoon tea, especially on a rainy or cold day? I don't refer here to tea in the formal English tradition, with watercress sandwiches and the whole works (though I've thoroughly enjoyed partaking of an English tea when I've had the chance). Rather, my idea of tea is a steaming pot of the herbal variety served with a little something sweet and enjoyed with a few friends or neighbors. I have borrowed the English idea of serving scones—these are most delightful served fresh from the oven. The quick breads don't suffer from being made ahead of time, but they, too, are very nice served warm with the tea.

oven, they are quite good with no embellishment, but a bit of black currant jam is nice.

2 cups whole wheat pastry flour
2 teaspoons baking powder
1/4 teaspoon salt
1/3 cup reduced-fat margarine
1/2 cup light brown sugar
2/3 cup currants
1 egg, beaten
1/4 cup low-fat milk

Preheat the oven to 350 degrees.

Combine the first 5 ingredients in the bowl of a food processor and pulse on and off until the mixture resembles coarse crumbs. Transfer to a mixing bowl and stir in the currants. Beat the egg together with the milk. Make a well in the center of the flour mixture and pour in the egg. Mix in, work together with well-floured hands to make a soft dough, then form into a ball.

On a well-floured board, roll the dough out into a 1/2-inch-thick round. Place on a floured baking sheet and with a sharp knife cut into 8 wedges halfway through the dough. Bake for 15 to 20 minutes, or until golden on top. Serve warm.

Calories: 223	Total fat: 3 g	Protein: 5 g
Carbohydrate: 42 g	Cholesterol: 27 g	Sodium: 145 mg

STRAWBERRY OAT BRAN SCONES

Makes 16 to 18 scones

Scones with fresh fruit baked into them are not common, but the result is moist and flavorful. Think of these for a rainy spring afternoon, once fresh strawberries are available.

2 1/4 cups whole wheat pastry flour
1 cup oat bran
1/2 teaspoon salt
1/2 teaspoon baking soda
1 1/2 teaspoons baking powder
1/3 cup reduced-fat margarine, softened
1/2 cup light brown sugar

1 cup hulled, finely diced (about ¼ inch) firm,
    sweet strawberries
1 egg, beaten
½ cup buttermilk

Preheat the oven to 350 degrees.

Combine the first 5 ingredients in a mixing bowl. Cut the margarine into the dry ingredients with a pastry blender, 2 knives, or fingertips until the mixture resembles coarse crumbs. Stir the brown sugar in until evenly distributed. Toss the strawberries with flour until they are thoroughly coated and stir gently into the flour mixture.

Make a well in the center of the mixture and pour into it the beaten egg and the buttermilk. Work together gently with hands to form a soft dough. If the dough seems too sticky, add a bit more flour.

Form the dough into a round, place on a well-floured board, and flatten. Roll out to ½-inch thickness. With a 2-inch round pastry cutter or a glass, cut 2-inch circles from the dough. Gather up and roll out scraps until all the dough is used. Arrange the scones on a lightly oiled baking sheet. Bake for 18 to 20 minutes, or until the tops are lightly golden. Serve hot.

Per scone:

Calories: 100	Total fat: 2 g	Protein: 3 g
Carbohydrate: 18 g	Cholesterol: 13 g	Sodium: 101 mg

CHOCOLATE CHIP PEAR BREAD

Makes 1 loaf

Rich with chocolate mini-chips, this melt-in-your-mouth loaf has become one of my standards, not only for afternoon tea, but as a dessert bread or a hostess gift. It's wonderful with almond tea.

1 ¾ cups whole wheat pastry flour
1 ½ teaspoons baking powder
1 teaspoon baking soda
½ teaspoon salt
¼ teaspoon ground nutmeg
¼ teaspoon ground cardamom, optional

"What should mightily recommend the use of tea to gentlemen of a sprightly genius, who would preserve the continuance of their lively and distinct ideas, is its eminent and unequalled power to take off, or prevent, drowsiness and dullness, damps and clouds on the brain and intellectual faculties. It begets a watchful briskness, dispels heaviness; it keeps the eyes watchful, the head clear, animates the intellectual powers, maintains or raises lively ideas, excites and sharpeneth the thoughts, gives forth vigour and force to invention, awakes the senses, and clears the mind."

—Dr. Thomas Short
Discourse on Tea, 1750

1 egg or 2 egg whites, beaten
1/2 cup packed light brown sugar
1/2 cup buttermilk
1/2 cup vanilla nonfat yogurt
1 teaspoon vanilla extract
1 cup bosc pears, cored and cut into 1/4-inch dice
1 cup semisweet chocolate mini-chips

Preheat the oven to 350 degrees.

In a mixing bowl, combine the first 5 ingredients plus the optional cardamom. In another bowl, combine the next 5 ingredients and beat together. Make a well in the center of the dry ingredients and pour in the wet mixture. Beat together until smoothly combined. Stir in the diced pear and chocolate chips. Pour the batter into an oiled 9- by 5- by 3-inch loaf pan. Bake for 45 to 50 minutes, or until the top is golden and a knife inserted in the center tests clean.

Per 3/4-inch-thick slice:

Calories: 232	Total fat: 6 g	Protein: 5 g
Carbohydrate: 39 g	Cholesterol: 22 g	Sodium: 136 mg

ALMOND BANANA BREAD

Makes 1 loaf

The texture of oats and the fragrance of almonds separate this loaf from the standard banana bread.

1 3/4 cups whole wheat pastry flour
1/3 cup rolled oats
1 teaspoon baking soda
1/4 teaspoon each: salt, nutmeg, allspice
1 egg plus 2 egg whites, beaten
2 tablespoons low-fat milk or soymilk
1/2 to 2/3 cup light brown sugar, to taste
1 cup mashed bananas (about 2 medium)
1/4 cup vanilla nonfat yogurt
1 teaspoon vanilla extract
1/4 cup finely chopped almonds

Preheat the oven to 350 degrees.

Combine the first 3 ingredients in a mixing bowl. Stir in the salt and spices. In another bowl, combine the beaten eggs and milk with the sugar until it dissolves. Beat in the bananas, yogurt, and vanilla until the mixture is smooth. Make a well in the center of the dry ingredients and pour in the wet mixture. Stir together vigorously until completely combined. Stir in the almonds.

Pour the batter into an oiled 9- by 5- by 3-inch loaf pan. Bake for 45 minutes, or until a knife inserted into the center tests clean.

Per $^3/_4$-inch-thick slice:

Calories: 167	Total fat: 4 g	Protein: 5 g
Carbohydrate: 30 g	Cholesterol: 22 g	Sodium: 71 mg

COUNTRY BREAKFAST TREATS

Wheat Germ Buttermilk Muffins

Zucchini Raisin Muffins

Banana Date Muffins

Lemony Blueberry Muffins

Cornmeal and Blueberry Griddlecakes

Golden Squash Griddlecakes

Brown Rice and Cornmeal Griddlecakes

Crunchy Oat and Ancient-Grain Granola

Crunchy Millet Bread

WHEAT GERM BUTTERMILK MUFFINS

Makes 1 dozen

Serve these fresh from the oven with fruit-only preserves or apple butter.

What to serve overnight guests for breakfast can be a puzzler for hosts. You want to offer something a little different, and not everyone wants to start the day with a heavy, egg-laden meal anymore. Putting out the dry cereal and milk just doesn't seem like the thing to do, either. How do fresh, warm muffins sound, then, or a stack of whole-grain griddlecakes? No, you needn't wake up at the crack of dawn to start preparing—each of these hearty treats requires only that you whip up a batter.

In addition, I have here a chewy yeasted bread made with nutritious millet, and a crunchy granola that harks back to the sixties, yet looks to the future with the addition of recently rediscovered ancient "supergrains."

For more breakfast ideas, especially for summer, see Chapter 5, Mother's Day and Father's Day, pages 71 to 77.

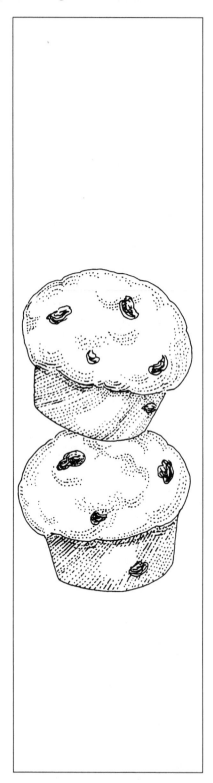

1 ½ cups whole wheat pastry flour
½ cup wheat germ
2 teaspoons baking powder
½ teaspoon baking soda
¼ teaspoon salt
1 egg plus 1 egg white, beaten
1 cup buttermilk
¼ cup honey
¼ cup toasted sunflower seeds

Preheat the oven to 375 degrees.

Combine the first 5 ingredients in a mixing bowl. In another bowl, beat together the remaining ingredients except the sunflower seeds. Make a well in the center of the dry ingredients and pour in the wet mixture. Beat together until smoothly combined. Stir in the sunflower seeds. Divide among 12 muffin tins and bake for 12 to 15 minutes, or until the tops are golden and a toothpick inserted in the center of a muffin tests clean. Cool on a rack and serve warm.

Per muffin:

Calories: 128	Total fat: 3 g	Protein: 6 g
Carbohydrate: 19 g	Cholesterol: 18 g	Sodium: 72 mg

ZUCCHINI RAISIN MUFFINS

Makes 1 dozen

Flakes of zucchini give these muffins a wonderful moistness and texture.

1 ½ cups whole wheat pastry flour
¼ cup oat bran or wheat germ
1 ½ teaspoons baking powder
½ teaspoon baking soda
½ teaspoon cinnamon
2 eggs, beaten
¾ cup plain low-fat yogurt
½ cup light brown sugar
1 cup firmly packed grated zucchini
½ cup raisins
¼ cup finely chopped walnuts, optional

Preheat the oven to 350 degrees.

Combine the first 5 ingredients in a mixing bowl. In another bowl, combine the next 3 ingredients and beat together. Make a well in the center of the dry ingredients and pour in the wet mixture. Beat together until smoothly combined. Stir in the zucchini, raisins, and walnuts. Divide the batter between 12 muffin tins and bake for 20 to 25 minutes, or until the tops are golden and a toothpick inserted in the center of a muffin tests clean. Cool on a rack and serve warm.

Per muffin:

Calories: 132	Total fat: 1 g	Protein: 4 g
Carbohydrate: 26 g	Cholesterol: 36 g	Sodium: 31 mg

BANANA DATE MUFFINS

Makes 1 dozen

Heavenly served warm with fresh-brewed coffee, cottage cheese, and fresh fruit.

1 ½ **cups whole wheat pastry flour**
½ **cup rolled oats**
1 **teaspoon baking powder**
1 **teaspoon baking soda**
¼ **teaspoon salt**
⅛ **teaspoon nutmeg**
1 **egg, beaten**
1 **cup well-mashed bananas**
½ **cup vanilla nonfat yogurt**
1 **teaspoon vanilla extract**
½ **cup finely chopped pitted dates**
⅓ **cup chopped almonds**

Preheat the oven to 350 degrees.

Combine the first 6 ingredients in a mixing bowl. In another bowl, combine the next 4 ingredients and beat together. Make a well in the center of the dry ingredients and pour in the wet mixture. Beat together until smoothly combined. Stir in the dates and nuts. Divide the batter among 12 muffin tins. Bake for 20 to 25 minutes, or until the tops are golden and a toothpick inserted into the center tests clean.

Per muffin:

Calories: 137	Total fat: 4 g	Protein: 5 g
Carbohydrate: 23 g	Cholesterol: 18 g	Sodium: 60 mg

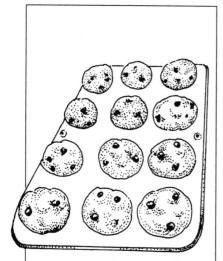

LEMONY BLUEBERRY MUFFINS

Makes 1 dozen

The subtle hint of lemon gives these classic muffins a nice twist. Be prepared to have them disappear quickly!

2 cups whole wheat pastry flour
2 teaspoons baking powder
1/4 teaspoon salt
1 egg, beaten
1/3 to 1/2 cup light brown sugar, to taste
1 cup lemon nonfat yogurt
1/4 cup low-fat milk
1 tablespoon lemon juice
2 teaspoons grated lemon rind
1 cup blueberries

Preheat the oven to 350 degrees.

Combine the first 3 ingredients in a mixing bowl. In another bowl, combine the remaining ingredients except the blueberries. Make a well in the center of the dry ingredients and pour in the wet mixture. Stir together vigorously until smoothly combined. Gently stir in the blueberries. Divide the batter among 12 oiled or paper-lined muffin tins. Bake for 15 to 20 minutes, or until the tops are golden and a toothpick inserted in the center of a muffin tests clean.

Per muffin:
Calories: 124   Total fat: 0 g   Protein: 5 g
Carbohydrate: 24 g   Cholesterol: 18 g   Sodium: 75 mg

CORNMEAL AND BLUEBERRY GRIDDLECAKES

Makes about 24 3-inch griddlecakes, or 4 to 6 servings

1 1/2 cups stone-ground cornmeal
1 teaspoon baking soda
1/2 teaspoon salt
2 eggs, beaten
1/2 cup whole wheat flour
1 1/4 cups buttermilk
1 cup blueberries

extra whole wheat flour
reduced-fat margarine for griddle
maple syrup

Combine the cornmeal with 1 ½ cups of boiling water in a mixing bowl and stir until smoothly combined. Let stand 10 minutes. In a small bowl, combine the flour, baking soda, and salt.

Stir the beaten eggs and buttermilk into the cornmeal mixture, then stir in the flour.

Place the blueberries in a food processor. Pulse on and off until they are coarsely chopped. Transfer to the bowl that held the flour. Toss with extra flour until lightly coated, then stir gently into the batter.

Heat a nonstick griddle and melt just enough margarine on the surface to coat it very lightly. When the griddle is hot enough to make a drop of water sizzle, ladle the batter onto it in scant ¼ cupfuls. Cook on both sides until golden. Keep the griddlecakes warm in a covered casserole in a 200-degree oven until all are done. Serve hot with maple syrup.

Calories: 263	Total fat: 3 g	Protein: 10 g
Carbohydrate: 47 g	Cholesterol: 87 g	Sodium: 275 mg

GOLDEN SQUASH GRIDDLECAKES

Makes about 24 3-inch griddlecakes, or 4 to 6 servings

The sunny color of these griddlecakes will cheer your guests on a cold winter morning. This is a great way to use up leftover squash.

¾ cup whole wheat flour
¼ cup cornmeal
1 teaspoon baking soda
½ teaspoon cinnamon
¼ teaspoon ground ginger
2 eggs, beaten
½ cup buttermilk
1 cup well-cooked, smoothly mashed butternut squash
reduced-fat margarine, for griddle
maple syrup, applesauce, or fruit butter

Combine the first 5 ingredients in a mixing bowl. In another

For many moons, my experience with griddlecakes was limited to reading about them because I thought they were just too complicated an undertaking for the morning. How wrong I was! Once I began making whole-grain griddlecakes, I realized how simple a task it really is, and I now have a number of favorites in my repertoire. Few things will earn a host as many oohs and aahs from guests as serving stacks of hot griddlecakes. For sweetening, pure maple syrup, not the imitation type, is a must. As an alternative, serve all-fruit preserves or applesauce.

You'll notice a common thread running through the griddlecakes—cornmeal and buttermilk. Cornmeal gives texture, and buttermilk lifts the flavor so that it isn't flat. Those on dairy-free diets can substitute soymilk for the buttermilk, bearing in mind that the results won't be quite as flavorful. For more pancake ideas, see Pancake Breakfast for Mom or Dad, pages 75 to 77.

bowl, combine the eggs, buttermilk, and squash and stir together until smooth. Make a well in the center of the dry ingredients and pour in the wet mixture. Stir together until completely combined, but do not overbeat.

Heat a nonstick griddle. Melt just enough margarine to coat it lightly. Pour the batter onto the griddle in scant $1/4$ cupfuls, enough to make 3-inch cakes. Cook on both sides until golden. Keep the griddlecakes warm in a covered casserole dish in a 200-degree oven until all are done. Serve at once with maple syrup, applesauce, or fruit butter.

Calories: 143	Total fat: 3 g	Protein: 7 g
Carbohydrate: 23 g	Cholesterol: 86 g	Sodium: 43 mg

BROWN RICE AND CORNMEAL GRIDDLECAKES

Makes about 18 griddlecakes

Adapted from a classic nineteenth-century deep-South recipe, these wholesome griddlecakes are filling and flavorful.

$1/2$ cup cornmeal
$1/2$ cup whole wheat flour
$1/2$ teaspoon baking soda
$1/4$ teaspoon salt
1 cup well-cooked brown rice
2 eggs, beaten
1 cup buttermilk
reduced-fat margarine for griddle
maple syrup, honey, or all-fruit preserves

In a mixing bowl, combine the first 4 ingredients. Stir in the rice until it is evenly distributed within the meal, then add the eggs and buttermilk and stir vigorously until the mixture is well blended.

Heat just enough margarine to coat the bottom of a non-stick griddle. Ladle the batter onto the hot griddle in scant $1/4$ cupfuls, enough to form thin 3- to 4-inch cakes. Cook on both sides until golden brown. Keep the griddlecakes warm in a covered casserole dish in a 200-degree oven until all are done. Serve hot with maple syrup, honey, or all-fruit preserves.

Calories: 52	Total fat: 0 g	Protein: 2 g
Carbohydrate: 9 g	Cholesterol: 24 g	Sodium: 44 mg

CRUNCHY OAT AND ANCIENT-GRAIN GRANOLA

Makes about 2 quarts

With a slight bow to those crunchy granolas that took off in the sixties and never faded away, this version is updated with the addition of recently revived super-nutritious ancient grains, amaranth and teff. Look for them in your natural food store.

4 cups rolled oats
1/2 cup raw amaranth or teff seeds, combination
1 cup untoasted wheat germ
3/4 cup chopped, untoasted almonds
1 tablespoon canola oil
1/3 cup honey
1/4 teaspoon cinnamon
1 cup raisins

Preheat the oven to 275 degrees.
Combine the first 4 ingredients in a large mixing bowl. In a small bowl, combine the oil, honey, and cinnamon. Toss thoroughly with the grain mixture. Spread on a lightly oiled cookie sheet or 2 and bake until golden, stirring occasionally, about 25 to 30 minutes. Let cool. Mix with raisins and store in jars. Serve as a breakfast cereal with milk or soymilk.

Per 1/2-cup serving:
Calories: 226	Total fat: 7 g	Protein: 8 g
Carbohydrate: 34 g	Cholesterol: 0 g	Sodium: 4 mg

CRUNCHY MILLET BREAD

Makes 2 loaves

Ever since a friend first brought this textured bread to my house for a dinner, I've treasured the recipe. Start your day with it, then serve it for dinner with your soup!

1 cup raw millet seeds
1 package active dry yeast
1/4 cup canola oil

2 tablespoons honey or molasses
4 cups whole wheat flour
1 cup unbleached white flour
1 ½ teaspoons salt
¼ teaspoon each: ground ginger, turmeric
2 tablespoons toasted sunflower seeds
½ cup raisins or chopped dried apricots, optional

Toast the millet in a hot, dry skillet, stirring frequently, for about 5 to 7 minutes, or until the grain smells nutty and is a shade darker.

Combine the yeast with ½ cup of warm water in a mixing bowl and let stand 10 minutes, or until dissolved. Stir in 1 ½ cups more warm water, the oil, and honey or molasses.

In a large mixing bowl, combine the flours, salt, and spices. Stir in the toasted millet. Make a well in the center and pour in the wet mixture. Work together into a dough, first with a wooden spoon, then with hands. Work in the sunflower seeds and optional raisins or apricots.

Turn the dough out onto a well-floured board. Knead for 10 to 12 minutes, adding more flour as needed until the dough loses its stickiness. Form into a round, place in a floured bowl, and cover with a tea towel. Place in a warm place and let rise until doubled in bulk, about 1 to 1 ½ hours. Punch down, then divide the dough into 2 parts and shape into loaves. Place in loaf pans and set in a warm place to rise until the dough reaches over the top of the pans, about 45 minutes. Score the top of the loaf with a sharp knife, and brush the top with warm water to encourage a crisp crust.

Bake in a preheated 400-degree oven for 10 minutes, then reduce the heat to 325 degrees. Bake for an additional 35 minutes, or until the tops are nicely browned and the loaves sound hollow when tapped.

Cool on racks, then wrap in foil, then in plastic bags to store. This is delicious served fresh and warm but is also very good sliced and toasted.

Per ¾-inch-thick slice:

Calories: 187	Total fat: 4 g	Protein: 5 g
Carbohydrate: 33 g	Cholesterol: 0 g	Sodium: 163 mg

Appendix
BASICS

KITCHEN EQUIPMENT FOR EASIER ENTERTAINING

You need not have a fancy kitchen nor fancy equipment to entertain, but there are a few items I find indispensable, either because they save so much time and effort or because they help achieve predictable results when you wish to impress your guests!

Electric Mixer

Since I tend to use whole wheat pastry flour in my relatively simple baked goods, I don't expect to desire fluffy, high-risen results. Nevertheless, using the electric mixer for cake batters seems to aerate them enough to create lighter textures. The mixer is also a lifesaver for whipping egg whites, especially when you don't have the time to bring them to room temperature.

Food Processor

I consider this the most indispensable appliance that a cook can own. Certain tasks that can be almost unbearably messy and tedious, such as grating beets for borscht, can be accomplished in seconds. Though food processors don't puree quite as smoothly as do blenders, they are more than adequate, and when you own the former, you don't need the latter.

BASIC VINAIGRETTE

Makes about ¾ cup

¼ **cup olive oil**
¼ **cup canola oil**
¼ **cup white wine vinegar**
juice of ½ lemon
2 teaspoons Dijon mustard
freshly ground black pepper to taste
1 teaspoon mixed dried herbs

Combine all the ingredients in a cruet and shake well. Shake well before each use.

Per 2-teaspoon serving:
Calories: 55	Total fat: 5 g	Protein: 0 g
Carbohydrate: 0 g	Cholesterol: 0 g	Sodium: 16 mg

VARIATIONS:

Garlic Vinaigrette: Add 1 or 2 cloves garlic, to taste, cut in half lengthwise or crushed, to the above dressing. Allow to marinate overnight before using.

Nutty Vinaigrette: Replace the olive oil with an equivalent amount of a good nut oil, such as walnut, hazelnut, or unrefined peanut oil.

GRAINY MUSTARD VINAIGRETTE

Makes about 1 cup

⅓ **cup canola oil**
3 tablespoons olive oil
⅓ **cup red or white wine vinegar**
juice of ½ lemon
2 to 3 tablespoons grainy mustard, to taste
1 clove garlic, crushed, optional
½ **teaspoon dried dill**
¼ **teaspoon each: dried tarragon, savory, and basil**
freshly ground black pepper to taste

Combine all the ingredients in a cruet and shake well. Shake well before each use.

Per 2-teaspoon serving:
Calories: 43	Total fat: 4 g	Protein: 0 g
Carbohydrate: 0 g	Cholesterol: 0 g	Sodium: 44 mg

FRENCH DRESSING

Makes about 1 cup

Make this dressing at least an hour before it is needed. It can also be made several days ahead of time, as it keeps well under refrigeration.

⅓ cup tomato juice
¼ cup light olive oil
2 tablespoons red wine vinegar
1 tablespoon plus 1 teaspoon reduced-fat mayonnaise
    or soy mayonnaise
2 teaspoons honey or light brown sugar
1 teaspoon paprika
freshly ground pepper to taste
1 to 2 cloves garlic, split lengthwise

Combine all the ingredients in a small mixing bowl and whisk together until smoothly combined. Use garlic according to how garlicky you like dressings—2 cloves steeped in the dressing for a day or more will produce a fairly pungent garlic flavor.

Transfer to a covered container or cruet and refrigerate until needed.

Per 2-teaspoon serving:
Calories: 28	Total fat: 2 g	Protein: 0 g
Carbohydrate: 1 g	Cholesterol: 0 g	Sodium: 16 mg

TOFU MAYONNAISE

Makes about 1 cup

1 cup mashed soft tofu

The processor can be an endless help in the kitchen and is a wonderful time saver when preparing full meals for company. With the steel blade you can make mayonnaise, create dips and pâtés, grind nuts, and puree soups. With the grating blade you can shred cheeses and hard vegetables; with the plastic blade, making pastry crust is a cinch. All these little tasks are easily accomplished and add up to a lot less work for the cook who likes to entertain.

Griddle

If you enjoy making griddlecakes and pancakes for breakfast, you can make a bigger batch at one time on a griddle than on a skillet, thus lessening the problem of keeping them warm while cooking the rest of the batter. A 12- or 14-inch skillet can be used instead, but a griddle cooks pancakes more evenly and efficiently. A nonstick surface is preferable. A griddle is also useful for cooking croquettes, making griddle scones, and heating tortillas.

Kitchen Scale

When making a recipe to serve a precise number of people, it's useful to have a scale if you need to measure exact quantities of certain items. For example, it can make more sense to call for a pound of zucchini, rather than 2 medium zucchinis, since "medium" can be a rather vague term in a recipe that requires a specific outcome in quantity of servings. It's also nice to be able to weigh items like dried mushrooms and sun-dried tomatoes, since many recipes, not just the ones in this book, specify amounts in ounces.

Oven thermometer

I remember how much I relied on this item when I had an older gas oven. These ovens can be notoriously inaccurate and can spell doom when exact baking temperatures are needed. For instance, a delicate soufflé should be baked at no more than 325 degrees, while corn bread needs to be baked quickly at a high temperature of 425.

Silverstone skillets and saucepans

I like Silverstone-lined skillets and pans, not only because they clean easily, but because the nonstick finish greatly reduces the amount of fat needed in cooking. For cooks who want to make a bigger investment in their cookware, Calphalon cookware is even more durable.

juice of 1/2 lemon
1 teaspoon prepared mustard
1/2 teaspoon salt, or to taste

Combine all the ingredients in the container of a food processor or blender. Process until velvety smooth.

Per 1-tablespoon serving:
Calories: 6	Total fat: 0 g	Protein: 1 g
Carbohydrate: 0 g	Cholesterol: 0 g	Sodium: 10 mg

ROASTED PEPPERS

8 to 10 servings

4 green bell peppers
2 yellow bell peppers
2 red bell peppers
2 tablespoons olive oil
1 tablespoon red wine vinegar
dash salt

Place the peppers on a foil-lined baking sheet under a preheated broiler. Broil on all sides, turning with tongs, until the skins are blackened, then remove. Divide the peppers between 2 paper bags. Fold the bags shut and let the peppers steam for 30 minutes, then slip the skins off. Remove and discard the stems, seeds, and fibers. Cut the peppers into strips. Place in a serving or storage container and toss with the remaining ingredients. Serve at room temperature.

Calories: 43	Total fat: 2 g	Protein: 0 g
Carbohydrate: 3 g	Cholesterol: 0 g	Sodium: 2 mg

HERB "BUTTER"

Makes about 2/3 cup

1/2 cup (1 stick) reduced-fat margarine or tub margarine, at room temperature
1/4 cup to 1/3 cup minced fresh herb of your choice, or a mixture of herbs

1 tablespoon minced fresh chives
1 clove garlic, minced, optional
dash lemon juice
freshly ground pepper to taste

Combine the margarine, herbs, and optional garlic in a small bowl. Sprinkle in the lemon juice and add a grinding or two of pepper. Work together with a fork until thoroughly combined. Pat into a crock, cover, and refrigerate until needed.

Per 1-tablespoon serving:
Calories: 37   Total fat: 2 g   Protein: 0 g
Carbohydrate: 3 g   Cholesterol: 0 g   Sodium: 2 mg

VARIATION:

Basil Butter: Use 1/4 cup minced basil leaves instead of mixed herbs.

HERBED CREAM CHEESE

Makes about 1 cup

8 ounces reduced-fat cream cheese, at room temperature
1/4 to 1/3 cup mixed minced herbs of your choice
(include some fresh chives and parsley; fresh dill is also delicious in cream cheese)

Combine the cream cheese with the herbs in a small bowl and work together with a fork. For a finer spread, combine in the container of a food processor and process until the herbs are tiny flecks. Pat into a crock, cover, and refrigerate until needed.

Per 1-tablespoon serving:
Calories: 40   Total fat: 4 g   Protein: 2 g
Carbohydrate: 1 g   Cholesterol: 14 g   Sodium: 58 mg

Wok

When making a large-quantity vegetable dish, a wok is considerably more comfortable than even a 14-inch skillet, especially for dishes that need to be stirred often. Don't limit the use of the wok to stir-fries; it works well for slower-cooked vegetable dishes like curries, too.

TIME-SAVING MICROWAVE TIPS

The microwave oven, arguably the greatest boon to come along for the busy cook, is an even more valuable tool for the cook who likes to entertain. Here are some tips to help you make the most of your microwave oven, if you own one, particularly in the context of the menus in this book. Or use these tips to help you decide whether to get one if you've been thinking of it. No specific cooking times will be given, since they vary according to the exact wattage and capacity of your unit.

- Long-cooking vegetables *like potatoes, beets, and winter squashes can be done in minutes.*

- Delicate vegetables *such as asparagus and string beans steam beautifully in the microwave. I like to arrange the vegetables in a casserole dish, with just enough water to keep the bottom moist, then cover and cook. I go for the minimum amount of time I think necessary, then I check and cook longer if need be, just until I get perfectly crisp-tender results.*

- Corn-on-the-cob *cooks beautifully in the microwave, and retains more flavor, since none is leached into cooking water. Cooking fresh corn in the microwave makes most sense when 2 to 4 ears' worth of kernels are needed in a recipe. Microwave husked ears in a covered casserole with about ½ inch of water on the bottom.*

- Breads, muffins, and cakes *that you wish to bake ahead of time in your conventional oven can be frozen, once cooled but still fresh, then defrosted in minutes in the microwave. They will taste fresh-baked.*

- Getting grilled foods started *is a useful function performed by the microwave. Some vegetables, such as onions and potatoes, need a head start before they go on*

BASIC PASTRY CRUST

Makes 1 9-inch pastry crust; double the recipe for 2-crust pies

1 cup whole wheat pastry flour
½ teaspoon salt
⅓ cup very cold reduced-fat margarine, cut into bits
4 to 5 tablespoons ice water

To make by hand, combine the flour and salt in a mixing bowl. Cut the margarine into the flour with a pastry blender, 2 knives, or the tines of a fork until the mixture resembles a coarse meal. Work the ice water in, 1 tablespoon at a time, until the dough holds together. Shape into a smooth ball.

To make in a food processor, place the flour and salt in the container fitted with the metal blade or the dough blade. Add the margarine and pulse on and off several times until it "disappears." Add the water, 1 tablespoon at a time, through the feed tube, until the dough masses together.

Chill the dough for at least 30 minutes to an hour.

Roll the dough out evenly into a circle on a well-floured board until large enough to fit a 9-inch pie pan. Line the pan with the crust and trim the edges. Crimp the edges and fill as directed in recipes.

Per ⅛ piecrust:

Calories: 75	Total fat: 3 g	Protein: 2 g
Carbohydrate: 11 g	Cholesterol: 0 g	Sodium: 191 mg

LIGHT VEGETABLE STOCK

Makes about 6 cups

This basic stock may be used in place of water in almost any meatless soup to give added depth of flavor.

1 large onion, coarsely chopped
1 large carrot, sliced
2 large celery stalks, sliced
handful of celery leaves
1 medium potato, scrubbed and diced
1 cup coarsely shredded cabbage
3 sprigs parsley

5 peppercorns
1 teaspoon salt

Combine all the ingredients in a large soup pot with 7 cups of water. Bring to a boil, then simmer, covered, over low heat for 40 to 45 minutes. Let the stock stand off the heat for 1 hour, or, if not using immediately, until cool, then strain through a fine sieve.

Per 1-cup serving:

Calories: 38	Total fat: 0 g	Protein: 1 g
Carbohydrate: 9 g	Cholesterol: 0 g	Sodium: 375 mg

BEAN BASICS

In recipes calling for beans, I give the option of using canned or cooked beans. Cooking your own beans has the advantages of being more economical and having control over how much salt to use. The high salt content of canned beans is, in fact, their major drawback. Otherwise, they are a boon to the busy cook preparing an entire meal for guests and are great to have in the summer when the long cooking required for beans is less desirable. I recommend buying canned beans with no additives, and rinsing the salty broth away before use.

If you'd like to cook your own beans, especially for recipes calling for a large quantity, say, 4 cups, follow these basic steps. Remember that beans generally swell to about 2 1/2 times their raw volume when cooked. So, if you need 2 cups of cooked beans, you'd start with 3/4 cup raw. But as long as you are going through the effort, it's worthwhile to cook more than you need for just one recipe, and freeze the extra beans for later use.

Here are the basic steps:

1. Rinse and sort carefully to remove grit and small stones.

2. Combine the beans in a large pot with 3 to 4 times their volume of water. Cover and soak overnight. Or, bring to a boil and let stand off the heat, covered, for an hour or 2 for a quicker soaking method.

the grill, so they won't char on the outside before they get cooked on the inside. And during warm grilling weather, it's nice to have a way to cook vegetables that won't warm up the kitchen.

- "Bring to room temperature before serving," *says the recipe, and you forgot to! No problem—heat in the microwave for 30 seconds to 1 minute, and the job is done.*

- Leftovers *of those delicious dishes you made for company can be reheated easily and neatly the next day.*

COOKING TIMES FOR LEGUMES USED IN THIS BOOK

Black beans: 1 to 1 ½ hours
Black-eyed peas: 1 to 1 ¼
    hours
Chick peas (garbanzos):
    2 ½ to 3 hours
Great Northern (cannellini)
    beans: 1 ½ to 2 hours
Kidney or red beans: 1 ½ to
    2 hours
Lentils, brown: 45 minutes
Lentils, red: 30 minutes
Navy beans: 1 to 1 ½ hours
Pinto beans: 1 ½ to 2 hours

3. Drain the soaking water. Though some vitamins may be lost, draining the soaking water also eliminates some of the complex sugars that many people have trouble digesting. Fill the pot with fresh water, about double the volume of the beans. There needn't be an exact amount, just plenty of room for them to simmer.

4. Bring the water to a boil, then lower the heat to a gentle simmer. Cover and leave the lid slightly ajar to prevent foaming. Cook the beans slowly and thoroughly to let them develop flavor, to prevent the skins from bursting, and to assure better digestibility. A bean that presses easily between the thumb and forefinger is done.

5. Add salt only when the beans are done. Salt tends to harden the skins and thus prolong cooking time.

INDEX